GW01401322

DEMOCRACY UNVEILED,

OR,

TYRANNY

STRIPPED OF THE
GARB OF PATRIOTISM

BY THOMAS GREEN FESSENDEN
(A.K.A. CHRISTOPHER CAUSTIC)

————Cœlum domus scelus omne retexit

You rogues! you rogues! you're all found out
And, "WE THE PEOPLE," I've no doubt,
Will Put a period to your dashing,
And *honest men* will come in fashion.

London
Spradabach Publishing
2024

Spradabach Publishing
BM Box Spradabach
London WC1N 3XX

Democracy Uncovered,
or, Tyranny Stripped of the Garb of Patriotism

First published in 1806
First Spradabach edition published 2024
© Spradabach Publishing 2024

Interior design by Alex Kurtagic

ISBN 978-1-909606-51-7

All rights reserved. No part of this publication may be reproduced,
stored in a retrieval system, or transmitted, in any form, or by any means
(electronic, mechanical, photocopying, recording, or otherwise) without
the prior written permission of the publisher. Any person who does any
unauthorised act in relation to this publication may be liable to criminal
prosecution and civil claims for damages.

British Library Cataloguing-in-Publication Data:
A catalogue record for this book is available from the British Library.

This book is sold subject to the condition that it shall not, by way of
trade or otherwise, be lent, hired out, or otherwise circulated without the
publisher's prior consent in any form of binding or cover other than that
in which it is published and without a similar condition including this
condition being imposed on the subsequent purchaser.

B E IT REMEMBERED, That on the fifth day of December, in the Thirtieth year of the Independence of the United States of America, Thomas Green Fessenden, of the said district, hath deposited in this office the title of a book, the right whereof the claims as a proprietor, in the words and figures following, to wit,

Democracy Unveiled, or Tyranny Stripped of the Garb of Patriotism

By Christopher Caustic, L. L. D. &c. &c. &c. &c. &c. &c. &c. &c. &c. &c. &c. &c.

Cœlum domus scelus omne retexit.

You rogues! you rogues! you're all found out
And, "WE THE PEOPLE," I've no doubt,
Will put a period to your dashing,
And *honest men* will come in fashion.

In Two Volumes, Vol. I. Third Edition, with Large Additions.

IN CONFORMITY to the Act of Congress of the United States, entitled "An Act for the encouragement of Learning, by securing the Copies of Maps, Charts and Books to the authors and proprietors of such copies during the times therein mentioned," and also to an act, entitled "An Act, Supplementary to an Act, entitled "An Act for the encouragement of Learning, by securing the copies of Maps, Charts and Books to the Authors and Proprietors of such copies during the times therein mentioned; and extending the benefit thereof to the Arts, Designing, Engraving, and etching Historical Prints."

EDWARD DUNSCOMB,
Clerk of the District of New York.

Table of Contents

Note on This Edition

T he text in this volume is based on the third edition with large additions, published in New York, in 1806, by I. Riley & Co. It appears here in its entirety.

The punctuation, spelling, and capitalisation have been left as in the original. So have the italics, except where the title of the works cited or referred to appeared between quotation marks; these titles were set in italics, as per modern convention.

The footnotes have been renumbered, so that they start counting from the beginning of each chapter, as opposed from the beginning of each volume (both original volumes are included in this one). Accordingly, internal references to previous footnotes have been adjusted to match.

Extensive quotes have been set as block quotes.

A full index has been generated and appended at the end of this volume.

Preface

With a solicitude to contribute to the amount of what my exertions can effect, for the welfare of my country, I have ventured to appear before the Tribunal of the American Public, in the character of an author. I hope I shall receive credit for the assertion, when I assure my countrymen, that my motives arise from a deep conviction, that our civil and political rights—all that can stamp a value on Society—are menaced by bad men now dominant, and bad principles, inculcated by the demagogues and philosophists of the day.

I am fully aware, that this publication will make me not a few inveterate personal enemies; but a wish to be serviceable to my country, is paramount to every other consideration.

I have indeed shown but little lenity to those men whom I have thought deserving of the lash. But I have been careful to bring forward no "railing accusation" against any man; and I am confident that these volumes contain nothing which is calculated to convey incorrect ideas of our public men and public measures.

In our Government, time was not allowed for the consolidation of its parts, nor was the value of the "machine" fairly tested by being put completely in motion, before our Gallatins began to clog "its wheels," and our Randolphs and Nicholsons now threaten to pull it to pieces, and to throw us into a state of society bordering on that of the savage. An exposition of their arts is absolutely incumbent on every man who possesses the means of information, and who holds the pen of a writer.

The people cannot be materially injured in their interest, unless they are deceived, and they cannot long be deceived, if as great efforts are made to enlighten thera by their true friends, as by their pretended friends to keep them in ignorance. It would be, indeed, a most infamous aspersion on the People of the United States, to insinuate, that *if they had known*, that many men who now fill the highest offices in government, were destitute of common honesty, they would have honoured them with their suffrages. Yet it is a fact, that the characters of many of them are stained with crimes of the deepest dies, and instead of being placed at the head of government, they deserve to be arraigned at the bar of justice.

With respect to the manner in which I have executed this Poem, I am sensible I shall not escape the shafts of the small critics, and doubtless, my faults will deserve the animadversion of those who are qualified successors of Louginus.[1]

---

1 Gentlemen of this description should not, however, pronounce a verdict without a proper attention to the merits of the cause. A Reviewer, in that respectable publication, the *Boston Monthly Anthology*, trips a little, in supposing that we have *stumbled* on an Anachronism.

"In the next Canto, Mobocracy," he tells us, "is an Anachronism of so little use that perhaps the author, so far from intercourse to derive advantage from it, in the hurry of comparison did not observe it. The rebellion of 1786 is perhaps one of the consequences of that spirit, excited by the revolutionary proceedings in France."

If the gentleman will examine that Canto more minutely, he will perceive that the spirit of the rebellion of 1786 is represented as *preparing the way* for the introduction of French revolutionary principles. It is true that the events alluded to in the Poem are not set down in chronological order, for that was not possible without destroying the connection of the Poem. The following lines will furnish him with a clue to the labyrinth of which he complains:

"Now, certain causes, most untoward.
Prepar'd the people to be fro ward," &c.
[P. 59, 1st & 2d edition.

After stating, among those causes, the half extinguished fire of rebellion in Massachusetts, the Poem proceeds:

"The smouldering flame in secret burn'd.

But do I then, (abjuring every aim)
All censure slight, and all applause disclaim?
Not so: where Judgment holds the rod, I bow
My humble neck, awed by her angry brow.
                                        GIFFORD.

I have divided the poetry, although of the Hudi-brastic kind, into four-line stanzas. For this singularity I am not positive I can justify myself. The division appeared to me to give the work an apophthegmatical appearance, and to facilitate the reading, and by (if I may be allowed an Americanism) locating each line with more precision than would otherwise be done, to assist the memory of the reader.

I am likewise aware, that I shall be accused of puns, alliterations, iterations, and other deviations from the precise path in which their reverences, the Critics, would fain have me walk.

With these grave fops, who, (bless their brains)
Most cruel to themselves, take pains
For wretchedness, and would be thought
Much wiser than a wise man ought
For bis own happiness to be,—
Who what they hear, and what they see,
And what they smell, and taste, and feel.
Distrust, "till Reason sets the seal."—

With whom

When Jefferson from France return'd," &c.
[P. 64, 1st & 2d edition.

xiv

"Not one idea is allow'd
To pass unquestion'd in the crowd,
But ere it can obtain a place
Of holding in the brain a place
Before the Chief in congregation,
Must stand a strict examination,"[2]

I shall not attempt to reason, but quietly await their sentence.

---

2   CHURCHILL.

Introduction

to

the Third Edition

The foregoing prefatory remarks were written for the first edition of the following Poem. The additions made to this impression, having doubled the size of the work, seem to require additional observations of an introductory nature. Some strictures, remarks, and hints for the improvement of this Poem, which were proffered on the appearance of the first edition, present, likewise, claims to attention, which I now respectfully beg leave to acknowledge, and will attempt to cancel.

I hate been accused of undue severity in the application of my satirical scourge; and some have affirmed that I appear disposed rather to *scarify* than to chastise in a reasonable manner those culprits, who are so unfortunate as to come under my lash. To such a charge I would reply in the language of Mr. Gifford, in his description of Anthony Pasquin, that some of the subjects of the following satire are *"so lost to every sense of decency and shame, as to he fitter objects for the headle than the muse."* Emollients, palliatives and even gentle caustics avail nothing when a gangrene has taken place; but when less powerful escharotics prove ineffectual, perhaps the clue application of *Lapis Infernalis* may preserve a defective limb from amputation.

To those whom I have thought myself in justice bound to expose on the Gibbet, I have no other apology to make for the treatment they have experienced than is contained in the following couplets:

>————————Enfin ton impudence
>Temeraire Viellard? aura sa recompence.[1]

>Miscreant, the scourge which you to day endure. Cuts to the bone—but then it cuts to cure.[2]

Those men, who hare "set the country and constitution in a blaze"[3] have no right to expect any thing eminently civil in return for such a favour. The Duanes, the Cheethams, and ihe Pasquins of

---

1   Boileau.

2   Gifford.

3   Hon. Fisher Ames.

our distracted country are as little entitled to that civility which regulates the intercourse of *gentlemen*, as are a band of night-prowling banditti to the courtesy of chivalry.[4]

It has likewise been urged that I have displayed but little of the "spirit of poetry"[5] in this produc-

---

4   "In a state of refinent an avoidance in company, a look of contempt, a silent glance of Indiginalion may prove a sufficient restraint to a person susceptible of the nicer feelings";* but a horde of Calmucks, or a gang of Democrats must be disciplined with more severity.

    * Chipman's *Principles of Government*.

5   So says a writer in the *Baltimore Evening Post* of July 24th, 1805. My excuse lor taking notice of such a compound of malice and stupidity may be found in page 7th note 11th of the following work. An English Satirist, in apologizing for having stooped to attack a malignant scribbler, declared, in substance, that it was not consistent with the true interests of literature that ignorant and malicious blockheads of that description should be forgotten—that they ought to be gibbetted for the scorn of the wise and the terror of fools.

    I should not, however, have been induced by the *folly* merely of this *Baltimore Evening Post* man to expose him, but his *sheer knavery*, demands the lash. A witling, who will *misquote* from iin autlior, in order to find fault with absurdities which did not originally exist, but were manufactured by the critic for the occasion, would not hesitate to comn it any other species of forgery, could fee hope to do it with impunity.

    After a *quantum sufficit* of prefatory nonsense, in which, among other things, he hugs himself for his sagacity in not calling "quotations" "criticisms," he vaults upon his Pegasus.

    That limps along, so heavy moulded.
    That *Sternhold's* self seems out-Sternholded.

    Here they go!

tion; have not poured from my

Other folks shall sound his fame
Who have or have not heard his name,
Ages unborn shall chaunt his praise.
And *Butler*'s self *begin* the lays.

He next accuses the author of *Democracy Unveiled* of tautology, because theorised and theorising both occur in the same Canto!

This man would, no doubt, have proved Pope a most egregious tautologist, for he says,

Where *wigs* with *wigs*, with *sword-knots sword-knots* strive.
Beaux banish *beaux*, and *coaches coaches* drive.

Of *various* habit and of *various* die, &c.

This forni'dable Critic proceeds to pass sentence of condemnation upon the rhymes, which happen not to suit his fancy. This is a specimen of his carping:

Philosophists Illuminati,
Beings of whom at any rate I.

If you sound (says he) the 'a' in 'illuminati' as in 'far' you will be sure not to make a rhyme."

In justification of this rhyme I shall not rely on the licence allowed in Hudibrastic verse, but shall give examples of greater liberties taken by the best architect of rhymes among the English Poets.

Of man, what see we but his station *here*.
From which to reason or to which *refer*

Pleas'd to the last he crops the flowery *food*,
And licks the hand just rais'd to shed his *blood*

O blindness to the future! kindly *given*,

That each may fill the circle mark'd by *heaven*.

Oh thou! whatever title please thine *ear*.
Dean, Drapier, Buckersiaff, or Gulli*ver*!

Now will this mole-eyed scribbler pretend that Pope did not understand rhyming; or would he have us believe that the rhymes must be more exact in Hudibrastic poetry, than in English Hexameter.

Again he informs us that "now how" and " pow wow," manage ill, and "ansel," "sedulity" and "credulity," "Louisiana" and "rainy," "Calcutta" and "about a," "nation" and "oppugnation," "treaty" and "yet he," are bad rhymes.

But we find such licences can be justified by the authority of authors of acknowledged merit, who have written the same species of poetry. In *Hudibras* we have the following:

When pulpit, drum *ecclesiastic*
Was beat with fist instead of *a stick*.

Quarrel with minc'd pies and *disparage*
Their best and dearest friend, plumb *porridge*.

Thus was he gifted and *accoutred*.
We mean on th'inside not the *outward*.'

It doth behove us to say *something*
Of that which bore our valiant *bumpkin*.

The bear is safe and out of *peril*,
Though lugg'd indeed and wounded very *ill*.

They count a vile abomi*nation*.
But not to slaughter a whole *nation*,

Instances of similar licences may be produced from Prior, Swift and Huddesford; but I forbear to enlarge; and should not have troubled the reader with these remarks had I not heard

————Big breast's prolific zone,
A proud poetic fervour, only known
To souls like theirs.

---

such objections urged by critics of more respectability than this Baltimore dabbler: But the malignity discovered by the misquotations shows that in him the heart of a Jacobin is united with the head of a sciolist.

In the first editions of *Democracy Unveiled* the following couplet occurs:

> Is it not true, he left no stones
> Unturn'd for—— Gabriel Jones.

The horizontal stroke, was intended to supply the place of a word descriptive of Jefferson's conduct in his transaction with Mr. Jones. But this honest critic has misquoted the couplet by leaving out the stroke, and declared that the defect was in the poem as it originally stood! Again he misquotes the following couplet:

> A single Jacobin, or scarce one
> More mischievous than this said *parson*,

the last word of which he has *altered* to "*person*," in order to find fault with the rhyme.

He next states what is not true about the English Reviews of "Terrible Tractoration," which he says "the English Reviewers mention in very vague terms indeed." The testimonies subjoined to this work will show the *falsehood* of that assertion. But I wash my hands of this

> Unfinish'd thing, one knows not what to *call*.
> His generation's so equivo*cal*;*

and if his folly is not superior to his malignity, he will keep out of my path in future.

* Pope's *Essay on Criticism*.

Or, in other words, have exhibited no signs of that madness, which half-wits mistake for poetic inspiration. To such I would beg again to reply in the words of Mr. Gifford:

> —————————————My lays
> That wake no envy, and invite no praise.
> Half creeping, and half flying, yet suffice
> To stagger impudence and ruffle vice.

Or, if my own language will be acceptable, I will repeat what I once before observed, when engaged in hunting down certain demagogues.

> Although my rambling muse, so airy,
> Is wild as Oberon the fairy.
> Her ladyship is forc'd to stoop,
> To hit the Jacobinic group,
> Must dig, and delve or take her aim
> A thousand leagues above her game.

I have preferred rhyme as a vehicle of my sentiments, chiefly, because I could express more, and impress certain, axioms, with more energy in the same number of words in rhyme than in prose. But flights of fancy were out of the question in wading through the disgusting details of individual enormity, which an attention to my subject rendered necessary. For the abundant use which I have made of notes, I have the example of some of the best English satirists, and may, perhaps, be allowed the apology of the author of the *Pursuits of Literatures*, who, speaking of satire, says, "as it is a view of life, designed to be presented to other times, as well as those in which it is written, the necessity of an author's furnishing notes to his own composition is evident, to clear up such difficulties as the lapse of time would unavoidably create."

I have been not a little amused by the suggestions of my friends respecting what might and ought to have been done for rendering this poem more complete. Some would have had me fabricate a production in the mock heroic stile, and fashioning a hero after the model of Don Quixotte, send him a tilting and tournamenting thro' the world, assailing the windmills, giants and dragons of democracy in the true stile of chivalry. Others would have me sit down and in sober sadness attempt to imitate the *Pursuits of Literature*. But with becoming deference to the opinion of such sage advisers, an author must be allowed the privilege of consulting his own genius, for "no man." says Swift, "ever made an ill figure, who understood his own talents, nor a good one who mistook them."

It has been objected to this poem, that the connection of its different parts is not sufficiently obvious: But in embracing a field so extensive as I have chosen, it would be found extremely difficult to proceed step by step like a mathematical demonstration. I am sure that the greater part of what I have written will be found to tend directly or indirectly to the main object of the poem, to strip the mask from democracy, and expose in their true colours the men, who are either ignorantly or maliciously busied in prostrating the pillars of social order, and whose disorganizing efforts threaten to deliver America, bound hand and foot, to domestic usurpers or foreign tyrants.[6]

I have followed no model in the construction of this poem, excepting so far as to observe the general rules of composition for Hudibrastic poetry. In my rhymes, I think I have been as exact as the best English authors, who have written poetry of this description. Indeed I hope the work, with all its faults, will serve as a sort of compendium of Federal principles, a key to facts, and a concise exposition of the arts of demagogues, and may enable some honest federalists to give a reason for the political faith which they profess.

I have, probably, been indebted for some of my ideas, and, possibly, some of my expressions, to authors to whom I may have omitted to give credit for their performances.[7] No man, however, has a more thorough contempt for a plagiarist than myself; but in the hurry of composition, I may have,

---

6   "There may be much diversity in the process, but the result is nearly the same; the chief difference is, that small states, generally, call in a master from abroad, and great nations make a master for themselves."
         Governor Strong's Speech

7   An acknowledgment to the Rev. Seth Parson, for some passages extracted from his tract, entitled *Proofs of the existence and dangerous tendency of Illuminism*, was, through accident, omitted in this edition.

inadvertently, stumbled on the sentiments of others, without being able to distinguish them from my own conceptions.

Repetitions of ideas and of words, in the following poem, frequently occur, and will, perhaps, subject me to the censure of critics. I thought, however, that it might be useful in some instances "to give line upon line." If I am wrong, in this particular, it is not owing to carelessness, but defect in judgment.

Many passages in the following pages will, perhaps, be thought of too trifling import to be allowed a place in a work which treats of some of the most important topics which can interest humanity. But for this I shall borrow an apology from Horace:

> Ego si risi quod ineptus Pastillos Rufillus olet,
> lividuset mordax videar?[8]

I believe there is no law in the code of legitimate criticism, which prohibits a poet from an *occasional* traffic in trifles. Besides the powers of serious argument and invective against our political back-sliders have been long since exhausted by the essayists of the day. Ridicule seems to be the only weapon which has not fallen blunted from the brazen buckler of Democracy, like the dart of Pria from the bosses of Pyrrhus.

---

8   I smile because the stupid Rufillus is scented with perfumes, must I be stigmatized as a man of an envious and malicious disposition.

I am sensible that I have presented to view some frightful pictures of political and moral depravity; but as they are drawn from the life, I cannot be implicated in their disgusting appearance. To those, who are inclined to suppose any part of the following publication libellous, I would observe that I, have not written with a view "to create animosities and disturb the public peace."[9] It is time that the community were well and truly informed of the characters of the principal performers on our political theatre; and if we cannot draw the curtain without the appearance of a "Castle Spectre" let us in earnest set about exorcising the land of the demons which infest us.

Every man, who has any thing at stake in society, is equally concerned with myself in the topics which are brought into view in the following production. Men of property, and men whose talents and industry afford them a reasonable prospect of its acquisition, are interested to the amount of their possessions and prospects in a regular, efficient and just government. If our *political rights* are undefined and insecure, our *civil rights*, among which is the right of property, will not long be respected. If the fountain head be contaminated, the streams cannot remain pure; and if our public affairs are badly conducted, individual distress will be the consequence. The anxiety which some of our luke-warm federalists show for the acquisition of property, while those institutions, which alone

---

9   Blacksiones *Com*, B, 4. Ch. I

can protect them in its enjoyment, are crumbling to pieces about them, is not unlike the sagacity of a *profound* gentleman, who, when his house was burning, was very active in placing for security his valuable effects in a closet which made a part of the edifice on fire. Professional men, men of education, all who possess talents or acquirements which entitle them to distinction in society, are called on to put a stop to the work of destruction commenced by the party now in power, and progressing under the auspices of our Randolphs, Nichoisons and Duanes.

The theme which I have chosen in the following work, has been not a little hacknied. The subject of American politics has commanded the attention of the philosophers and literati of all nations. It cannot, therefore, be expected that I have either exhausted the subject, or that my labours have produced any thing which can lay claim to the merit of novelty. My book contains but an abstract of what might be said, it is merely a sort of a horn-book of Federal politics, but I hope, so far as it goes, it is correct and will be useful. It has been the result of much investigation. I have taken great pains to ascertain facts, and I believe my allusions and assertions are always supported by them. I have not drawn my bow at random, but if I know my own heart, I have had a single eye to the public good, even in those attacks which are most personal. If I have offended one really good man it will be to me a subject of lasting regret, and I will make any reparation in my power. But bad men are fair game, and "I will not be intimidated by the war whoop of Jacobins and Democratic writers, or the feeble shrieks of witlings and poetasters,"[10] from attacking those who are foes to rational freedom and to my country.

I would have printed the additions which I have made to this impression separately, had it been consistent with the general plan of this work. But a *poetical appendix* would be truly an aukward appendage to a poem.—When I published the last edition, I did not contemplate making, *immediately* any additions to the work as it then stood. But finding in New-York sources of information of which I could not so conveniently avail myself in my former situation, and conceiving that I had, but glanced at many subjects, which required more mature consideration, I was induced to proceed without delay in the prosecution of the plan, which I had at first in view, provided the poem met with the patronage of the public.

In the second Canto, entitled Illuminism, I have attempted merely a sketch of those principles, which have given the democracy of our own times that dreadful and systcmatic malignancy, which distinguishes it from the revolutionizing efforts of former ages. I have likewise opposed, with the little powers I possess the torrent of infidelily, which threatens to overwhelm the moral world. I cannot but flatter myself that this part of my labours will

---

10   *Pursuits of Literature.*

meet with the approbation of those whose duly it is to warn their fellow-men against the "cold and flippant scepticism which damps our hopes, removes tjie sanctions of morality, chills domestic happiness, destroys the obligations of social order, and builds up the philosophy of vanity on the subversion of the altars of God."[11]

"Literature, well or ill conducted," (says that consummate writer, the author of the *Pursuits of Literature*) "is the great engine, by which I am fully persuaded all civilized States must ultimately be suppoited or overthrown." The word *Literature* ought to be taken in its most comprehensive sense, including whatsoever is presented to the world through the medium of the press. It was by the agency of prostituted presses that our demagogues have obtained their ruinous ascendency. It was by the means of the press that the impious tenets of the French philosophists prepared the way for those desolating scenes of anarchy, which cannot be paralleled in history. It was the interposition of the press;—the patriotic exertions of such writers as Edmund Burke, and the author of the *Pursuits of Literature*, aided by the timely efforts of a few individuals, which prevented similar scenes in Great Britain. It is only by a servile press that tyrants and demagogues can, in the present state of society, support themselves in power. I re-

---

11   Henry Yorke, Esq. quoted from the oration of Mr. Lewis, pronounced before the Connecticut Society of Cincinnati, July 4, 1799.

peat it, no people can be enslaved unless they are *deceived.*—How great then ought to be the force of public indignation against those men, who prostitute literan tal ents to the purposes of a party. An Editor of a party paper, who, knowingly, gives currency to falsehoods, ought to be shunned as a monster of crime; for, if we are to estimate the enormity of a criminal from the consequences which his crimes produce in society, one such editor with the kind of abilities which even Democrats ascribe to their friend Duane, is more to be dreaded *than a whole colony of convicts.* The *people* ought immediately to put it out of the power of such wretches to injure society, by withdrawing from them their confidence, and refusing to pay for their vehicles of falsehood. If the voice of public opinion should not pronounce a sentence of outlaivry against such enormous culprits, we shall soon find ourselves "*fooled* out of our security, *fooled* out of our happiness; and when we have lost every blessing *beyond recovery,* we shall look round at each other in a stupid despair, clashing our chains and unable to shake them off, and ask, "How has all this been brought about?"[12]

The pillars which secure the fabric of society in America are placed on a less solid foundation than in older countries. In England, in a particular manner, there are certain *estahlished* principles, which are considered as the *basis* of their government; not written article by article like a Bill of Rights, but

12   *Pursuits of Literature.*

their evidences rest in writing, sanctioned by the practice of ages, understood and respected, and no Randolph or Nicholson dare infringe on them. In America *public opinion* must, in a great measure, supply the place of long established precedents, and form the chain which binds together society. It is, therefore, all-important, that the public mind should be correctly informed, and any attempt to misinform, and by that means mislead the public, should be considered as a blow aimed at the vitals of society, and the propagators of such falsehoods ought to be esteemed as foes to their country, to freedom and to mankind.

I consider myself as having brought a set of culprits to trial before the tribunal of *public opinion*. Their guilt is clear beyond all dispute, for I come armed with proofs and documents, which must make it manifest to every capacity. If there is not virtue and independence enough in the *court* to condemn them, the country is ripe for that despotism, which will not fail to await us, preluded by *anarchy*, and accompanied by all the horrors, which attend a revolutionary slate of society.

The Tocsin

The wight, who led the Royal College
To furious fight, which all acknowledge
Exceeded, nineteen times to one,
All battles else beneath the sun.
Commences war with certain brats.
Who style themselves *good* Democrats,
Although in ten there's more than nine,
Just nine times worse than Cataline!
And first begins, sans any coaxing,
To sound his ruin-boding tocsin;
An awful prelude to the battle.
He means to wage with such vile cattle.

Devoid of influence or fear,
I trace Democracy's career,
And paint the vices of the times,
While bad men tremble at my rhymes;

And I'll unmask the Democrat,
Your sometimes this thing, sometimes that,[1]

---

1   I here have reference to the different appearances, which our
     Antifederalists, alias Democrats, alias Republicans, alias "gen-
     uine" ditto (for the man who manages the Aurora makes two
     divisions of these self denominated friends to the people) have
     assumed in the evanescent stages of their political existence.
     But more of this hereafter.

Whose life is one dishonest shuffle,
Lest he pechance the mob[2] should ruffle;

And who by *public good*, intends
Whatever subserves his *private* ends,

---

2   I would make a distinction, which I think of the highest im-
portance, between the *people*, and the *mob*, or *populace*. By
the latter, I would designate certain of the lowest class in the
community, who are alike destitute of property and of prin-
ciple, and may be emphatically stiled the rabble. These, in
America, consist principally of imported desperadoes, who
have made this country an "asylum," and having nothing to
lose, are wishing

> . . . . "To turn the world up-
> Side down to put themselves a top."
> *Trumbulls's Mc Fingal.*

These are the kind of beings to whom the Mantuan Bard
alluded in the following naost exquisite simile:

> *Ac veluti magno in populo cum scepe coorta est,*
> *Seditio, sævitque animis ignobile vulgus;*
> *Jamque faces et saxa volant; furor arma ministrat.*

> As when in tumults rise th' ignoble cVowd,
> Mad are their motions, and their tongues are loud:
> And stones and brands in rattling volleys fly,
> And all the rustic amis which fury can supply;
> *Dryden.*

By the people, I mean the great body of American farmer's,
merchants, mechanics, &c. who, possessing habits of industry,
and our primitive New England manners, may be considered
as the *stamina* of republicanism.

And bawls for freedom, in his high rant,
The better to *conceal the tyrant*.[3]

Determin'd I'll do what I can do,
And pray what more can mortal man do?
For weal and welfare of our nation,
And this backsliding generation.

I'll blow my shrewd satiric horn,
The taunting finger point of scorn
A *vice* and *folly, fools* and *knaves*;[4]
It *must be done or we be slaves.*

In Tom Paine's *Rights of Man* no smatterer[5]
The people's *friend?*, but not their *flatterer*;

---

3   In characterising the now prevailing party, I would not af-
    firm that they are at heart *all tyrants*, but that their leaders
    are, generally speaking, haughty and imperious demagogues.
    Like the genuine-republican-slave-driving-nabobs of Virgin-
    ia, who would fain conceal their designs of domination be-
    neath the mask of liberty, and a pretended zeal for the rights
    of the people.

4   "Satire never can have effect without a personal application. It
    must come home to the bosoms, and often to the offences of
    particular men."
        Pursuits of Literature.

5   Nothing ever yet written, can be more directly calculated for
    sapping the foundations of society, than the productions of
    this demoralizing scribbler. He has indeed mixed *some truth*
    with his falsehood, and *now and then correct reasoning* with
    his *school-boy sophistry*. But his writings, in general, are
    much better calculated for *dissolving*, than for cementing the
    social compact.

I'll not electioneer nor job,
Adore sage Mammoth, nor king mob.

For Chronicle abuse I care not;[6]
But I will cry aloud and spare not,
The tyrant Democrat unveil,
Though damn'd for such a damning tale.[7]

Those who assume, at Faction's call,
A Right t' infringe on rights of all,[8]
Who swear all honesty a hum,[9]

---

6 The author has been honoured somewhat liberally with the abuse of the *Chronicle* scribblers. They have, among other lies affirmed that he was imported," under "British influence," &c.

7 I would not use the epithet damn'd, in a profane sense, but in the sense it is used when we speak of temporal evils only, or in the sense of Mr. Gifford, who speaking of the productions of illiterate scribblers, says, they are

"Works damn'd, or to be damn'd."

8 See a Charge delivered lo the Grand Jury in Pennsylvania, by the Honourable Alexander Addison, in which the distinction between liberty and licentiousness, the dangers to be apprehended from the tyranny of the MANY, ever more dreadful than thatof the FEW, are pointed out in a perspicuous and masterly manner.

9 Declarations to this effect, I have repeatedly heard made by those who stiled themselves good Democrats, friends to the people, real patriots, &c. &c. That there is no such thing honesty in politics; that in the scramble for power, bad means were justifiable to obtain the good end in view, to wit, the aggrandizement of the party making use of such means; that they have ever acted in conformity to these tenets, an impartial history of the party will amply testify.

Who rise because the'y are the scum.[10]

May hide their heads, for I determine,
To set my foot upon the vermin,
Except some creeping knaves exempt,
Who have not risen to contempt![11]

A mortal foe to fools and rogues,
Your Democrats and demagogues,
Who've sworn they will not leave us a brick.
Of freedom's blood cemented fabric.

---

10   "When the political pot boils, the scum rises."

11   Such little things, for instance, as Anthony Haswell, editor of a newspaper at Bennington, Vermont, parson Griswold, the Walpole *Observatory*-man, upon whom I could wish never to be under the disagreeable necessity of wasting a line. I may, however, be compelled to bestow some share of my attention on these and other animalculæ of the fry of sedition. An asp is an animal apparently quite insignificant, but its bite may be as fatal af the paw of a lion. Perhaps Federalists have carried their contempt of these grub worms of faction too far. There are many, among both our great and little vulgar, who cannot *comprehend* a sentence of correct English, if it chance to contain an idea; but are quite "up to any thing," which may be drivelled from the noddle of Tony Haswell, or Do. Pasquin. The attempting to hew blocks with razors, is a very foolish affair. The more *knowing* Democrats, who lead by the nose the simpletons of the party, are sensible of it. They therefore work upon their thick-headed supporters, with such sorry tools as the pair of Tonies aforesaid, parson Griswold, &c.

    The attempting to hew blocks with razors, is a Yery foolish affair. The more *knowing* Democrats, who lead by the nose the simpletons of the party, are sensible of it. They therefore work upon their thick-headed supporters, with such sorry tools as the pair of Tonies aforesaid, parson Griswold, &c.

I'll search in Democratic annals,
Elicit truth from dirty channels,
Describe *low* knaves in *high* condition,
Though speaking truth[12] is deem'd sedition.

I would not, willingly, omit
One *scoundrel*, high enough to hit,
But should I chance to make omission,
I'll put him in my next edition.

But still with caution will refrain
From giving *honest people* pain;
And only *private vice* unmask,
Where *public good* require the task.

I would not wantonly annoy . . . .
No good man's happiness destroy;

---

12   It is indeed wonderful, (if any thing in the annals of Democracy can be so) that Democrats should, without a blush, affirm that the Sedition Law was "Law against Constitution." Yet they have not only frequently asserted this among other lies, but have represented it as a most horrible engine of tyranny, fabricated by the Federalists, for no other purpose but to oppress the people! And this was once among many other still more atrocious falsehoods, which has formed the basis of their political consequence. The fact is, that this law not only mitigated the rigour of Common Law on that subject, but guarantied to the American Citizen an important riprht, which, under the drmination of the now ruling party, he is not permitted to exercise.

     A prosecution has been instituted against Harry Croswell, for a libel, but our Democratic liberty and equality gentlemen in office, would not permit the defendant to prove the *truth* of the matter alledged to be libellous!!

None lives, I say, with honest pride, who
Despises *slander* more thaft I do.

But when *vile convicts* make pretence
To power and public confidence,
The indignant Muse of satire urges
he *honest bard* to ply her scourges.

And therefore be it known to all,
That though the risk I run's not small,[13]
I'll lash each knave that's now in vogue,
Merely because he is a rogue;[14]

And hope at least to pull the pride down,
Of those, who our best men have *lied* down,[15]

---

13 The person who in these times dares to rend the veil of Democracy, and disclose the demon in his naked deformity, must expect that the worshippers of that infernal idol, will vow vengeance on his devoted head. The sword of the duellist, it is to be feared, may merely precede the dagger of the assassin. But it is the duty of every real Republican, to be ready, like the Roman Curtius, to plunge into the gulf, and sacrifice himself to save his country.

14 I am no farther a foe to any of the characters who are the subjects of the following Satirical Strictures than as they are foes to good order, morality, and to my native country. Personal animosity is not among the motives which produced this Poem.

15 Reader, I will here present thee with one among nany specimens, of the adroitness of our self-styled friends to the people, in the art and mystery of political lying.

At the time that our Envoys to France, Messrs. Marshall, Pinckney and Gerry, were insulted by those infamous propositions, from the French Directory, made through the medium

And have contriv'd, the rogues, to rise
By arts, which honest men despise.

Unite your force then, Chronicleers,
Withthosewhohave,orhavenot . . . .ears . . . ,
The Ægis-man, and both the Tonies,
May join with half a dozen Honees.

Come, Cheetham, Duane, Smith and Pasquin,
In presidential favour basking;
With all your scoundrel gang affords,
Who straddle poles, or wear wood swords;

Imported patriots, whose fit station
Should be that kind of elevation,
Which happens oft to rogues, less callous,
When they're *exalted* on the gallows;

I hope your *knaveships* won't refuse,

---

of X. Y. and Z. which justly excited the indignation, not only of
America, but of all Europe, it was promulgated by good Dem-
ocrats among their ignorant supporters, that the dispatches
from our Plenipotentiaries, were forged by Federalists at Phil-
adelphia, for the purpose of throwing an odium on our great
and magnanimous sister republic!! This impudent falsehood
answered good democratic purposes. A full bloode'd Jacobin
was sent to Congress, in retaliation of the aforesaid Federal
forgery!!

This however is only one in a million. A long life devoted to
the express purpose of detecting the falsehoods of the deceitful
demagogues, who have crowded themselves into consequence,
would be too short a period for that purpose; but

"Half the tale must be untold."

To *honor* me with your abuse;
But let not these, my *modest* lays,
Be blasted by a scoundrel's praise; . . . .

For since my country's good demands
Thig piece of *justice* from my hands,
I'll string you up, *sans ceremonie*,
From Duane down to dirty *Tony*.[16]

No threats, nor growling, shall prohibit
My hanging you on satire a gibbet;
Expos'd in dolorous condition,
Like flies impall'd by old Domitian.[17]

Now, since ye are a ruffian crew
As honest Jack Ketch ever knew;
Have chang'd your names, as well as courses,
Like folks who trade . . . . in stealing horses;

I'll take each Demo, and expose his
Form in his each metempsychosis,
Though he assumes as many shapes
As Jove for managing his rapes.

As Tories many of you vex'd us;[18]

---

16 These pure patriots shall receive, with those men.

17 We are informed by historians, that this Emperor amused his
    leisure hours, by impaling flies on the point of a needle.

18 Nothing can exceed in impudence the Democratic falsehood,
    sooften repeated, that the Federalists were Tories under Brit-
    ish influence &c.; when the truth is, that the Federalists were,

As Antifederals then perplex'd us;
And, ever bent upon confusion,
Oppos'd the Federal Constitution;

And then, camelion like, vile brats!
You call'd yourselves good Democrats;
And next to drive deception's game,
Self-styl'd Republicans . . . . For shame!

And when by dint of different phases,
You crowd into your betters' places:
Republicans, by process curious,
Are split to "genuine" and "spurious."

But after all these shifts . . . . you rogues!
You're nothing more than demagogues,
And bawl for freedom, in your high rant,
The better to conceal the tyrant![19]

---

most generally, active supporters of American Independence, while Jefferson was hiding himself in the cave of the mountain, and Tench Coxe was piloting the British army into Philadelphia.

19   This couplet has before occurred, but our predecessors, Homer and Virgil, were much addicted to iterations of this kind. The reader may please to consider it as the *Incite Mixnalios mecum mca tibia versus* of this Poem.

Illuminism[1]

We now the origin will trace
Of that dire pest to human race,
That freedom, with which France was curst,[2]
Ere Bonapart, the bubble burst:
The fiend exorcise from our land,
Who erst, with desolating hand,
Bade Democrats, a horrid train,
Half Europe "heap with hills of slain."

here was a gaunt Genevan priest,[3]
Mad as our New Lights are at least,[4]
Much learning had, but no pretence

---

1 No doubt every hound in the Democratic pack, will open upon
me, for introducing in this place they would call the phantom
of Illuminism. But *scriptæ literæ manent*. There are certain
damning facts, which, with all their shuffling ingenuity, and
sneaking evasions, will ever stare them in the face. They nev-
er have been able to prove, that either the Abbe Barruel, of
Professor Robison, (who with a great number of other credible
witnesses have testified to the existence of Illuminism and its
damning tendency) were weak or wicked men, were deceived
themselves, or entertained a wish to deceive others. Besides,
the documents which have been adduced, and the multitude
of corroborating circumstances, which go to prove that this
mystery of iniquity has a real existence, cannot fail to enforce

To wisdom, or to common sense.

conviction on the minds of the most credulous. How far the developement of the plans of the Illuminati by Professor Robison and others may have induced them to defer the execution of their nefarious projects, it is impossible to determine. They may, perhaps, be resting on their oars, and watching, till the popular current, shall set m their favour. It certainly behoves those who wish well to society, who prefer the social to the *savage state*, and who would not wish that America should realize all the horrors of the most bloody revolutions recorded in history, to keep a watchful eye over the motions of this most infernal of all JUNTOS.

I know there are many of our politicians, who seem determined not to believe that Illuminism to any dangerous extent has ever existed in America, and that its influence in Europe has been much less than has by many been apprehended. I wish for the honor of human nature that there was less proof of the existence of such a combination. As the fact of the existence, or at least of the pernicious tendency of Illuminism, is by our democrats generally denied, I shall confine myself in this note to the establishment of the credibility of one of the principal witnesses in convicting this nefarious gang of their diabolical conspiracy.

As Dr. Robison is a principal evidence in the cause now pending, it will be necessary to enquire, whether we have a just view of the man. The result of this inquiry, will serve to give the public some idea of the means which have been made use of to discredit Illuminism, and how benevolently disposed some among us are, to prevent their countrymen from being misled by what are called, the ridiculous reveries of Robison. The reader's patience, it is feared, will be exhausted by the detail of credentials which the effrontery of his accusers have rendered necessary; but the character of a witness is of the first importance. The following sketch of the principal events of the life of Dr. Robison, was drawn up from authentic documents,

This crazy wight, by some mischance,

received directly from Edinburgh, through a respectable channel.*

The father of the Professor, a respectable country gentleman, intended him for the church, and gave him eight years of an University education at Glasgow. Prefering a different profession, he accepted an offer of going into the Navy, with very flattering prospects. He was appointed Mathematical Instructor to his Royal Highness the Duke of York. In that office, he accordingly entered the Navy in February, 1759, being that day twenty years old. He was present at the siege of Quebeck. With the late Admiral Knowles, he was particularly connected, and his son, afterwards captain Knowles, one of the most promising young officers in the British Navy, was committed to his charge.

In 1761, he was sent by the board of Admiralty, to make trial of Harrison's Watch at Jamaica. At the peace of 1763, he returned to College. In 1764, he was again appointed by the Admiralty to make trial of Harrison's improved Watch at Barbadoes; but his patron, Lord Anson, being dead, and the conditions not such as pleased him, he declined the employment, returned again to College, and took under his care the only remaining son of his friend, Sir Charles Knowles. This son is the present Admiral Sir Charles Knowles.

In 1770, Sir Charles was invited by the Empress of Russia to take charge of her Navy. He took Mr. Robison with him as his Secretary. In 1772, Mr. Robison was appointed superintendant of the education in the Marine Caslet Corps, where he had under his direction about 500 youth, 350 of whom were sons of noblemen and gentlemen, and 26 masters in the different studies. The Academy being burnt, Mr. Robison, with his pupils, removed to an ancient palace of Peter the Great at Constradt, a most mis-

Had rights to prosecute in France;

erable, desolate island, where, finding no agreeable society, he availed himself of the first opportunity, of quitting so unpleasant a situation, and accepted an invitation from the Magistrates of Edinburgh, to the Professorship of Natural Philosophy in the University in that city, which ranks among the first Universities in the world. To this very honorable office he acceded in August, 1774, and from that time continued his lectures, without interruption, till 1792, when illness obliged him to ask for an assistant. To enable him to give such a salary to his assistant, as would make the place worth the acceptance of a man of talents, the King was pleased to give him a pension of 100l. a year. After five years confinement, by a painful disor der, he resumed his chair, in 1797.

In 1796, he was elected a member of the Philosophical Society at Philadelphia, of which Mr. Jefferson is President; and in 1797, a member of the Royal Society of Manchester. In 1799, after the publication of his book, the University of Glasgow, where he received his education, conferred on him, unsolicited, the honor of a Doctor's degree in Law, in which, contrary to the usual custom in these cases, is given a very particular and flattering account of his nine years studies in that University. This peculiar evidence of esteem and respect was given in this way, in order that his Diploma might have all the civil consequences which long standing could give. When he published his book, in 1797, he was Secretary of the Royal Society of Edinburgh. In April, 1800, without solicitation of a single friend, he was unanimously elected a Foreign Member (there are but six) of the Imperial Academy of Sciences, at St. Petersburg, which, in point of reputation, is esteemed the third on the continent of Europe in the room of the much lamented and highly celebrated Dr. Black. To prepare for the press and superintend the publication of the Che mical writings of

By legal subterfuge was cheated,

this great man, required the ablest Chemist in Great Britain. This distinguished honour has been conferred on Professor Robison, who has undertaken this important work. This appointment, for which no man perhaps is more competent, together with the numerous, learned, and copious articles which he has furnished for the *Encyclopedia Britanica*, fully evince that in reputation and solid learning, he ranks among the first literary characters in Europe. Add to all this, *he sustains a* MORAL *character, so fair and unblemished, that any man may safely be challenged to lay any thing to his charge of which an honest man need be ashamed.*

The following account of Professer Robison, is from a work entitled *Literary Memoirs of Living Authors of Greet Britain*, 8cc. in two volumes, 8vo, published in London, 1798, for R. Faulder:

John Robison, Esq. M. A. Secretary of the Royal Society at Edinburgh, and Professor of Natural Philosophy, in the University. Professor Robison is distinguished for his accurate and extensive knowledge, especially on subjects of science. He contributed to the *Encyclopedia Britanica* the valuable articles. Physics Pneumatics, Precession of the Equinoxes, Projectiles, Pumps, Resistance of Fluids, River, Roof, Rope-making, Rotation, Seamanship, Signals, Sound, Specific Gravity, Statics, steam, Steam-Engine, Strength of Materials, escope, Tide, Articulating-Trumpet, Variation of Compass, and Water-works, also Philosophy, in association with Dr. Gleig.

In the autumn of the year 1797, Professor Robison published an octavo volume, entitled *Proofs of a Conspiracy*, &c. This volume has been favourably received, and although too hasty a performance for a work of so much consequence, is well entitled, both

By pettifogging knaves, mal-treated;

from its subject and its authenticity, to the serious attention of every reader. It arrives at the same remarkable conclusion as the celebrated *Memoirs* of the Abbe Barruel, illustrating the history of Jacobinism, though the authors were perfectly unconnected with each other, and pursued their enquiries in very different ways. It has raised (we are sorry for such an appearance) a considerable clamour and enmity against the Professor; though it was written, we are fully convinced from the best of motives. We cannot conclude this article without observing that the principles, and honest zeal which Professor Robison has displayed upon this occasion, are highly creditable to him, and merit the warmest acknowledgments from society in general.

*   Concerning the facts contained in this historical sketch, which were communicated to Dr. Erskine, he writes thus; "The most important facts in it I have had access to know, being first settled at Kirkintillock, the neighbouring parish to Boderoch, where lay the estate of his worthy father. For the few facts of which I know less, full and unexceptionable vouchers can be produced."

2   I shall in the additional notes at the end of the volume endeavour to point out the connection between Illuminism and those causes which produced the French revolution, and the present establishment of tyranny in France.

3   Jean Jaques Rousseau, the father of modern Democracy. For some further account of the levelling tenets of this profligate wretch, see Abbe Barruel's *History of Jacobinism*, vol. 2. chap. iii. and Rosseau's *Confessions*.

4   By New Lights, I mean not merely the particular sect or denomination of fanatics, who are known exclusively by that appellation; but all your itinerant, ignorant, bawling, field and barn preachers, whatever may be their professed tenets, who go about "creeping into men's houses, leading captive silly women," exerting themselves to destroy regular and estab-

Found foppish Frenchmen as they were
Delineated by Voltaire;[5]
Polish'd their manners, yet insidious,
Professing friendship, still perfidious.

But since they were, by reputation,
A most polite and gallant nation,
And since the fickle, fluttering elves,
Were almost worshipp'd . . . . by themselves;

'T was thence concluded, by Rosseau,

---

lished societies, alienating the minds of the people from their established pastors, to their sacred office. These wretches are generally demagogues, and the characters of most of them stained with vices.

Fanatics have ever been, like Cromwell and his faction, fomenters of that spirit of turbulence and insurrection which leads to anarchy, and invariably terminates in despotism.

Most of the *bawling* Itinerants who have fallen within the sphere of our observation, are perfectly French in their politics. They have been correctly-described in the following lines:

> Most true it is, though passing odd,
>   That this our godly band,
> Have join'd the men WITHOUT A GOD,
>   And imps of Talleyrand.

But we have-another pill for them in our 5th Canto.

5 Voltaire, in some of his writings, has affirmed in substance, that his countrymen were a strange compound of the subiilty of the Monkey and the ferocity of the Tiger. That in his time, they were amusing themselves and others by their apish airs, but that he foresaw the time in which they would put off the Monkey and put on the Tiger, to the infinite annoyance of mankind. Here it seems that "Saul was among the prophets!"

17

That *all refinement* did but go
To alter nature's simple plan.
And *scoundrelize* the creature man . . . .

From whence he madly theoriz'd,
That man were best *uncivilized*,
Like those philosophers, who prate.
Of Innocence in savage state.[6]

---

6   I cannot resist the temptation of transcribing, from Guthrie's
     [*A*] *Tour* [*performed in the Years 1795-96*] *through the Tau-
     rida, or Crimea, the ancient kingdom of Bosphorus,*" &c. the
     following remarks, relative to this savage sort of innocence,
     with which the founders of Democracy in Europe, and our
     American Jacobins, seem so highly enamoured.

         We saw nothing in passing lliis extensive stept
     or plain, but an immense extent of pasturage, well
     adapted for the wide range of these Nomades, (sav-
     age inhabitants) with their flying camps and numer-
     ous herds. But it is by no means with a mind at case,
     that one passes through the country of a people, who
     have kept the surrounding nations, for ages, in con-
     tinual alarms by their predatory excursions.
         It is imposible, in a tour through the wilds of
     Scythia, not to smile at the ideas which speculat-
     ing philosophers, from their cabinets, have spread
     abroad on the innocence and happiness of the pasto-
     ral state; probably by confounding men who follow
     the occupation of shepherds in civil society, with the
     shepherds of Holy Writ, and the pastoral Tartars or
     Arabs, who have, at different periods, drenched the
     world in blood, and put whole nations to the sword.
     This ridiculous ignorance is of a piece with the eu-
     logiums of the same speculatists on man in a state
     of nature, whorn we are sorry to acknowledge, after
     the new light thrown on the subject by our late cir-
     cumnavigators, joined with other circumstances, to

E'en took it in his crazy noddle,
A *savage* was *perfection's* model;
And nature without cultivation,
The *ne plus ultra* of creation.

Anticipated, happy dealings,
When mankind *rul'd* by *social feelings*,[7]

---

be the most savage and dangerous animal in nature,
often feeding on his vanquished enemies. *We find
however what he is always mild, humane, and ra-
tional, in proportion to his ad vancement to civili-
zation; although even that seems to have its limits,
after which he again becomes a savage.* OF THIS WE
HAVE A RECENT INSTANCE IN THE MOST HIGHLY POL-
ISHED NATION OF EUROPE, DESTROYING ALL HUMAN
AND DIVINE INSTITUTIONS.

The state of society which is here described, *is precisely that
which Democracy let loose, would introduce into this coun-
try.* But our most refined Democrats appear to have a wish to
save the intermediate stages which the French have passed;
and, by "Destroying all human and divine institutions," step
into a *state of nature* at once.

7 See Rousseau's *Emilius*, Godwin's *Political Justice*, and oth-
er writings of the canting philosophists of the same school.
It is one of the inconsistencies of these black-hearted, and
wrong-headed enthusiasts, to be ever prating about maintain-
ing society without law or subordination, by the *social feelings*
while they are busily employing themselves to annihilate those
feelings. But I cannot better express my ideas on this subject,
than in the following words of Professor Robison:

    Indeed of all the consequences of Illumination,
    the most melancholy, is the revolution which it
    seems to operate in the heart of man. The forcible
    sacrifice of every affection of the heart to an ideal di-
    vinity, a mere creature of the imagination. It seems

Would be perfected, sans a flaw,
Without the *Tyranny of Law.*

From such *sagacious* theorizing,
Was form'd a plan of his devising,
By which society destroy 'd
Perfection might be unalloy'd.

Indeed this arch illuminator
Seem'd fitted by the hand of Nature
To change the tone of public mind.
And revolutionize mankind.

Good reader we'll attempt to etch
A short characteristic sketch

---

a prodigy, yet it is a matter of experience, that the farther we advance, or vainly suppose that we do advance in the knowledge of our mental powers, the more are our moral feelings flattened and done away. I remember reading, long ago, a Dissertation on the Nursing of Infants by a French Academician, Le Cointre, of Versailles. He indelicately supports his theories, by the case of his own son, a weak, puny infant, whom his mother was obliged to keep continually applied to her bosom, so that she rarely could get two hours of sleep during the time of suckling him. M. Le Cointre says, that she contracted for this infant, *une partialité tout á-fait deraisonable.* Plato, Socrates, or Cicero, wquld probably have explained this by the habitual exercise of pily, a very endearing emotion. But our Academician, better illuminated, solves it by *stimuli*, on the papillae, and on the nerves of the skin, and by the meeting of the humifying aura, &c. and does not seem to think that young Le Cointre was much indebted to his mother.

Of this strange compound of a man.
Prime mover of the illumin'd clan.

But will not represent the elf,
Worse than he has pourtray 'd himself.
What time he utter'd his concessions,
His Edmund Randolph-like "Confessions."[8]

---

8   Rousseau wrote a book, with the title of *The Confessions of J. J. Rousseau*, and a very precious legacy is therein bequeathed to mankind. The outlines of our short sketch of his character are taken chiefly from these memoirs. A writer in the *Encyclopaedia Britannica* has the following remarks on that performance.

"In the preface to these memoirs, which abound with characters well drawn, and written with warmth, with energy, and sometimes with elegance, he presumes" (says M. Palissot)

> like a peevish misanthrope, who boldly introduces himself on the ruins of the world, to declare to mankind, whom he supposes assembled upon these ruins, that in that innumerable multitude, none could dare to say I am better than that man. This affectation of seeing himself alone in the universe, and of continually directing every thing to himself, may appear to some morose minds a fanaticism of pride of which we have no examples, at least since the time of Cardan. But this is not the only blame which may be attached to the author of the *Confessions*. With uneasiness we see him, under the pretext of sincerity dishonour the character of his benefactress, lady Warrens,

&c. Again the same writer remarks. "It is certain that if Rousseau has given a faithful delineation of some persons, he has viewed others through a cloud, which formed in his mind perpetual suspicions. He imagined he thought and spoke truly; but the simplest thing in nature," says M. Servant, "if distilled through his violent and suspicious hand, might become poison."

He was, by 's own account, at once
An artful, and a stupid dunce,
Fickle and sullen, airy, grave,
A fool, philosopher, and knave.[9]

A very proper person truly to write political essays, "Social compacts," &c. to which mankind are to have recourse for standards in forming a government, and political societies.

9   The odd mixture of heterogeneous qualities, which distinguished this singular character is thus described by himself. Speaking of an Interview with a patron, who designed to promote him if found worthy of promotion, he thus describes his own behaviour and that of his friend.

He took an excellent method of making me chatter, spoke freely with me, put me under as little restraint as possible, talked to me of trifles and on all sorts of subjects; all without seeming to observe me, without the least affectation, and as if pleased with me, he would converse without restraint. I was delighted with him. The result of his observations was, that, whatever my exterior and ray animated physiognomy might promise, I was if not absolutely a fool, at least a boy of very little sense, without ideas, almost without acquirements; in a word, a very shallow fellow in all respects, and that the honor of becoming the parson of a village, was the greatest fortune I ought to aspire to. This was the second or third time I was thus judged, it was not the last.

He explains this stupidity in the following manner:

Two things almost inalliable, unite in me, without my being able to perceive the manner. A constitution extremely violent, impetuous and lively passions, and ideas slowly produced, confused, and which never offer till after the proper time. Yon would think my heart and mind do not belong to the same indi-

A mixture odd of jarring qualities

vidual. Sentiment, quicker than light fills my soul, but instead of enlightening, fires and dazzles me. I feel every thing and see nothing. I am transported but stupid; I must be cool to think. What astonishes is that I have my feeling pretty sure, penetration, and even delicate wit, provided they'll wait for me: I can make an excellent impromptu, at leisure, but in an instant I never wrote or said any thing clever.

Thence comes the extreme difficulty I find in writing. My manuscripts scratched, blotted, mixed, not legible, attest the trouble they cost me. Not one, but I was obliged to transcribe four or five times before it went to the press. I never could do any thing, the pen in hand, opposite a table and paper: 'twas in my walks, amidst rocks and woods; 'twas in the night, during my slumbers I wrote in my brain, you may judge how slowly, particularly to a man deprived of verbal memory, and who in his life never could retain six verses by heart. Some of my periods have been turned and winded five or six nights in my bead before they were in a state for going on paper.

I am not only troubled to render my ideas, but also in receiving them. I have studied mankind, and think myself a tolerable good observator: nevertheless I cannot see any thing in that I perceive. I see clearly that only which I recollect, and I have no knowledge but in my recollections,

&c. Thus it appears this philosopher's wits were always a wool gathering. He possessed undoubtedly what Dr. Darwin would style the temperament of genius, which might qualify him for a smooth and pretty writer of "Reveries," but that best boon of heaven common sense is never the lot of such a genius.

I may perhaps seem unjustifiably harsh in applying the epithet knave to this great modern philosopher. But if the reader will please to consult his confessions he will find a sorry story, which he tells of himself, which is sufficient to justify me in bestowing on him appellations still more severe. He will there

Still toss'd about by strange fatalities,
Was now all lead, was now a bubble,
But ever happiest, when in trouble.[10]

---

find that our great philosopher stole a ribband, and attributed the theft to a servant girl, by which she was ruined. Ingratitude is likewise a trait in his character etitirely consistent with his sublime sentiments and perfect philosophism.

10 In this he was not quite alone in the world, there appears to be an order of beings, whom nothing but the stimulus of being in distress can give energy. Some of the English poets were of that description of character. Thomson proposed to write a poem on the man *who loved to be in diatress*, and if we are to judge of the character by the conduct of many of his tuneful brethren, they courted, rather than shunned misfortune, perhaps that they might enjoy the *luxury of being pitied*. Pope, Addison, Swift, and many others, however, were willing enough to be exempted from the iron hand of the relentless power yclep'd ADVERSITY, to whom Gray has addressed one of the finest odes in the English language. But to return to Rosseau, he gives this account of his circumstances, while a vagrant in France.

Being reduced to pass my nights in the street, may certainly be called suffering, and this was several times the case at Lyons, having preferred buying bread with the few pence I had remaining, to be- stowing them on a lodging; as I was convinced there was less danger of dying for want of sleep than of hunger. What is astonishing, while in this unhappy situation, I took no care for the future, was neither uneasy or melancholy, but patiently waited an answer to Madamoiselle du Chatelet's letter, and laying in the open air, stretched on the earth, or on a bench, slept as soundly as if reposing on a bed of roses. I remember particularly to have past a most delightful night at some distance from the city, in a road which had the Rhone, or Saone, I can't recollect which, on one side, and a range of raised gardens,

Never the same two hours together
In passion's hurricane a feather,
The lightest football now of folly,
Now sunk in morbid melancholy.[11]

---

with terraces on the other. It had been a very hot day, the evening was delightful, the dew moistened the fading grass, no wind was stirring, the air was fresh without chillness, the setting sun had tinged the clouds with a beautiful crimson, which was again reflected by the water, and the trees that bordered the terrace were filled with nightingales who were continually answering each other's songs. I walked along in a kind of extacy, giving up my heart and senses to the enjoyment of so many delights, and sighing only fiom a regret of enjoying them alone. Absorbed in this pleasing reverie, I lengthened my walk till it grew very late, without perceiving I was tired; at length, however, I discovered it, and threw myself on the step of a kind of niche, or false door, in the terrace wall. How charming was the couch! the trees formed a stately canopy, a nightingale sat directly over me,, and with his soft notes lulled me to rest: how pleasing my repose, my awaking more so. It was broad day; on opening my eyes I saw the water, the verdure, an admirable landscape before me, I arose, shook off the remains of drowsiness, and finding I was hungry, retook the way to the city, resolving, with inexpressible gaiety, to spend the two pieces of *six blancs* I had yet remaining in a good breakfast. I found myself so chearful that I went all the way singing; I even remember I sang a cantata of Baptistin's called the *Baths of Thomery*, which I knew by heart.

11 Thomson has given us no bad picture of Rousseau and some other pretended philosophers of the visionary cast in his personification of Hypochondria.

His head a wilderness of schemes,
A magazine of madman's dreams,[12]
Was stuff'd with many a paradox,
Like plagues in Dame Pandora's box.

But still his eloquence was winning
As his, who tempted Eve to sinning,
And us'd too oft the self same way
To lead the human race astray.

And oft his Jack-o-lantern head
Its owner many a goose chase led
Stretch'd on the tenters of anxiety
By blunder crime or impropriety.

So wild a scheme in politics

And moping here did Hypochondria sit
Mother of spleen, in robes of various dye,
Who vexed was full oft with ugly fit,
And feme *her frantic deem'd*, and some *her deem'd a wit.*

Madness is frequently mistaken for *inspiration*, and want of *common sense*, is often thought a proof of I krow not what *sublime sense*. Thus the ravings of Della Crusca and the moon struck tribe of sonneteers in the same school, have been thought to be the perfection of poetry. Indeed Della Crusca's poetry and Rosseau's politics are different diagnostics of the same disease, and the poor creatures who are affected with these symptoms are absolutely mad!

12 Some of these lay scatter'd here and there in his *Confessions.* It appears that this geat man, first ran away from his father, then from his patroness and mistress Madame de Warrens, and that he was ever and anon eloping from his benefactors in pursuit of some chimerical project.

Seen never was on this side Styx,
As his rude harum scarum plan
Of his new social savage man.[13]

---

13   Rousseau's *Emilius* and *Social Contract* are proofs in point of our assertion. A regular critique upon these publications would exceed our limits. A word or two, however, upon the latter may not be useless, especially as this is the fountain from whence Pain and other Sciolists of the new school appear to have derived their political principles.

"Man" (say Rousseau) "is born free and yet we see him every where in chains." *Social Contract.* Book I. Chap. 1. Again in the same Chapter he observes,

"If I were only to consider force, and the effects of it I should say that, when a nation is constrained to obey and does obey it does well; but whenever it can throw of the yoke, and does throw it off it does better."

Now this profound philosopher does not attempt to tell us what he means by the term yoke, but he says that *man is every where in chains*, and we are led to conclude that those nations who mean to "do better" than "well" will immediately set themselves about overturning their governments.

After a great number of paradoxical observations, the substance of which had been before made by Montesquieu, and have since been enlarged upon by Tom Pain and his disciples, we are presented with paradox of paradoxes, as follows,

Where shall we find a form of association which will defend and protect with the whole aggregate force the person and the property of each individual and by which every person, while united with ALL, shall obey only HIMSHLF. and remain as free as before the union?

Book 1 Chap. 6
Hic labor, hoc opus est. I have my doubts whether all this will ever be found.

Rosseau however says,

Every malefactor who; by attacking the social
right becomes a rebel and a traitor to his country
ceises by that act to be a party in willing the laws
and makes war, in fact, with himself.

Book 2. Chap. 5.

Here we learn that the criminal who is condemned by the
laws of his country, has signed his own act of condemnation
by consenting to become a member of the society from which
he is cut off as an excrescence, and if he is executed for crimes
commited against the society of which he is a member, he is
guilty of a *felo de se*, in having consented to become a member
of such society.

We likewise in Book 2. Chap. 3. are informed that the general
will cannot err, (*vox populi, vox dei*) and that it tends invaria-
bly to the public advantage. Yet we are told almost in the same
breath that the people, a majority of whose suffrages compose
this infallible general will are often deceived. That is that the
expressions of the will of a *fallible* body are always *infallible*.

The French revolutionary jargon about liberty and equality
is borrowed from this production.

But we shall not fatigue our readers by a detail of of all the
absurdities, and contradictions, with which this treatise is teem-
ing. The author appears to think that a nation is a kind of ma-
chine, and may be governed by mechanical principles, but has
no clear idea of the wonderful mechanism which he attempts
to explain. Hence we are every where lost in a jargon of words
without meaning, and perplexed by distinctions without dif-
ference. He was certainly correct in complaining that his ideas
were *confused*. But it is really astonishing that the vain *philoso-
phy* of this and similar writers, should have the effect of exciting
the mad million to overturn all existing systems, without any
distinct idea of what they were to substitute in the place of what
they destroyed. They would demolish a palace before they had
provided materials for erecting even a hovel on its site.

The author of the *Pursuits of Literature* has the following
remarks on this writer,

Like other Democratic sages
He spurn'd the wisdom of all ages
And found perfection had beginning
In systems of his own dear spinning

That whatsoever *is*, is wrong
Was still the burthen of his song,
From whence his inference seem'd to be
Whatever *is* must cease to be:[14]

Rousseau, by the unjustifiable, arbitrary and cruel proceedings against him, his writings and person in France, where he was a stranger and to whose tribunals he was not amenable, was stimulated to pursue his researches into the origin and expedience of *such* government, and of such oppression, which, ot'herwist; he probably never would have discussed; till he reasoned himself into the desperate doctrine of Political equality, and gave to the world his fatal present the *Social Contract*. Of this work the French since the revolution have never lost sight. With them it is first, and last, and middle, and without end in all their thoughts and public actions. Rousseau is, I believe the only man to whom they have paid an implicit and *undedeviating* reverence; and without a figure have worshipped in the Pantheon of their new idolatry, like a new Chemos, the obscure dread of Gallia's sons.

14 Let us grant to our revolutionists that all the *powers which be* were originally founded on oppression, and that by tracing the titles, we shall find some defect which in the opinion of casuists like Rousseau, ought to weaken their claims. Yet they must allow there ought to be power *somewhere* in society, which shall be sufficient to coerce, restrain and punish the turbulent and vicious; and those who are solicitous to pull down and destroy such power, ough surely to be able to establish a better claim in those who are to succeed in its possession. Be-

And therefore Throne and Principality,
In gulph of Jacobin equality,
Must topsy turvy, down be tumbled
And all the powers which *be*—be humbled.

Of modesty he loos'd the zone
And made the female world his own,
By Chesterfieldian-like civility
And softening *lust* to *sensibility*.[15]
And set the head upon the whirl

---

sides power is more frequently abused by an upstart, who has intrigued, forced and perhaps assasinated his way into office, than by one who enjoys it by more justifiable means. The head of a man not accustomed to elevation is apt to be giddy if he is exalted, and the little finger of a Buonaparte is generally heavier than the loins of a Louis.

15 The following beautiful lines are from "Jacobinism," a poem printed in England 1801.

> With subtlest passion to inflame the heart
> The Swiss magician wakes his wondrous art,
> How throbs the unpractised bosom, warm and frail,
> O'er Eloisa's soft seductive tale!
> Soft as the music of the vocal grove,
> He pours the thrilling strains of lawless love;
> Soft as enamour'd virgin's melting lay,
> Or Zephyr panting on the lap of May.

To this quotation we are tempted to add one from Coleman's *Broad Grins*, which although expressed 'in a very different stile, is not less to the purpose: than the preceding.

> Were I a pastor of a boarding school,
> I'd quash such books *in toto*;—if I could'nt,
> Let me but catch one Miss that broke my rule
> I'd flog her soundly; dam me if I would'nt."

Of many a vain, and giddy girl,
Who weds her father's coachman since
She can't so well command a prince.

A gang of Sophists him succeed,
French Democrats, detested breed,
Encyclopedists, justly dreaded,[16]

---

16 The arts of which the French Encyclopedists made use, for dis-
seminating the poison of their principles, are detailed at large
by the Abbé Barruel, vol. 1. chap. iv. to which we must refer the
reader who wishes for more ample information on this subject.
Some of the tricks, however, of these Illuminees, were so pev-
fectly similar to those of the shuffling Jacobins of the present
period, who mutilate, garble, and misquote Adams' Defence of
the American Constitution, in order to show that the author
of a treatise, written in defence of a Republican form of gov-
ernment, is at heart a monarchist, that we think it cannot be
malapropos, to exhibit a few of their mischievous devices.
   "Look for the article God, (Genevan edition) and you will
find very sound notions, together with the direct, physical and
metaphysical demonstration of his existence; and indeed, un-
der such an article, it would have been too manifest, to have
broached any thing bordering on Atheism, Spinonism, or Epi-
curism; but the reader is referred to the article Demonstration,
and there all the physical and metaphysical cogent arguments
for the existence of a God disappear. We are there taught, that
all direct demonstrations *suppose the idea of infinitude, and
that such an idea cannot be of the clearest, either for the nat-
uralisty or the metaphysician.* This, in a word, destroys all
confidence the reader had in the proofs adduced of the exist-
ence of God. There again, they are pleased to tell you, that a
single inject, in the eyes of a philosopher, more forcibly proves
*the existence of a God, than all the metaphysical arguments
whatever*; (*ibid.*) but you are then referred to Corruption,
where you learn how much you are to beware of asserting, in
a positive manner, that corruption can never beget animated
bodies; and that such a production of animated bodies by cor-

Steely nerv'd, and cobweb-headed.

ruption seems to be countenanced by *daily experiments*; and it is from these experiments precisely, that the Atheists conclude that the existence of God is unnecessary, either for the creation of man or animals. Prepossessed by these *references* against the existence of God, led the leader turn to the articles of ENCYCLOPAEDIA, and EPICURISM. In the former, he will be told. *That there is no being in nature that can be called the first or last, and that a machine, infinite in every way, must be the Deity.* In the latter, the atom is to be the Deity. It will be the primary cause of all things, by whom, and of whom, every thing is active essentially of itself, *Alone Unalterable, Alone Eternal, Alone Immutable*; and thus the reailcr will be insensibly led from the God of the gospel, to the Heathenish fiction of an Epicurus, op of a Spinosa.

The same cunning is to be found in the article of the Soul. Where the sophisters treat directly of its essence, they give the ordinary proofs of its *spirituality, and of its immortality.* They will even add to the article BRUTE, that the soul cannot be supposed material nor can *the brute be reduced to the quality of a mere machine, without running the hazard of making man an automato.* And under NATURAL LAW, we read, That if the determinations of man, or even his oscillations arise from any thing *material extraneous to his soul, there will be neither good nor evil, neither just nor unjust, neither obligation nor right.* Then *referred* to the article LOCKE, in order to do away all this consequence, we are told. That it is of no importance *whether matter thinks or not, for what is that to justice or injustice, to the immortality of the soul, and to all the truth of the system, whefher political or religious.* The reader, enjoying the liberty and equality of his reason, is left to doubt with regard to the spirituality, and no longer know whether he should not think himself *all matter.*

But he will decide, when under the article ANIMAL, he finds, *That life and animation are only physical properties of matter*; and lest he should think himself debased by his resembling a plant or an animal, to console him in his fall, they will tell him, article ENCYCLOPEDIA and ANIMAL, That the only difference between certain vegetables and animals such as us, is that they sleep, and that we wake, that we are animals that feel, and that they are animals that feel not; and still further in article ANIMAL That the sole difference between a stock and a man, is, that the one never falls, while the other never falls after the same manner.

After perusing these articles *bonâ fide*, the reader must be insensibly drawn into the vortex of materialism.

In treating of Liberty or Free Agency, we find the same artifice. When they treat it directly, they will say, "Take away liberty, all human nature is overthrown, and there will be no trace of order in society. Recompense will be ridiculous, and chastisement unjust, The ruin of liberty carries with it that of all order of police, and legitimates the most monstrous crimes; so monstrous a doctrine is not to be debated in the schools, but punished by the magistrates," &c. Then follows a portion of Demoeratic rant: "Oh, liberty," they exclaim, "Oh, liberty, gift of Heaven! Oh, liberty of action! Oh, liberty of thought! thou alone art capable of great things!" (See article AUTHORITY, and the PRELIMINARY DISCOURSE.) But at the article CHANCE, (fortuit) all this liberty of *action* and of *thought*, is only a *power that cannot be exercised, that cannot* be known by actual exercise; and Diderot, at the article EVIDENCE, pretending to support Liberty, will very properly say, "This concatenation of causes and effects, supposed by the philosophers, in order to form ideas representing the mechanism of the universe, is as fabulous as the Tritons and the Naiads." But, both he and D' Alembert, descant again on that concatenation, and returning to CHANCE (fortuit) tell us, That though it is imperceptible it is not less *real*; that it connects all things in nature, that all evens depend on it; just as the wheels of a watch, as to the motion, depend on each other: that from the first moment of our existence, we are *by no means masters of our motions*; that were there a thousand worlds similar to this, and simultaneously existing, governed by the same laws, every thing in them would be done in the same way; and that *man, in virtue of these same laws would perform at the same time, the same actions*, in each one of these worlds." This will naturally convince the uninformed reader, of tne chimara of such liberty

With these unite a German swarm,
Of *devils*, guis'd in human form,
Cold-blooded and *wrong-headed* wights,
Weishaupt's detested proselytes;[17]

Philosophists, Illuminati,
Beings, of whom at any rate, I
May well affirm a viler set,
Ne'er this side Pandemonium met.

Though scores of volumes would not hold.
What might of them with truth be told;
Though setting forth this horrid tale,
May make New England men turn pale; . . . .

---

or free agency, which cannot be exercised. Not content with this, Diderot, at the article FATALITY, after a long dissertation on this concatenation of causes, ends, by saying. That it cannot be contested either in the physical ivorld, or in the moral and *intellectual world.* Hence, what becomes of that liberty, without which there no longer exists *just* or *unjust obligation or right?"*

These examples will suffice to convince the rea- der of the truth of what we have asserted, as to the artful policy with which the Encyclopedia had been digested; they will show with what cunning its authors sought to spread the principles of Atheism, Materialism and Fatalism; in fine, every error incompatible with that religion, for which they professed so great a reverence at their outset.

17   The character of this abominable wretch, who debauched his wife's sister, and attempted to murder her, together with the fruits of their illicit commerce, is but a type of that of many leading Jacobins in this country. His intimate friends and disciples, were all monsters of iniquity. See Robison's *Proofs*, p. 114. and 130.

Some of their tenets we will trace,
Which one would think could ne'er have place
This side the Democratic club,
Whose President is Beelzebub.

With other things, which mark the *fiend*,
That *means* are sanction'd by the end;[18]
And if some *good end* we would further,
No matter if the *means* are *murther*!

That in this philosophic æra,
A God is found a mere chimæra,[19]

---

18 "Nothing was so frequently discoursed of" (in the German Lodges) "as the propriety of employing for a good purpose, the means which the wicked employed for evil purposes."

ROBISON's *Proofs.*

This abominable tenet of the Illuminati, appears to have been the principal rule of action of the monster, Roberspierre, who made France an aceldama for the purpose of introducing his fancied perfection.

19 Freret, whose writings were recommended by the Illuminati, tells us expressly, "The universal cause, that God of the Philosophers, of Jews, and of Christians, is but a chimæra, and a phantom." The same author continues, "Imagination daily creates fresh chimeras, which raises in them that impulse of fear, and such is the phantom of the Deity."

To the opinion of these philosophists, might be opposed that of a host of real philosophers. But the fallowing observations of Professor Robison, are so apposite, that we think they supercede our own remarks.

Our immortal Newton, to whom the philosophers of Europe look up as the honor of our species, whom even Mr. Bailly, the president of the National Assem-

By priests created but for wildering

bly of France, and mayor of Paris, cannot find words
sufficiently energetic to praise; this patient, saga-
cious and successful observer of nature, after having
exhibited to the wondering world, the characteris-
tic property of that principle of material nature, by
which all the bodies of the Solar system are made
to form a connected and permanent universe; and
after having shewn that this law of action alone was
adapted to this end, and that if gravity had deviated
but one thousandth part from the inverse duplicate
ratio of the distances, the system must, in the course
of very few revolutions, have gone into confusion
and ruin; sits down, and views the goodly scene; and
then closes his principles of natural philosophy with
this reflection, (his *scholium generale.*)

This most elegant frame of things could not have
arisen, unless by the contrivance and the direction of
a wise and powerful being; and if the fixed stars are
the centres of systems these systems must be simi-
lar; and all these constructed according to the same
plan, are subject to the government of *one* Being. All
these he governs, not as the soul ofthe world, but as
the Lord of all; therefore, on account of his govern-
ment he is called the Lord God. . . . Παντοϛατος;
for God is a relative term, and refers to his subjects.
Deity is God's government, not of his own body,
as those think who consider him as the soul of the
world, but of his servants. The Supreme God, is a
being, eternal, infinite, absolutely perfect. But a be-
ing, however perfect without goernment, is not God;
for we say, my God, your God, the God of Israel. We
cannot say my eternal, my infinite. We may have
some notions indeed of his attributes, but we can
have none of his nature. With respect to bodies, we
see only shapes and colour; hear only sounds; touch
only surfaces. These are attributes of bodies; but of
their essence we know nothing. As a blind man can
form no notion of colours, we can form none of the

Fools, ignoramusses and children;

That worlds of *mind* may be explored,
By lights, which *matter* can afford,
And Power Omnipotent must bend,
To what a *worm* can comprehend.[20]

That by some accidental clatter,
Of pristine, crude, chaotic matter,
(But how, an Atheist only knows)

---

manner in which God perceives, and understands,
and influences every thing.

Therefore we know God only by his attributes.
What are these? The wise and excellent structure,
and final aim of all things. In these, his perfections,
we admire him and we wonder. In his directions or
govern pent, we venerate and worship him; we wor-
ship him as his servants; and God, without domin-
ion, without providence, and final aims, is Fate; not
the object either of reverence, of hope, or of fear.

These are the sentiments of a *real* philosopher, not a Tom
Pain, a Godwin, or a Voltaire.

20 It has ever appeared to us as the essence of folly, for those who
pretend to be philosophers, to deny the being of a God, be-
cause they cannot comprehend how he exists. As well might
they deny the existence of the atmosphere, because it is invisi-
ble. Will these presumptuous mortals affirm that the magnetic
needle does not point towards the pole, because they cannot
develope the cause of the magnetic influence! Then may they
affirm, that because they cannot

Trace the secret mystic links which bind
The *world of matter* to the *world of mind*,

that there is no God and no mind in the universe.

37

This beauteous universe arose.[21]

That there is nothing like reality,
In future life and immortality;[22]
When death our thread of fate shall sever,
We go to rest, and sleep forever.

That actions are, or are not virtuous,
As they conduce most good or hurt to us,[23]
The agent judging their propriety.
And operation in society.

And maxims hammer'd out for steeling
The mind against each social feeling,
To gain attainable perfection,

---

21 "The author of *Good Sense*, which D'Alembert wishes to see abridged, in order to sell it for five pence to the poor and ignorant, says, That the phenomena of nature, only prove the existence of God, to a few prepossessed men; that the wonders of nature, so far from speaking a God, are but the necessary efforts of matter, infinitely diversified."
BARRUEL.

22 Boulanger tells us, "That the immortality of the soul, so far from stimulating men to the practice of virtue, is nothing but a *barbarous*, *desperate* and fatal tenet, and contrary to all legislation." "In the lodges, (of the Illuminati) death was declared to be an eternal sleep."
ROBISON'S *Proofs*.

23 Helvetius says, "That the only rule by which virtuous actions are distinguished from *vicious ones*, is the law of princes, and public utility. That *virtue*, that *honesty*, with regard to individuals, is no more than the *habit of actions personally advantageous*, and that self interest is the scale by which the actions of those can be measured."

Would root out natural affection.[24]

Maintain'd that fathers, children, brothers,
No nearer are to us than others;
And as for that frail being, *woman,*
They held, she should *be held* in common;[25]

---

24   "The commandment of loving father and mother, is more the
work of education, than of nature."

HELVETIUS.

25   By a decree of the French National Convention (June
6, 1794) it is declared that there is nothing criminal
in the promiscuous commerce of the sexes, and
therefore nothing that derogates from the female
character, when woman forgets that she is the de-
positary of all domestic satisfaction, that her honor
is the sacred bond of social life—that on her modesty
and delicacy depend all the respect and confidence
that will make a man attach himself to society, free
her from labour, share with her the fruits of all his
own exertions, and work with willingness and de-
light that she may appear on all occasions his equal,
and the ornament of all his acquisitions. In the very
argument, which this selected body of senators has
given for the propriety of this decree, it has degrad-
ed women below all estimation. 'It is to prevent her
from murdering the fruit of unlawful love, by remov-
ing her shame, and by relieving her from the fear of
want.' The senators say, 'the Republic wants citizens,
and therefore must not only remove this temptation
of shame, but must take care of the mother while she
nurses the child. It is the property of the nation and
must not be lost.' The woman all the while is con-
sidered only as the SHE ANIMAL, the breeder of Sans
cullottes. This the just morality of Illumination.

ROBISON'S *Proofs*, p. 374-5.

These degrading ideas of the female sex are pre cisely the

That vice, in all the horrid shapes
Of *murder, perjury, theft and rapes*,
Is right in those, who can invent,
A mode t' escape from punishment;[26]

That man should have no more remorse
For evil actions than his horse,
Because what vulgar folks call conscience,
Is nothing more than vulgar nonsense;

That modesty is all a trick
And chastity a fiddlestick,
A vile, old fashion'd sort of trimming
Meant to set off your pretty women;[27]

Like sly finesse in *fille de joye*;
Who pleases more by being coy
Than if she came with air voluptuous
Sans ceremonie dancing up to us;

---

same, which were taught in the German lodges, and furnish
proof of the connection between Illuminism, and the causes
which excited the French Revolution.

26   "The man who is above the law, can commit without remorse
the dishonest act, which serves his purpose."
                                                   HELVETIUS.

27   "Modesty is only the invention of refined voluptuous-
ness." . . . Helvetius. The French women have, however, pretty
well divested themselves of this appendage. Madam Tallien, ac-
companied by other beautiful women, laying aside all modesty,
came into the public theatre, presented themselves to public view,
with bared limbs a la sauvage as the alluring objects of desire.
                                          ROBISON's *Proofs*, p. 197.

That thrones and powers must be demolished
And all things sacred be abolish'd,
Each man be all, and every thing,
A Subject, Magistrate and King;[28]

Such principles as here are stated
By philosophs are propagated,
Sans intermission, or fatigue,
By open force, and dark intrigue.

The monsters made it still there aim
So fit for deeds without a name
Their pupils, train'd with wondrous art
To play the fell assassin's part.

The ties of nature disregarding
'Twas still there aim the heart to harden,
And make a murderer of man[29]

---

28 The object of the Illuminati, as appears from Barruel and Ro-
bison, was not only anti-christian, anti-monarchical, but an-
ti-social. They wished to annihilate every thing which went to
strengthen the bands of society, and reduce man to a state of
nature. The candidate for the degree of epopt, or priest, was
informed by his sufierior, that *These secret schools of phi-
losophy shall one day retrieve the fall of human nature, and
princes and nations shall disapear from the face of the earth;
and that with out violence. Reason shall be the only book of
laws, the sole code of man.*"

29 A candidate for reception into one of the highest
orders, after having heard many threatenings de-
nounced against all who should betray the secrets
of the order, was conducted to a place where he saw
the dead bodies of several who were said to have
suffered for their treachery. He then saw his own

To propagate perfection's plan.

brother tied hand and foot begging his mercy and intercession. He was informed that the person was about to suffer the punishment due to his offence, and that it was reserved for him (the candidate) to be the instrument of this just vengeance, and that this gave him an opportunity of manifesting that he was completely devoted to the Order. It being observed that his countenance gave signs of inward horror (the person in bonds imploring his mercy all the while) he was told that in order to spare his feelings a bandage should be put over his eyes. A dagger was then put into his right hand, and being hoodwinked, his left hand was laid on the palpitating heart of the criminal, and he was then ordered to strike. He instantly obeyed; and when the bandage was taken from his eyes he saw that it was a lamb that he had stabbed. Surely such a trial and such wanton cruelty are only fit for training conspirators.

ROBISON'S *Proofs*, p. 299.

No wonder that people trained to blood in this manner should have been guilty of the most horrid excesses. Nothing in the annals of history can equal the cruelties committed by Illuminees and Philosopbists. Well might the Abbe Barruel affirm,

It was the principles of the sect tnat made Barnave, at the sight of heads carried on pikes, ferociously smile and exclaim, "*was that blood then so pure that one might not even spill one drop of it?* Yes, it was those principles that made Chappellier, Mirabeau, and Gregoire, when they beheld the brigands surrounding the Palace of Versailles in sanguinary rage, thirsting after murder, and particularly after the blood of the Queen, exclaim *the people must have victims.* It was these principles that even smothered the affection of brother for brother, when the adept Chenier, seeing his own brother delivered over to the hands o the public executioner, coolly

No kind of care nor pains were stinted

said, If my brother be not in the true sense of the revolution, let him be sacrificed . . . . that eradicated the feelings of the child for his parents, when the adept Philip brought in triumph to the club of Jacobins *the head of his father and mother!!* This insatiable sect calls out by the mouth of the bloody Marat for two hundred and seventy thousand heads, declaring that before long it will count only by millions. They knew well that their systems and last mysteries of equality can only be accomplished in their full extent by depopulating the world; and by the mouth of Le Bo, it answers the inhabitants of Montauban, terrified with the want of provisions, *"Fear not*; France has a Sufficiency for twelve millions of inhabitants. All the rest (that is the other twelve millions) must be put to death, and then there will be no scarcity of bread.

BARRUEL, vol. IV. p. 271.

We are likewise told by the historians of that disastrous period that new words were invented to denote the butcheries which took place. Whole hecatombs of victims were shot *en masse*, and this was stiled *Fusillades*; hecatombs were also drowned, and this species of murder was called *Noyades*.

One of their own waters, a republican, gives the following description of the cruelties practised by these adepts in iniquity.

Under the name of a revolutionary government, all the public functions were united in the committee of public safety, where Robespierre had for a long time dominated. Then it was that this committee became dictatorial, hurried into the departments that horde of ferocious pro-consuls, whom we have seen betraying and slaughtering the people, whose servants they were, and to whom they owed their political existence; sometimes carrying with them in their murderous circuits, the *guillotine*, at others declaring it *permanent*, which was saying in

To poison every thing that's printed,

other words, that the executioner was not to have
a moment's rest. These monsters in mission, these
Colossusses of crime, these phœnomena of cruelty,
hunted men as a German baron hunts wild boars.
The despotic Turk, when he makes his equal expire
under the bastinado of a Pacha or by the chord of
the mutes, does not say to his victim, *thou art free.*

We have already said that all tyrannies resemble
each other; all tyrants have, like our decemvirs, em-
ployed the arm of terror; and it is not in this point of
view that the history of the epoch of our revolution
is new; but what has never yet been seen, and what
probably will never be seen again, is a great and en-
lightened people, who during six months were mu-
tilated, decimated, shot, drowned, and *guillotined*
by their representatives; it is the extreme ferocity of
so many public functionaries butchering those from
whom they received their commissions. Rome had
a series of tyrants in succession, or at least at short
intervals; but France had at one and the same time
a host of Caligulas. Tacitus himself would have bro-
ken his pencil with regret at not being able to paint
all the crimes which sprung from the monstrous
junction of the ferocious Robespierre with the san-
guinary Couthon; of the barbarous Billaud with the
gloomy Amar; of the tiger Collot, with the tiger Car-
rier; of the cut-throat Dumas with the cut-throat
Coffinhall; and a thousand subalterns submissive to
their orders. Mirabeau undoubtedly foresaw a part
of these horrors, when he said, *liberty slept only on
maitrasses of dead carcases.*

What a picture! the waves of the ocean swelled
by the mangled bodies, which were secretly commit-
ted to the bosom of the Loire; blood flowing in tor-
rents down the streets of every town; the dungeons
of a hundred thousand bastiles groaning under the
weight of the victims with which they were incum-

By modes, which other men would scorn.
From folio, down to book of horn.[30]

Among these human Demons were
Condorcet, Diderrot, Voltaire,
And other shrewd, self-boasting sages,
Whose names shall not disgrace our pages.

Now they appear in varied guise,
Like their great prototype of lies,
Who erst adroitly to deceive
In serpent's form accosted Eve.

In Paris many a democrat

---

bered; the threshold of every door stained with gore; and as the height of insult, the word humanity engraven on every tomb, and associated to death! such was the lamentable aspect which France presented! On every frontispiece were to be seen the contradictory words of Liberty, Fraternity, or Death. Alas! the last was the only one which was realized.

PAGE'S *French Revolution*, vol. II. p. 166, 7, 8.

Here we have the faint outlines of a picture of the horrors of the French revolution, drawn by a Frenchman and a democrat. This is the kind of liberty and equality which illuminated philosophers prepare for mankind.

30   Infidelity is now served up in every shape that is likely to allure, surprise, or beguile the imagition; in a fable, a tale, a novel, a poem, in interspersed and broken hints; remote and oblique surmises; in books of travels; of philosophy; of natural history; in a word, in any form rather than that of a professed and regular disquisition.

PALEY.

In dark, infernal concrave sat,
Brooded on eggs of curs'd confusion,
And hatch'd the Gallic revolution.[31]

---

31 I do not pretend to affirm that the French revolution was alto-
gether the *immediate* and *direct* effect of the operations of the
Illuminati. But I believe that the principles inculcated in the
lodges of these terrene infernals, and which were circulated by
them, and by those who were connected with them, paved the
way to those enormities, which rendered the French revolu-
tion by far the most bloody recorded in history. There were no
doubt many, who without ever *perceiving it themselves* were
under the influence of principles taught in these lodges. There
was a great differnce between the systematical ferocity of the
leaders in the French revolution, and the desultory efforts of
the common Jack Cades and Wat Tylers of rebellion. Many of
them had thoroughly *reasoned* themselves into a belief that
their massacres were laudable, and would eventually redound
to their own honor and the great good of the human species.
The following anecdote will, I think, corroborate my assertion.

To give an idea of the temper of the people at Paris,
it is proper to remark, that at the same instant when
the multitude with bloody fury were massacring the
menial servants in the palace, (on the memorable
10th of August 1792) and could scarcely be restrained
from offering violence to the Swiss who were made
prisoners, they would suffer no acts of pillage to go
unpunished. Several attempts of this kind were ac-
cordingly followed by the instant death of the crim-
inals. The plate, the jewels, and money found in the
Thuilleries were brought to the National Assembly,
and thrown down in the hall. One man, whose dress
and appearance bespoke extreme poverty, cast upon
the table an hat full of gold. . . . But the minds of
these men were elevated by enthusiasm; and they
considered themselves as at this moment the cham-
pions of freedom, and objects of terror to the kings
of the earth.

Anon their black atrocious band
Skulk in disguise though every land,
Rebellion propagate, by stealth
Through City, Kingdom, Commonwealth.

Thus the fell fiend of yellow-fever,
Hurls viewless arrows from his quiver,
Hovers in darkness dire, and flings
Distruction from mephitick wings.

Nor were their efforts bent alone
Against the altar and the throne,
But were intended for prostration
Of order, law, and civ'lization.

They fought as bold as Bonapart's
To level science and the arts;
Bid mankind list beneath the scrub
Of strongest arm, and largest club.

And swore to have the pure reality.
Essence of Jacobin equality,
That freedom, which no more nor less is,
Than wolves enjoy in wildernesses.[32]

---

32 The following extract from an address to the French people by
    the adepts Drouet, Babieuf, and Longelat, exhibits a correct
    specimen of Jacobin equality.

> *We are all equal.* . . . That principle is incontest-
> able. . . . very well! We mean in future to live and
> die as we are born. We will have real equality or
> death. . . . That is what we want, and we will have

Their leading tenets tally nicely,
In many things the same precisely
Unfolded by that fish of odd fin,

---

that real equality, cost what it will. *Woe be to those whom ive shall meet between it and us!* Woe to the man who shall dare oppose so positive a determination! The French revolution is but the forerunner of a revolution greater by far and much more solemn; and which will be the last.

What do we ask more than the equality of rights? Why, we will not only have that equality transcribed in the declaration of the rights of man, and of the citizen; we will have it in the midst of us, under the roofs of our houses. We consent to every thing for the acquisition of it, even to clear decksy that we may possess it alone; perish the arts, if requisite, provided we do but preserve a real equality!

Legislators and governors, proprietors, rich and fbowelless, in vain do you attempt to paralyze our sacred enterprize, by saying we are only re-producing the Agrarian law that has been so often asked for before.

Calumniators I hold your peace in ybiir turn, and in the silence of confusion hearken to our pretensions dictated by nature and grounded on justice. " The Agrarian law, or equal partition of lands, was the momentary wish of a few soldiers without principles, of a few clans, actuated rather by instinct han by reason. We aim at something more sublime, far more equitable, GOODS IN COMMON, or the COMMUNITE OF ESTATES! *No more individual properties in land, for the earth belongs to nobody.* We demand and will enjoy the goods of the earth in common. The fruits belong to all. *Disappear now, ye disgusting distinctioris of rich and poor, of higher and lower, of master and servants of* GOVERNING AND GOVERNED! *for uo Other distinctions shall exist among mankind than those of age and sex.*

The Jacobinic William Godwin.[33]

---

33   Were it not true that our American Jacobins arc very great ad-
mirers of this disorganizing philosophist, I would not waste a
syllable on his productions. His Political Justice is held in utter
abhorrence by all men of sense and erudition on either side of
the Atlantic. But as it is unfortunately the case that some men,
who are neither men of sensenor erudition, are very aspiring
characters, the said William Godwin is toasted in democratic
clubs, and many of the y men now in power, shape their con-
duct according to the models of this principal pedlar of French
manufactured morality.

I would premise, however, that I shall not attempt to trace
the sorry sophist through all his labyrinths of "desolating non-
sense." A concise sketch of some of the most prominent fallacies
which we have observed in his Political Justice, must suffice.

He commences his theory of political justice, with a de-
scription of the "evils existing in political society," then at-
tempts to prove that these devils are to be ascribed to public
institutions and next proposes to inform us, how such evils are
to be removed!

Under the head of evils existing in society, we Ire presented
with much conMion place declamation, about fraud, robbery,
wars, &c. To these succeed several arid chapters, relative to
innate principles, antenatal innpressions, instincts, &c. all of
which is either very trite, or very nonsensical. We are next in-
formed that our voluntary actions are invariably the result of
reason. That passion and appetite cannot counteract its man-
dates . . . . that "truth is omnipotent" . . . . that when a
rational being *knows* what is right, he will invariably act ac-
cording to his knowledge.

Hence we have nothing further to do in performing the
process of perfecting man, than merely to illuminate him with
some of philosopher Godwin's lucid displays of truth, as ex-
hibited, for instance, in his political Justice, and he will be so
perfect, that the now *"necessary evil"* of government may be
annihilated.

Here, however, some slight difficulties in our progress to
perfection intervene. But these cannot long retard Philosopher

49

Who held society was needing

Godwin. He acknowledges that there are some soils in which the plant, *perfectibility*, will not flourish. The influences of luxury, of climate, &c. oppose something like obstacles. But these vanish before plenipotent philosopher Godwin. "For," quoth he, "if truth, when properly displayed be omnipotent, then neither climate nor luxury are invincible obstacles." No, our philosopher is not to be put down by trifles. He will contrive "moral causes," to overpower all physical impediments. The shrivelled Eskimaux, or the parched African, are alike capable of perfection, and of consequence, of dispensing with the formality of government.

We are next presented with a curious chapter on "Justice." In the we are informed that the "distribution of justice should be measured by the capacity of its subject." That is, that in measuring such justice, we are not to consult the claims of the persons to whom it is *due*, but the good of the mass of mankind, abstractedly considered. Whence it follows, that if I owe a sum of money to A. but B. to whom I am not indebted, would, *in my opinion* make a better use of that money than A. I am bound, in justice, to pay it to the former. It seems to be the object of this singular being to consider justice as a sort of abstract quality, an undefinable *something,* due to the "system of nature," and to distributed where it will contribute most to the mass of enjoyment now existing, or which may hereafter exist in the universe.

Hence it appears that Mr. Godwin's Justice is not unlike Dr. Darwin's "universal philanthropy," which is consoled for the loss of thousands of human beings, by the reflection that the matter of which they were organized might be profitably employed in the manufacture of myriads of insects, the sum of whose happiness might be equal to that of the slaughtered armies, to whose destruction these flying and creeping things owed; their existence. *Phytologia.*

But to return to Mr. Godwin. In proving all these fine things, however, our wonderfully profound philosopher, as might be expected, not unfrequently contradicts himself. Truth is sometimes represented as "Omnipotent," and sometimes as totally imbecile, although by its agency all his perfection is to be brought about. For we are informed, that

A little salutary bleeding,

Self deception is of all things the most easy. Whoever ardently wishes to find a proposition true, may be expected insensibly to veer towards the opinion that suits his inclination. It cannot be wondered at, by him who considers the subtilty of the human mind, that belief should scarcely ever rest upon the mere basis of evidence, and that arguments are always viewed through a delusive medium, magnifying them into Alps, or diminishing them to nothing.*

We are afterwards told of conscientious assassins and persecutors, who are to be governed by this "Omnipotent Truth," but how all this will be brought about, no body but a philosophist can determine.

Mr. Godwin now proceeds to explode rights, and unshackle his unlimited morality,† till at length we are presented with a new set of "Principles of Government," in which "Omnipotent Truth," sanctioned by justice *without coercion* is to regulate society according to a *new order of things*, and introduce a political millenium. When this happy æra commences, every man in every action, will consult at once his own happiness, the happiness of his neighbours, of the world of mankind, and the present and future good of the universe. Here our modern philosopher is placed in a situation a million times as puzzling as that of the schoolman's ass between two equally attractive stacks of hay; for if he moves but his little finger in any way not conducive to the introduction of universal felicity, the whole of Mr. Godwin's fine fabric is annihilated.

The next thing worthy of notice in the course of this gentleman's destructive career, is an attack upon the Obligation of Promises. In this he would have a philosopher be the opposite to the just man, described by Dr. Watts, who,

Though to his own hurt he swears.
Still he performs his word;‡

And because it is lawful to take, in some cases, what is not our own, to satisfy hunger, he argues thus;

To kill one half mankind were best,

The adherence to promises, therefore, as well as their employment, in the first instance, must be decided by the general criterion, and *maintained only so far as upon a comprehensive view it shall be found productive of a balance of happiness.*

Here it is to be observed, that the *promissor* is to be the *judge*, in his own case, how far the observance of his promise may be "Productive of a balance of happiness." And with regard to the facility with which an honest man, making a promise, may deceive himself respecting this "balance of happiness," we would refer our reader to the passage already quoted from book II. chap. iv. p. 133.

Our scheming politician is not contented with having made an end of promises, but in his second volume, *Oaths of Office*, are declared not only useless, but execrable. But I fear I shall trespass on the patience of my reader, by pursuing this visionary writer through the mazes of his "vain philosophy." I shall therefore take leave of Mr. Godwin, with a quotation or two; and, 1st, from his own book, exemplifying the means by which Mr. Godwin would be willing to obtain his *perfection*; and, 2ndly, from the *Pursuira of Literature*, expressing the apprehensions which that great writer, in common with all men of science and reflection, have felt from the effects of such poisonous principles.

Perhaps no important revolution was ever bloodless. It may be useful in this place to recollect in what the mischief of shedding blood consists. The abuses which at present exist in all political societies, are so enormous, the oppressions which are exercised so Intolerable, the ignorance and vice they entail so dreadful, that possibly a dispassionate enquirer might decide, that, if their annihilation could be purchased by an instant sweeping of every human being now arrived at years of maturity, from the face of the earth, the purchase would not be too dear. It

And then philosophize the rest.
Some say one might say with propriety
They were like our St. Tam. Society;[54]

is not because human life is of so considerable value,
that we ought to recoil from the shedding of blood.
Death is in itself among the slightest of human evils.
An earthquake, which should swallow up a hundred
thousand individuals at once, would chiefly be to be
regretted for the anguish it entailed upon survivois;
in a fair estimate of those it had destroyed, it would
often be comparatively a trivial event.

In this sentence we have Illuminism completely unmasked.
This was the principle, which actuated the blood-thirsty tygers
of the French revolution.

I cannot better conclude my remarks on this work, than
by quoting from the *Pursuits of Literature*, a passage, which
evinces the apprehensions which the author of that poem en-
tertained from the prevalence of these and similar tenets of
modern philosophy.

My conviction and my fears on this most awful
subject (while it may yet avail us to consider) some-
times overpower me, till I absolutely sink under them.

I have heard it asserted that Godwin has retracted some of
the tenets advanced in this horrid production. But the recan-
tation, if such exists, has not been made sufficiently public to
serve as an antidote to the poison contained in the principles,
and our American democrats still pretend to admire the de-
structive sophisms with which that work abounds.

* Book II. chap. iv, p. 133.
† Book II. chap. iv.
‡ Book II. chap. iii.

54 There is a society established in New-York, called the St. Tam-
many Society, who personate the aboriginal savages very suc-
cessiuliy in our opinion.

But, as I know not whom I may hit,
Of course I shan't presume to say it

Vile propagands in every city
Make smooth the path of French banditti,
And Jacobin illiimin'd savages
Prelude fell French fraternal ravages.

Kings, nobles, priests, besotted elves
Strangely combin'd against themselves,[55]
Oppos'd with blind infuriate zeal
There own as well as publick weal.

But scarce the bard, in half a century,
Could mark the progress of this gentry,
Nor trace illuminated guilt
Through seas of blood by madmen spilt.

But well the reader knows, I fancy,
How freedom *alamode de Francois*
Was forc'dto choose for her protector
The Corsic despot to perfect her;

Surrendered all her harlot charms
To murderer Buonaparte's arms,
And now is doubtless safe enough, in

---

55 Among the sovereigns who were wheedled into the plans of
the conspirators, were Joseph II. Emperor of Germany, Cath-
erine II. Empress of Russia, Christiern VII. King of Denmark,
Gustavus III. King of Sweden, and Poniatowskj, King of Po-
land, together with princes and princesses too numerous in
this place to mention.

The churches of that ragamuffin.[56]

---

56 Among the many astonishing instances of tht wilful, or stu-
pid blindness of the party, who arrogate to themselves the
appellation of republicans, may be included their persevering
eulogies of Bonaparte, long after the mask of republicanism
was thrown off by that usurper. Notwithstanding well au-
thenticated accounts were received in America, of the infer-
nal means by which he was accomplishing the end of enslav-
ing that country, still he remained the subject of democratic
demi-adoration. But our limits will not allow us, in this place,
to give a full length portrait of the *republican* Emperor of the
Gauls. A few sentences from an English publication, the con-
ductors of which, we know, will not give currency to a false-
hood, shall suffice.

Trace this man of blood, from his first entrance
on his revolutionary career, to the present mo-
ment, (July, 1803.) Behold him, after contributing
to the murder of that sovereign, to whose liberality
he had been indebted for his education and sup-
port, acting a conspicuous part with his friend, the
late minister of police, Fouche, as an agent of the
National Convention at Toulon, where, after its
evacuation by the English, he superintended the
massacre of the loyalists; then follow him to Paris,
see him placed by Barras, at the head of the con-
ventional army, and murdering seven thousand of
the citizens of the metropolis, for daring to exer-
cise a constitutional right, by the election of their
own repre sentatives; next observe him, accept-
ing, as a reward for this sanguinary act, from the
contemplation of which every honest mind revolts
with horror, the hand of the mistress of Barras,
with the command of a banditti, destined to over-
run the fertile plains of Lombardy; view him in his
destructive progress, dealing death and desolation
around, and involving, in one mass of complicat-
ed ruin, the prince and the peasant, the young and

When first the boding storm began

the old, the woman and the child; mark his conduct during his progress at the village of Tenasco, where one of his soldiery, instigated by brutal lust, (in the unrestrained gratification of which his troops were, and still are, SYSTEMATICALLY indulged) entered the cottage of a peasant, and attempted to violate his daughter, scarcely arrived to years of maturity, the resentment of which by the father, produced a scuffle, which ended in the death of the military ruffian . . . . see Bonaparte, whose head-quarters were near by, revenge this deed of justice by ordering the whole village of Tenasco to be reduced to ashes, and its innocent, unprotected inhabitants, to be put to death without distinction of age or sex, an order, which was instantaneously and most mercilessly obeyed . . . . pursue this monster in human shape to the shores of Egypt; there hear him publicly renounce his Redeemer, reject the proffered salvation of his God, order the wanton massacre of thousands of the helpless people of Alexandria, merely to *strike terror into their countrymen* . . . . then trace him to Jaffa, to the cold-blooded murder of 3,800 captured Turks; follow him in his disgraceful retreat, when driven by British valour from the walls of Acre, and observe, him calmly directing the poisoned bowl to be administered to five hundred and eighty of his sick soldiers,

&c.

Hence we see a short sketch of the character of the man, whom our democrats have ever idolized; and to similar scenes would unrestrained democracy lead, in this or any other country. It is in vain for the favourers of Frenchmen and French measures, in this country, to deny the existence of the facts here disclosed. They have been repeatedly published, both in England and America, and never contradicted by the friends and admirers of the *genuine*-republican, who is now king of the Gauls.

To threaten civil, social man,
When vials of Illumination
Were pour'd abroad on every nation.

Great Britain felt the fated shock,
But Pitt was her salvation's rock,
Like Calpe's mound amid the waves
He stems the tide, his country saves.[57]

He sees the aims, and thwarts the plans
Of democratic partizans,
Breaks down nefarious coalitions
Of self-created politicians.

Since writing the above I have perused a tract entitled Bonaparte and the French people, written with considerable ability by a German, resident in France. This work contains many proofs of the despicable despotism to which the French nation is now reduced under the domineration of the Corsican usurper. Splendor without magnificence, luxury without taste, caprice, suspicion and cruelty beyond example, characterize the court of the mimic emperor. A cotemporary writer says the author has well observed:

> Thus every thing has returned, after an unfortunate round-about way, to the very point from which it set out; yet with this difference, that in former times an opposition of the independent states and bodies, might be shewn to the royal plea- sure.

57 Mr. Pitt in early life was somewhat led astray, as young men most frequently are, by the illusory phantoms of democratic liberty and equality. Time and experience, however, corrected his error, and perhaps it was owing chiefly to his exertions, that the revolutionary phrenzy did not take effect in England, and lead to enormities, similar to those, which, in France, surpassed every thing heretofore recorded in history.

Now every man of sense agrees
That democrats, Illuminees,
Are birds obscene, and of a feather,
Should therefore all be class'd together.

They all object to the propriety
Of law and order in society,
Think reason will supply restraints,
And make mankind a set of saints.[58]

These principles excite to action

---

58 Such is the *slang* of the faction from felon Burroughs to phi-
losopher . . . . The former of these
democrats, who appears as highly to appreciate, and as fully to
understand the true principles of fieedom as the latter, speak-
ing of the *cruelty* of establishing jails in a *free country*, says:
"How is this, says I to myself, that a country, which has stood
foremost in asserting the cause of liberty, that those who have
tasted in some measure, the bitter cup of slavery, should, so
soon after obtaining that blessing themselves, deprive others
of it?" p. 126. Again, speaking of another *democratic gentle-
man*, imprisoned for theft, he informs us that, "This man, by
mistake having taken some cattle not his own, and appropri-
ated them to his own use, some people were so impolite as to
charge him with *theft*." p. 130. Assisting another to break jail,
he observes, "Truly, said I, this conduct has been guided by the
principles of philsophy," p. 131. When confined at the castle in
Boston harbour, he reselved to rise on the garrison, and blow
up the magazine, he remarks, "Such were the outlines of my
plan; I determined to make one powerful effort to carry it into
execution; either to lose my life in the cause of *liberty*, or else
gain a *glorious* freedom."
   Here is *genuine* republicanism of the true Aurora stamp.
Duane himself could go but little farther in the theory and
practice of his wild-Irish sort of liberty.

The restless Pennsylvania faction,
While *tertium quids* oppose in vain,
The daring demagogue Duane.[59]

Such principles, alas, will flood
Columbia's "happy land" with blood,
Unless kind Providence restrain
These demons of the hurricane.

---

59 The "lamentable comedy," acting on the political theatre of
Pennsylvania, although at present it seems replete with "mar-
vellous pleasant mirth," will, it is to be feared, terminate with
a most tragical catastrophe. Were it otherwise, it would be
not a little amusing to be a looker on the struggle between the
Duanites and the Dallasites, alias the "*genuine republicans*,"
Rnd the *tertium quids*. These things would be comical enough,
were it not that the foundations of society are thereby shaken
to their centre, and were it not probable that this earthquake
of faction will ingulph our blood-bought liberties, and inhume
every thing which can render society of any value.

.

CANTO III

Mobocracy

ARGUMENT

I sing French freedom wafted o'er
From frantic Gallia's blood-stain'd shore,
And how th' accursed wild-fire found
"*Asylum*" in Columbian ground;
How honest yeomen, bold and rough.
For lack of liberty enough,
Seduc'd by bold, ambitious bad men,
Behav'd, *I'm loth to say*, like mad men;
And form'd democracy's inflections.
In Shays' and whiskey-insurrections . . . .
With other matters you'll discover.
Good reader, when you've read them over.

When democrats, from public papers,
Learn'd how the French were cutting capers,
They lost the little wits they had,
And were, *poor things*, completely mad;

Good reader, though it may embarrass one,
We'll conjure up some bright comparison,
Somewhat to liken to the revels
Of democratic demi-devils:

Such as were held in celebration
Of crimes of our good sister nation,
To gratulate vile *sans cullottes*
On cutting one another's throats.

Pray, Sir, dids't ever stop and stare
At showman with a dancing bear,
Whipping dull bruin round a stake, or
Dids't ever see a shaking quaker?

Or New lights dancing pious jigs,
Spinning like tops, their dismal rigs,
On one heel whirling, spirit-driven,
A precious way to go to heaven?

Dids't ever hear a story which is
Most horrible! about the witches!
Bedevil'd! (so they say) in Salem,[1]

---

[1] We do not wish to be satirical in our remarks on the once famous Salem witchcrafts. Hutchinson says that

> The great noise, which the New England witchcraft made throughout the English dominions proceeded more from the general panick, with which all sorts of persons were seized, and an expectation that the contagion would spread to all parts of the country, than from the number of persons who were executed; more having been put to death in a single county in England, in a short space of time, than have suffered in all New-England.
>
> Hutch. *His. Massachusetts*, vol. II. p. 15.

But the allusion is opposite to our subject in a philosophical as well as poetical point of view. It shews how liable mankind are to be seized with *mental epidemicks* and to *run mad in concert*. The crusade mania, the witchcraft mania, but worst of all the Gallic-democratic-Tom-Pain mania have been terrible diseases, and the last mentioned in particular much more destructive in its consequences than the yellow fever or even the plague itself.

And what the devil else could ail 'em?

Dids't ever hear of heathen gods,
Who, drunk with nectar, fell at odds,
Broke a crown's worth of good glass bottles.
And would have cut each other's throttles.

Had not the good old blacksmith Vulcan
Appeas'd the riot with a full can,
Made them shake hands both whig and tory
As Gaffer Homer tells the story?

Hast read in Ovid's Metamorphoses
What a most sorry scrape was Orpheus's
When tipsey hags, with other matters
Tore the old fiddler all to tatters?[2]

Dost know how Hercules once behav'd,
Ranted and rended, roar'd and rav'd,[3]

---

2   The conduct of the female Bacchantes, who demolished the
     Thracian band (see Ovid's *Metamorphoses*, Lib. xi. Fab. i.) has
     been far exceeded by the French Revolutionary female fiends
     at Paris. Mad with Jacobinic fury, the beautiful, the tender
     sex with the most savage fury actually gnawed the amputat-
     ed limbs of their wretched countrymen, whom the mob had
     butchered in the cause of liberty and equality. Such is the spirit
     of democracy. Even the fair sex without the restraints of reli-
     gion and government, become more ferocious than tigers, and
     man the most savage animal in existence.

3   *Dum potuit solita gemitum virtute repressit,*
     Victa malis postquam patientia repulit aras;
     Impevitque suis nemerosum vocibus Oëten.
                              OVID, *Met.* Lib. ix. Fab. 3

What time his wife, a jealous flirt,
Sent him her sweet-heart's brimstone shirt?

What riot erst had been in hell
About the time that Adam fell,
If democrats, (so Milton makes
It plain) had not been turn'd to snakes?[4]

---

[4] The reception which the arch democrat met with on his return
from that expedition which brought "death into the world,"
and his Metempsychosis on that occasion are thus described
by the first of poets.

> So having said, a while he stood expecting
> Their universal shout, and high applause,
> To fill his ear, when contrary he hears
> On all sides from innumerable tongues,
> A dismal universal hiss, the sound
> Of public scorn; he wonder'd, but not long
> Had leisure, wondering at himself now more;
> His vissage drawn he felt to sharp and spare,
> His arms clung to his ribs, his legs intwining
> Each other till supplanted down he fell
> A monstrous serpent, on his belly prone,
> Reluctant, but in vain, a greater power
> Now rul'd him, punish'd in the shape he sinn'd,
> According to his doom: he would have spoke
> But hiss for hiss return'd with forked tongue
> To forked tongue, for now were all transform'd
> Alike to serpents, all as accessaries
> To this bold riot.

That these serpents were democrats is plain, first from the
testimony of Butler, who says,

> The devil was the first of the name
> From whom the race of rebels came,
> Who was the first bold undertaker

Dids't ever know on fourth of July
With many a "*d . . . . n your eyes!*" and "*you lie!*"
Vile Irishmen, in bloody fray
Honor our Independence day?[5]

All these thou knows't, but not a scrape
Among them all, in any shape,
Could equal ox-head celebration

Of bearing arms against his maker.
BUTLER'S, *Misc. Thoughts.*

Secondly, we have the declaration of democrats vs. democrats, to be found in a semi-weekly electioneering handbill printed in New-York, entitled *The Corrector*, in which the Burrites, *good democrats* have drawn the Clintonians, likewise *good democrats*, as large as life and hung them up in what they very properly called THE PANDEMONIAN GALLERY. Some however, have very plausibly maintained that, although these paintings may be correct copies of the originals who appear to have sat for their pictures, yet in comparing them to the devils of Milton, they have caricatured the latter beyond all comparison.

5   The 4th of July 1805, was celebrated in a "*genuine republican*" stile by a number of the jolly sons of St. Patrick, collected for that purpose on the Battery in New-York. These brawny democrats undertook, by *pugilistical demonstration* to make it evident that fresh imported Irishmen were the only real *American soldiers* and "*genuine*" patriots of seventy-six. Those who had the hardihood to dissent from this doctrine were sure to be knocked down in a very convincing manner. These Hibernian logicians, finding however that there were *two sides* to the question even as they argued it, were at length obliged to yield to the more *impressive reasons* of their opponents assisted by the *ultima ratio* of the city police. On this great occasion the Declaration of Independence was with singular propriety read by an Irishman who had been lately imported.

In honor of the frantic nation.[6]

---

6   The following account of a feté of the Boston democratic party, we extract from *Remarks on the Jacobiniad*, an extremely well written publication, which appeared in Boston at the time that Americans were running into some of the French revolutionary excesses.

Though the adventures of the ox's head are well known in this metropolis, a short account of them may not prove unacceptable to such as have not the happiness of being our fellow citizens. We beg leave then to inform them, that on the retreat of the Duke of Brunswick, and the successes of our Gallic friends under Dumouriez, a Civic Feast was given in honor of these illustrious events. The subscription was liberal; a handsome entertainment was provided for the lovers of equality, in Faneuil Hall, whilst their "MAJESTIES THE MOB," were regaled with an ox roasted whole in the street. The supposition, that more than 3000 persons of all ages, sexes and descriptions, would quietly set down and wait till they were helped, was benevolent in the extreme: but their majesties very uncivilly disappointed the expectations of their patrons; for, unrestrained by the ties of gratitude, for the money expended for their amusement, they destroyed the benches provided for their accommodation, tore the poor ox piecemeal, broke the plates, and scattered the mingled fragments of beef and earthern ware in every direction, to the destruction of the neighbouring windows, and to the great annoyance of dogs, women, children, selectmen, &c. who were inactive spectators of this very interesting scene. The head of the animal was then fixed, in grinning majesty, on the pole of LIBERTY, and consecrated to that goddess, amidst the thunder of a tremendous *swivel*. In this state it remained until the fate of the unfortunate *Louis* was announced, when it was seen in mourn-

Now demos gave their feelings vent
In all parts of the continent,
And were as "brisk as bottled ale"
Or dog with shingle tied to's tail.

But time would fail to set forth now how
Full many a democratic pow wow.
Was held in bawling exultation
For crimes of our dear sister nation.

Nothing would suit the rogues beside
Your madcap freedom Frenchified,
Of which they vow'd t' import a cargo,
Though Washington had laid embargo.

And though 'twas shrewdly urg'd by some
That we had liberty at home,
Which like our Chief's religious stuff,

---

ing for that melancholy event. This was conceived
very dangerous to the French cause by some polit-
ical fanatics, and the head was in consequence, ig-
nominiously stripped of its "suit of solemn black."
In revenge for this insult, those who had furnished
the tourning, levelled the sacred tree of Liberty to
the ground, and with it fell the innocent cause of the
contest. The pole was put up and down . . . . and
up again . . . . to the no small amusement of all
unconcerned; whilst the head, if we are rightly in-
formed, being found, on examination of *Jacobinical*
strength and capaciousness, was converted into a
punch-bowl, (the two horns serving admirably for
handles) and is now used as the receptacle of grog
and flip, by the Democratic Society, in this our en-
lightened metropolis.

If not the best was "good enough,"[7]

Still demo's swore to have the frantic
Kind manufactur'd o'er the Atlantic,
Such as our secretary well knows
Suits whiskey-insurrection fellows.[8]

Thus nothing pleases *bon ton* ladies,
Which is their native country made is
But let a thing be e'er so frightlul,
Dear bought and far fetch'd, 'tis delightful.

Next we were punish'd for our sins
With clubs of crazy Jacobins,
Who, with pure freedom to content us,
Themselves appoint to represent us.[9]

---

7   "Religion is well supported," (to wit, in Pennsylvania and New-
    York) "of various kinds indeed, but all good enough."
    Notes on Virginia, p. 221. Bost. edit. 18mo.

8   One among the many wonders which democracy has achieved
    in favour of the liberties of the people, has been, to elevate to
    high and responsible situations, certain convicts, most gener-
    ally foreigners. The part which Mr. Gallatin took in the Pitts-
    burgh insurrection, which cost the United States a million of
    dollars, is well known, and it is probable that his present eleva-
    tion, is a reward for his patriotic services on that occasion. But
    more of this gentleman hereafter.

9   It is impossible to imagine a greater burlesque on the idea of a
    representative republic than the farcical conduct of our demo-
    cratic societies, who by virtue of no authority whatever except
    that of their own good will and pleasure, seated themselves in
    the magisterial chair, assumed the appellation of "*We the peo-
    ple*," and had the impudence to dictate and control the affairs
    of our national government.

Now certain causes most untoward
Prepared the people to be froward,
Form'd many plausible excuses
For mobocratical abuses.

But should I make in metre ginigle
Those causes operant all and single,
Which rais'd 'gainst government a few setts
Of Pittsburgh rogues, and Massachusetts,

The reader might compare with mine
Old Blackmoore's everlasting line,[10]
I'll therefore hint and glance along
Nor call a muse to aid my song.

But I'll purloin a little. . . . why not?
From classic history of Minot,
For *theft* can need no other plea
Than this, *Our government is free!*

Our demo's steal each others trash,
While Coleman plies in vain the lash,[11]
And prithee, therefore, why can I not
Steal my *Mobocracy* from Minot?

---

10   And Edwin eke out Blackmoore's endless line.

11   We allude here to the practice of our good democratic managers of newspapers of what Cheetham calls, "the arts of able editors" publish matter as *original* which they have stolen from some other paper. This trick has been exposed by the editor of the *New-York Evening Post*, whose exertions in bringing to light the *scoundrelism* of the faction, entitle him to the gratitude of every friend to the prosperity of his country.

Fas est ab hoste el doceri,
If that be true why then 'tis clear I . . . .
But gentle, reader, have you read it!
"Yes" . . . . then I'll give my author credit.[12]

---

12   The nature and operation of the causes, which led to the rebel-
lion in Massachusetts, are explained in a lucid and masterly
manner, in the history of George Richards Minot; the style of
which might rank its author as the Sallust of America. Accord-
ing to that writer, the commonwealth of Massachusetts was
in debt, upwards of 1,350,000*l.* private state debt, exclusive
of the federal debt, which amounted to above one million and
an half of the same money. And in addition to that, every town
was embarrassed by advances they had made to comply with
repeated requisitions for men and supplies to support the
army, and which had been done upon their own particular
credit. The people, he informs us,

> had been laudably employed, during the nine years
> in which this debt had been accumulating, in the de-
> fence of their liberties; but though their contest had
> instructed them in the nobler science of the rights of
> mankind yet it gave them no proportionable insight
> into the mazes of finance. Their honest prejudices
> were averse to duties of impost and excise, which
> were at that time supposed to be anti-republican, by
> many judicious and influential characters.
> The consequences of the public debt did not at
> first appear among the citizens at large. *The bulk of
> mankind are too much engaged in private concerns
> to anticipate the operation of national causes.* The
> men of landed interest, soon began to speak plainly
> against trade, as the source of luxury, and the cause
> of losing the circulating medium.

&c.

> Commercial men, on the other hand, defended
> themselves by insisting that the fault was only in the

And then proceed in rhyme and prosing,
Nor mind if you're awake or dosing,
In simple, homespun, manner shewing
What set *Mobocracy* a going.

When our wig champions fain would hit on
Successful modes for thwarting Britain,
Our leaders thought that they were right in
Whatever kindled ire for fighting.

To paint the ills, which power attend
Oar men of mind their talents lend,
But overlook the great propriety
Of *power* to guaranty society.[13]

---

regulations which the trade happened to be under.
&c.

The writer then proceeds to point out other causes which contributed to lead the people astray; and his history exhibits abundant proof, that the people at large are not always correct judges of what political measures may best subserve their own prosperity.

13   The *jealousy* of republicans against *delegating* power, has most generally been the cause of their destruction. No community can long subsist without authority to coerce and punish; but such authority ought to be marked by legal and well defined boundaries, and entrusted to such men only as have their characters established for *integrity* as well as *abilities*. The only method which can be devised to prevent the *assumtion*, by unprincipled men, of that power, which is *tyranny* in effect, whatever may be its name or disguise, is to delegate *legal power* without too much jealousy or reserve, of men, who will be a "terror to evil doers."

Hence, brave men who our battles fought,
Did not distinguish as they ought
The odds existing in a high sense
'Twixt Liberty and boundless license.

And when they found our chiefs intent
On building up a government,
And that one of its consequences
Would be some national expenses.[14]

Our honest clever country folks
Did not well relish such dry jokes,
But many a moody murmur mutter'd,
And words to this effect were utter'd:

"We thought that when the war was over
"Americans would live in clover,
"That nothing then would vex and harass us,
"No debts nor taxes to embarrass us.

---

14   There is nothing in which our democratic politicians are more
     profoundly absurd, than in their estimates of *national econ-
     omy*. The penny-saving maxims of Dr. Franklin, *injudicious-
     ly* applied to affairs of national magnitude, are of very mis-
     chievous tendency. Money paid for public purposes, which
     is expended among the inhabitants of a country, does not
     impoverish such inhabitants. It is paid by the people to the
     government, and by the government distributed among the
     people. If it be so distributed as to be a reward to merit, and
     give a proper tone to industry, there is little danger of being
     too lavish. The whole body politic becomes invigorated by its
     circulation; the farmer and the mechanic finding a ready sale
     for their commodities, are stimulated to that industry which
     constitutes the real wealth of a nation.

"We've fought a long and bloody war,
"But what have we been fighting for,
"If king George thrown off, we are loading
"Our backs with weight of one king Bowdoin,

"What, shall we sell our hoes and axes,
"For paying arbitrary taxes?
"No . . . . and for rulers, we don't need 'em
"In this good land of perfect freedom.

"With all our toil, and all our blood,
"One tyrant makes another good,
"Our boasted freedom is a sham,
"Not worth a single whisky dram."

Such sentiments had long been brewing,
And boded nothing less than ruin
To our still weak confederation,
Too novel for consolidation.

Thus stiff-neck'd Israelites of old
Were froward, insolent and bold,
With other Jacobin procedures
Full oft rebell'd against their leaders.

Now fann'd by Gallatins and Shayses,
The fire of civil discord blazes,
And breaks out in a vile rebellion,
Yea, two or three, which I might tell ye on.

But scampering off from Petersham

Without their wonted morning dram,
Their courage cool'd . . . . the rogues surrender'd
On easy terms, in mercy tender'd.

Though rebels, under Shays and Gallatin,
Received from government a malleting,
And social harmony seem'd ratified,
Too many still remained dissatisfied.

The mouldering flame in secret burn'd,
When Jefferson from France returned,
To aid the Factions' frantic schemes,
With fresh illuminated dreams.[15]

---

15   We have it from good authority that Mr. Jefferson actually be-
came initiated, while in Paris, into the mysteries of Illuminism,
and his writings and conduct, since his embassy to France, dis-
play "internal evidence" of his being infected with the poison of
illuminated principles. "Condorcet, likewise (a well known Illu-
minatus) was a particular friend of our American philosopher."*
His advocates, who would maintain that he imbibed no new
principles in France, which smack of Illuminism, must be under
the necessity of affirming, that *honesty never* was the *policy* of
a certain great man . . . . that he never did scruple about the
means provided the *end* could be obtained. His advice to Con-
gress, respecting the transfer of the debt due to France, to a com-
pany of Hollanders, is a proof in point. Instaling this, I shall have
recourse to the pamphlet of Mr. Smith, referred to above.

   Mr. Jefferson, says that writer, after mentioning an offer
which had been made by a company of Hollanders, for the
purchase of the debt, concludes with these extraordinary ex-
pressions:

> If there is a *danger* of the public payments not
> being punctual, I submit, whether it may not be
> better, that the discontents which would then arise,

should be *transferred* from a court, of whose *good will the have so much need, to the breasts of a private company.*

This letter was the subject of a report from the Board of Treasury, in February, 1787. The board treated the idea of transfer, proposed, as both UN-JUST and IMPOLITIC; *unjust,* because the nation would contract an engagement, which there was no well grounded prospect of fulfilling; *impolitic,* because a failure in the payment of interest on this debt transferred (which was inevitable) would justly blast all hopes of credit with the citizens of the United Netherlands, in future pressing exigencies of the union; and the Board gave it as their opinion, that it would be advisable for Congress, *without delay,* to *instruct* their minister at the court of France, to forbear giving his sanction to any such transfer.

Congress, agreeing in the ideas of the Board, caused an *instruction* to that effect to be sent to Mr. Jefferson. Here there was a *solemn act of government, condemning the principle as unjust and impolitic.*

If the sentiment contained in the extract which has been recited, can be vindicated from political profligacy, then *is it necessary to unlearn* all the ancient notions of *justice,* and to substitute some new fashioned scheme of morality in their stead.

Here is no complicated problem, which *sophistry* may entangle or obscure; here is a plain question of *moral feeling.* A government is encouraged on the *express condition of not having a prospect* of making a *due provision* for a debt which it owes to *concur in a transfer of that debt* from a *nation, well able* to bear the inconveniences of a failure or delay, to the *individuals* whose *total ruin* might have been the consequence of it; and that, upon the interested consideration of having need of the good will of the

In Weishaupt's school his lesson learn'd

creditor nation, and with the *dishonorable* motive, as is clearly implied of having more to apprehend from the discontents of that nation, than from those of disappointed and betrayed individuals? Let every *honest* and impartial mind-consulting its own spontaneous emotions, pronounce for itself upon the rectitude of such a suggestion.

An effort, scarcely plausible, has been heretofore made by the partizans of Mr. Jefferson, to explain away the turpitude of this advice.†

It was represented, that

A company of adventuring speculators, had offered to purchase the debt at a discount, foreseeing the delay of payment, calculating the probable loss, and willing to encounter the hazard.

But the terms employed by Mr. Jefferson, refute this species of apology. His words are,

If there is a danger of the public payments not being punctual, I submit, whether it may not be bettery that "the discontents which would then arise, should be transferred from a court, of whose good will we have so much need, to the breasts of a private company.

He plainly takes it for granted, that discontents would arise, from the want of an adequate provision, and proposes that they should be transferred to the breasts of individuals. This he could not have taken for granted, if, in his conception, the purchasers had calculated on delay and loss. Here we have the full effulgence of Godwinism bursting upon us! It was an attempt to implicate the government of America, in a sale of bad securities, the venders knowing them to be such. The "transfer," of "discontents," which Mr. Jefferson foresaw would arise from the French court, to the poor Hollanders, to the probable

76

He with pernicious ardour burn'd,

---

ruin of the latter, is somewhat similar in kind, to the *justice* which the author of Hudibras attributes to the first settlers of New-England.

> Our brethren of New England use
> Choice malefactors to excuse,
> And hang: the guiltless in their steady
> Of whom the churches have less need;
> As lately 't happen'd: in a town
> There liv'd a cobler, and but one,
> That out of doctrine could cut use,
> And mend men's lives as well as shoes,
> This precious brother having slain
> In time of peace an Indian,
> (Not out of malice, but mere zeal,
> Because he was an infidel)
> The mighty TOTTIPOTTYMOY,
> Sent to our elders an envoy,
> Complaining sorely of the breach
> Of league held forth by brother Patch
> Against the articles in force,
> Between both churches, his and ours;
> For which he crav'd the saints to render
> Into his hands or hang the offender;
> But they maturely having weigh'd.
> They had no more but him o' th' trade,
> A man that serv'd them in a double
> Capacity, to teach and cobble,
> Resolv'd to spare him; yet, to do
> The Indian Hoghan Moghan too
> Impartial justice, in his stead, did
> Hang an old weaver that was bed-rid!"

* *See a pamphlet, written by William Smith-Esq. of South Carolina, with the signature of* PHOCION.

† *See Jefferson's attempted vindication, in Dunlap's* Daily Advertiser, *of October,* 1792.

To introduce his *whimskalilies*,
And make them in our land realities.

Nature ne'er made a fitter man
To give effect to such a plan,[16]

---

16   Mr. Jefferson's pretensions to the station he holds, have been
frequently scanned by men, whose talents and opportunities
have given the peculiar advantages for the investigation. The
result has appeared to be somewhat unfavourable, unless for
the purposes of the party now predominant, he should be
thought *better* than a *better* man. But the principal traits in his
character, are so well exhibited in the pamphlet of Mr. Smith,
that we are tempted again to quote, from his production, the
following summary of the wonderful qualifications of our chief
magistrate.

We shall now take leave of Mr. Jefferson and his
pretensions, as a *philosopher* and politician. The
candid and unprejudiced, who have read with at-
tention the foregoing comments on his philosophi-
cal and political works, and on his public conduct,
must now be convinced, however they may hitherto
have been *deceived* by a *plausible* appearance and
specious talents, or misled by artful partizans, that
the reputation he has acquired is not bottomed on
solid merit . . . . that his abilities have been more
directed to the acquirement of literary fame, than
to the substantial good of his country . . . . that
his philosophical opinions have been capricious
and wavering, often warped by the most frivolous
circumstances . . . . that in his political conduct
he has been timid, inconsistent, and unsteady, gen-
erally favouring measures of a factious and disor-
ganizing tendency, always leaning to those which
would establish his popularity, however destructive
of our peace and tranquility . . . . that his political
principles are sometimes whimsical and visionary,

Nor do I think, with ten years pother,
That she could hit out such another.

Phlegmatic, cunning, and wrong headed
To visionary tenets wedded,
A writer, plausible, sophistical,
Never profound, but always mystical.

Possessed of that mysterious air,
Which makes the gaping vulgar stare,
And gives the weakest men dominion,

---

at others, subversive of all regular and *stable* government that his writings have betrayed a disrespect for religion, and his partiality for the impious *Paine*, an enmity to *christianity* . . . . that his advice respecting the Dutch company, and his open countenance of an incendiary printer, and of the views of a faction, manifest a want of due regard for *national faith* and public credit . . . . that his *abhorrence* of *one* foreign nation, and *enthusiastic devotion* to *another*, have extinguished in him every germ of *real national character*; and, in short, that his elevation to the presidency, must eventuate either in the *debasement* of the American name, by a whimsical, inconsistent and feeble administration, or in the prostration of the United States at the *feet of France*, the subversion of our excellent *constitution*, and the consequent *destruction* of our present *prosperity*.

Such is the character, who now presides in America, as drawn by a gentleman, who has held some of the most important offices in our government, and such the predictions, which we fear are beginning to be fulfilled in this country. The prostration of the Judiciary, and the sacrifice of the greater part of our navy, are alarming forerunners of the fulfilment of the prophecy.

Founded on popular opinion.

His native cunning to enhance,
He adds the dark finesse of France,
Reduc'd to system, by the rules
Of Jacobin-illumin'd schools.

Supported by the factious heads
Of ever restless anti-feds.
Rogues to true liberty a pest,
Who make her seat an hornet's nest.[17]

He begs the boon with vast humility
To introduce perfectibility.
For man, he's sure, unless we manage ill.
Will rise one link above the angel.

(This quack perfection still we find
Among the vilest of mankind
A favorite doctrine, sure the elves
Can't judge of others by themselves.)

And now the wicked faction join'd

---

17   We commenced the manufacture of this our poetical produc-
tion, with a determination, which we think all candid critics
will pronounce not a little laudable, to deduce, so far as con-
venient, our poetical and rhetorical flourishes from *Cis*-Atlan-
tic sources. And here we think that our reviewers will do us
the justice to acknowledge, that no poet's "eye in a fine frenzy
rolling" ever glanced at a prettier comparison than this of a
nest of those irascible insects with a commonwealth infested
by turbulent demagogues.

To tamper with the public mind.
Of liberty kept such a bawling
It seem'd the rogues would take us all in.

But honest people soon behold
That all which glitters is not gold.
Discern in sticklers of mobocracy
A deal of scandalous hypocrisy

That were not justice in arrears
These New school folks would lack their ears,[18]
Of course don't much admire their plan
For perfecting the creature man.

Our demos then with great propriety,

---

18   It is a truth, which we think even democrats themselves will
not have the effrontery to deny, that *the leaders* of their party
are men whose moral characters will not bear examination. Is
it not then astonishing, that Americans should trust their all
important political interests, upon which depends the enjoy-
ment of their lives, liberty, and property, to men with whom
they would have no dealings in their private capacity? It is not
too much to say, that many men who have the management of
our public concerns, or are patronized and pensioned editors
of newspapers, are known to be alike destitute of honour and
honesty. The infamous character of Pasquin the right hand
Chronicle man, is almost proverbial in England. The political
career of a certain honorable duellist, has been remarkable for
****, but as this gentleman is an excellent shot, and in con-
stant practice it may not be prudent to offend him. We wish,
however, that our readers would candidly and coolly compare
the qualifications of the federalists, with those of the demo-
crats, and not give the preference to the latter, merely because
they *style themselves* republicans.

Are hooted at throughout society,
And many a rascally curmudgeon,
Is nicely bang'd with satire's bludgeon;

Yes, many a chief whom now they boast.
Was tied to satire's whipping-post,
Their foremost partizans now dashing,
Had their deserts in many a lashing.[19]

The fed-wits serv'd the scoundrel fry as
Of old Apollo serv'd Marsyas,
What time his Godship did contrive
To skin the whistling chap alive.

But still determin'd not to yield,
Though trodden down, they kept the field.
Displayed of feeling less the powers
Than rogues, who have been hung for hours.[20]

---

19 It is notorious that the family of wit have ever been federalists. Most of the "half formed witlings," who have occasionally dashed in democratic newspapers, like your Cheethams and your Pasquins, are beings beneath notice in a literary point of view.

   Apollo views, with honest pride
   His favourites all on federal side.

   Hence these poor creatures have generally passively submitted to the Federal lash, and pretended to despise their opponents like a blustering bully? who brags though he is beaten.

20 You will find, gentle reader, by turning to *Terrible Tractoration*, p. 64, New-York edition, a notable instance of *sensibility*, expressed by a felon who had been executed for murder, who being somewhat "oppugnated" by a meddling philosopher,

When haply hit off to a tittle,
At first it nettled them a little,
But careless apathy now boastings
They quietly submit to roasting.

Thus Jack Ketch, having noos'd a paddy,
("Perhaps, O Sylph!" . . . . 'twas Duane's daddy![21]
Who made more growling than was fit,
And did not love to swing one bit; . . . .

A fellow sufferer by his side
A crum of comfort thus applied,
"Your blubbering, Pat, has no excuse to't,
"*You know, you Irish dogs are us'd to't!*"

---

with his Galvanic stimulants, *clenched his right hands*, and
exhibited other menacing symptoms of his being alive to the
affront. But our democrats, though spitted with the arrows
of satire, by the merciless wits of the age, and roasted before
the slow fire of public indignation, appear to possess as little
feeling as the "passive ox," that graced the democratic fete in
Boston, held in honor of the French revolution.

21　This petty piece of an apostrophe we hereby acknowledge to
have taken *verbatim et literatim* from one of Moore's songs.
We consider this Confession as a very proper proceeding on
our part; for having in our last edition inadvertently hit on one
of Butler's rhymes, a democratic scribbler in the *Baltimore
Evening Post* the *tertium quid* paper of that place has raised a
hue and cry against us, forsooth for *plagiarism*. As well might
the booby affirm that we had stolen our poetry from Cicero's
Orations, because we make use of the Roman alphabet. This
would-be critic has an undoubted right in a free government^
to be a *fool*, but if he has set up *for a wit*, his best way, as Swift
has it, is to *set down again*.

Nothing did demos any good
But *syllogisms* made of wood,[22]
But these applied with proper force,
Confounded Jacobins of course.

They found the basis of their grandeur,
Must be deceit, and lies, and slander,
The only possible foundation
Of democratic reputation.

Their crafty chief, with other fetches.
Hires a vile gang of foreign wretches,

---

22   The famous *spitting* affray, and the consequent cudgelling in
Congress hall, where are well known to every body. An *appeal*
to the *right of the strongest*, became in that instance *justifia-*
ble, if not *unavoidable*, in consequence of the obstinacy of the
party whose political sentiments agreed with the gentleman,
who in that rencounter had the honor to be the *cudgellee*. It
is to be feared, however, that the most *forcible* arguments of
this kind, will not always be sufficiently powerful to make a
lasting *impression* on the headstrong demagogues of this fac-
tion. Some political partizans, have shown themselves to be so
wilfully blind, obstinate, and ignorant, that the means which
we have mentioned in *Terrible Tractoration,*

    Of making sky lights to the mind,
    By boring a bole through the body,

seem to be the only practicable mode by which they can be
enlightened. But this method will not be adopted by the feder-
alists. The more violent demagogues of the now ruling party, it
is to be feared, will be the first to sacrifice their leaders, while
the latter, like Fayette in France, and like M'Kean in America,
strive in vain to hush the hurricane of their own exciting.

To lie down every man of merit,[23]
Of honesty and public spirit.

His sovereign friends the mob caresses
From twenty different hireling presses,
Who spread vile lies, with vast sedulity,
T' impose on honest men's credulity.

Gives foreigners our loaves and fishes[24]

---

23 The falsehoods, which Callender and others have been *paid* for propagating, the torrents of abuse which have been poured upon Washington and other patriots, are now, happily for the public, pretty generally traced to their filthy sources. The characters of the men who have been vilified by the scoundrel-gang of Mr. J . . . . . . n's hirelings, are found to be such as do honor to our country. But their calumniators . . . . who are they? Cheethams, Pasquins, Duanes . . . . men who (to talk like an Irishman) had they *lived* in their native country till *this time* would have *been hung, years ago.*

24 It is a truth which the political history of America makes abundantly manifest, that the principal disturbances which have convulsed the United States, have originated in the intrigues of "imported patriots." This is a circumstance, which is by no means remarkable, when we consider the habits, attachments, and situations of such foreigners in their native country. Few men are disposed to migrate from the land of their nativity, who are not thereto induced by *misconduct,* or a turbulent and aspiring disposition. The principle which is denominated *patriotism,* modern philosophers notwithstanding, is implanted in man by the hand of nature, and he who has divested himself of that principle, either by, *philosophizing,* or by any other still less justifiable means, must have rooted out those moral feelings which are the best security of society. Besides, foreigners who leave their native countries, with a determination to settle in America, are, generally, men who have been accustomed to be governed

'To bend our counsels to his wishes,
And *guillotine* the reputation
Of every good man in the nation.

Fellows, who sped away betimes
To seek "asylum" from their crimes,
In annals of Old Bailey noted,
Are in *"Freedonia"* promoted.[25]

Vile renegades of every nation
Are sure to gain an elevation,

---

themselves, and to the amount of their powers, to govern others with a strong arm . . . . have either themselves been hard pressed by the heavy hand of government, or have been, as members of such government, active in imposing a heavy hand on others. They have, generally, no definite ideas of that temperate liberty, which is as remote from licentiousness as it is from despotism.

All nations, except the American, have found it necessary to lay aliens under certain restrictions, disadvantages and liabilities, which, though they may appear to operate as an hardship on the individuals subjected thereto, are imperiously demanded for the purpose of securing the best interests of the communities in which such aliens reside. If such regulations are necessary in other nations, they will be found pre-eminently requisite in that of America, where, such is the want of power in our rulers, and so delicate is the mechanism of the government, that a single Gallatin may impede, if not stop its wheels. But this subject has been ably discussed in Congress, in the debates respecting the repeal of the alien Law.

25   Freedonia is a cant phrase, which certain small poets or prosaic scribblers, we forget which, would have us adopt as an appellative to designate the United States of America. At a time like this, when misrule and licentiousness are the order of the day, there can be but little propriety in coining new phrases to enrich the vocabulary of sedition.

But honesty and reputation
Are passports to a private station.

These wretches now announce hostility
To talents, virtue and civility[26]
Direct their vandalizing ravages
To make men like themselves, mere savages.

By creeping cunning overbalance
The weight of wisdom, and of talents.
Like Absalom, with wicked arts.
Contrive to steal the people's hearts.

The leading demos have their tools,

---

26 There always is something "rotten in the state of Denmark," if
men of the first abilities are decried by demagogues, and point-
ed out as proper objects for the jealousy of the people. That the
principal talents in America are now in disgrace because they
are federalists, none but the most brazen faced partizans will
deny. If by talents, however, we are to understand

> That low cunning, which in fools supplies,
> And amply too, the place of being wise;
>   CHURCHILL,

we must allow the dominant party are far from being deficient.
But wisdom and cunning are very distinct attributes, although
by many absurdly blended. The former qualifies its possessors
to aggrandize society, at the same time that it promotes the
interests of all its individuals. The latter is of no consequence
to any person but its possessor, and is by him usually em-
ployed to exalt himself at the expense of society, or of individ-
uals. Wisdom was well exemplified in Washington, cunning in
J . . . . . . n

A mongrel set, 'twixt knaves and fools,[27]
But I've not patience to examine a
Crew that's so destitute of stamina.

These, by arch demagogues are led on.
And futile promises are fed on,
Enjoying, by anticipation
Some post of profit in the nation.[28]

And now to make the people jealous,
The scoundrels undertake to tell us,
They are themselves the chosen band,
"Exclusive patriots" of the land.

Thus, when a swindler means to cheat you,

---

27   Your *half wits* are, by nature, formed for Democracy. Leaden
pated gentlemen, who vainly aspire to eminence in the learned
professions, quack-doctors illiterate clergymen, and blunder-
ing lawyers, are the Democracy of nature, and their opposites
are, sometimes, styled the Aristrocracy of nature. Between
these two sorts of candidates for eminence, there will always
exist a covert or an open war. Those who belong to that class in
society, which nature intended should move in a subordinate
and limited sphere, are rarely contented with their condition,
but by means of the little arts of little minds, elevate them-
selves to an artificial consequence, which terminates in their
disgrace and the public detriment.

28   The impossibility of realizing all these anticipations, must
create divisions and subdivisions among the now triumphant
demagogues. Those who have been honestly led astray, it is to
be hoped, will unite heart and hand with those who have con-
stantly trod the path of Federal rectitude, and form a union of
upright and intelligent men, who may yet preserve the nation
from the "abhorred gulf" of Democratic tyranny.

With vast civility he'll treat you,
In all his intercourse pretends
To be your very best of friends.

Such friendship Joab erst employ'd,
When his friend Abner he decoy'd,
And Judas such a friend as this,
Betray 'd his master with a kiss.

Now these Pat-Ryots join as one[29]
To thwart the plans of Washington,
And puff th' immaculate Thomas Jefferson
As Freedom's only great and clever son.

Yes . . . . Washington our pride and glory,
Vile denies dubb'd a British tory,[30]
And Duane undertook to blast him,
And prove no Nero e'er surpass'd him!

With bug-bear phantoms to alarm us
They conjure up huge standing armies,
With which, and Washington to lead 'em,

---

29 Dean Swift, in some of his writings, informs us, that the word
    Patriot, originated from one Pat-Ryot, a turbulent Irishman
    who was hung for rebellion, and as we are particularly fond of
    etymological deduction we have here rcitored the word to its
    original orthography.

30 It is fresh in the recollection of every person, who is in the
    smallest degree acquainted with the political history of the
    United States, that Washington did not escape the abuse of
    the faction now in power. He was said to have been partial to
    British interests, and reviled in the most unqualified terms, by
    the Aurora patriots.

The feds would bayonet our freedom.[31]

---

31 No measure of the federal administration, has called forth more abuse from their political opponents, than the raising of a sttanding army. But many who reprobate that step, and suppose that it led to that step in deep designs of domination, may, perhaps, be convinced that the motives from which it originated were pure, when they peruse the following letter from our beloved and im mortal chief, by which he signified his acceptance of the command of this army, which, say the Democrats, was destined to destroy our liberties. Mount-Vernouy July 13, 1798.

DEAR SIR,

I had the honor, on the evening: of the 11th instant, to receive from the hand of the secretary of war, your favour of the 7th, announcing that you had, with the advice and consent of the Senate, appointed me "Lieutenant-General, and Commander in Chief of all the armies raised, or to be raised, for the service of the United States."

I cannot express how greatly affected I am at this new proof of public confidence, and the highly flattering manner in which you have been pleased to make the communication. At the same time, I must not conceal from you my earnest wish that the choice had fallen on a man, less declined in years, and better qualified to encounter the usual vicissitudes of war.

You know, sir, what calculation I had made, relative to the probable course of events, on my retiring from office, and the determination I had consoled myself with, of closing the remnant of my days in my present peaceful abode; you will therefore be at no loss to conceive and appieciate the sensation I must have experienced, to bring myself any conclusion that would pledge me, at so late a period of my life, to leave scenes I sincerely love, to enter upon the boundless field of action, incessant trouble, and high responsibility.

It is not possible for me to remain ignorant of, or indifferent to recent transactions.

The conduct of the directory of France towards our country; their insidious hostility to its government; their various practices to withdraw the affec- tions of the people from it; the evident tendency of their acts, and those of their agents, to countenance and invigorate opposition; their disregard of solemn treaties and laws of nations; their war upon our defenceless commerce; their treatment of our ministers of peace; and their demands, amounting to tribute, could not fail to excite in *me* corresponding sentiments with those my countrymen have so generally expressed in their affectionate addresses to you. Believe me, sir, no one can more cordially approve of the wise and prudent measures of your administration. They ought to inspire universal confidence; and will no doubt, combined with, the state of things, call from Congress such laws and means, as will enable you to meet the full extent of the crisis.

Satisfied therefore that you have sincerely wished and endeavoured to avert war, and exhausted to the last drop, the cup of reconciliation, we can with pure hearts appeal tb Heaven for the justice of our cause, and may confidently trust the final result to that kind Providence, who has heretofore, and so often, signally favoured the people of the United States.

Thinking in this manner, and feeling how incumbent it is upon every person, of every description, to contribute at all times to his country's welfare, especially in a *moment like the present, when every thing we hold clear and sacred, is so seriously threatened*; I have finally determined to accept the commission of Commander in Chief of the armies of the United States, with this reserve only, that I shall not be called into the field until the army is in

Adams they styled a hoary traitor,[32]

---

a situation to require my presence, or it becomes indispensible by the urgency of circuitistances.

In making this reservation, I beg it may be understood, that I do not mean to withhold any assistance to arrange and organize the army, which you think I can afford. I take the liberty also to mention, that I must decline having my acceptance considered as drawing after it any immediate charge upon the public; or that I can receive any emoluments annexed to the appointment, before entering into a situation to incur expense.

The Secretary of War being anxious to return to the seat of government, I have detained him no longer than was necessary to a full communication upon the several points he had in charge.

With great respect and consideration,
I have the honor to be, dear sir,
your most obedient humble servant,
GEORGE WASHINGTON.

32   The infamous Callender, a tool and hireling of Mr. Jefferson, thus expresses himself in *The Prospect Before Us*:

"This hoary-headed incendiary (*Adams*) bawls out, to arms!" "Alas, he is not an object of envy,! but of compassion and . . . . of *horror!*" Again, "JOHN ADAMS . . . . that scourge, that scorn, that outcast of *America*."

"We have been governed by one of the most execrable of all SCOUNDRELS. He is, in private life, one of the most egregious fools on the continent."

"He (the future historian) will inquire by what species of madness, America submitted to accept as her President, a person *without abilities*, and *without virtue*; being alike incapable of attaching either tenderness or esteem,"

&c.

Pickering a public defalcator,
And that with other mischief done, he
Had stolen all our public money.

We might proceed through reams on reams
To set forth democratic schemes
Their midnight caucusses declare,
To shew what precious rogues they are.

Our pithy poem might enamel
By telling how they brib'd one Campbell,
(Which tale, O Gallatin, would pleasure ye)
To steal the books from public Treasury.

How Duane, Gallatin, and Smilie,
And other rogues in Co. went slily.
And drudg'd all night to ruin Pickering
And furnish documents for bickering.

But since our poem is a peg.
On which to hang our notes,[33] we beg,
This midnight matter to disclose
Without a trope, in simple prose.[34]

---

33 Democrats have so declared, but as the author of the *Pursuits of Literature* and some other writers of eminence are involved in a similar charge, we shall not attest to refute the accusation, but plead the custom of authors in the Court of Criticism in our own justification.

34 Among other malicious manceuvres of the faction, who have supplanted the friends and followers of Washington, may be numbered the mean attempt to stigmatize Col. Pickering, by corrupting a clerk in one of the public offices. Anthony Camp-

bell, the tool of the party on this occasion, was in 1800 a re-
cording clerk in the office of the Auditor of the Treasury, all
accounts having been previously *audited* and *examined* by the
principal clerk, were registered in the books then entrusted to
Campbell. The monies drawn by the Secretary of State were
charged to him in those books, but the credits for the appli-
cation not entered till vouchers were produced of the manner
in which the sums were disbursed. Months and sometimes
years necessarily expired before vouchers and receipts relative
to the expenditures of money destined to the payment of our
Ambassadors, and other public pur- poses in Europe, could
be procured from the persons to whom they were transmitted.

Campbell informed some of the *deep ones* among the dem-
ocrats, that the books of his department exhibited a large un-
expended balance in the hands of Mr. Pickering. Campbell,
together with one Gardner, was prevailed upon to become
an instrument in the hands of the faction, and give Colooel
Pickering's political opponents a view of the books: For this
purpose under the pretext of personal accommodation he ob-
tained leave to sleep in the office. A meeting of pure patriots
was held at Israel Israel's, corner of Third and Chesnut street,
Philadelphia, among whom were Gallatin, Smilie, Duane, and
some others amounting to eight or ten. The books of the Treas-
ury were taken by night to Israel's, the accounts afterwards
published in the Aurora transcribed by these scriveners, and
the books returned before day light.

The remarks which appeared in the *Washington Federalist*
of April 21, 1802, accompanying a developement of this dark
transaction, are so pertinent to the subject that we cannot re-
sist the temptation of transcribing them.

> Can it be supposed that Gallatin, and many oth-
> ers, when they examined these accounts did not
> know their unsettled state, and the imperfect view
> which they gave of the disbursement of the public
> money? And when Mr. Wolcott in his letter dated
> 23d day of June 1800, in answer to the charge in
> the Aurora, explained the nature of these accounts,

Although in any foreign land,

could any one have doubted a moment that the statements published were imperfect? And yet we find the Aurora with matchless impudence repeating those charges. Towards Campbell we feel pity and contempt, that he should so far forget his duty as to violate the most sacred obligations of honor and perjure hiniself to become the tool of a party. But what emotions does the conduct of those excite who instigated him to such infamous practices, who could not only resort to means so base to obtain those documents, but likewise employ them in the manner they did, knowing them to be imperfect. If they were convinced that the charges were just, why did they not at once bring forward an impeachment against Mr. Pickering, or appoint a committee to examine into his accounts? Because they knew the result would be what every subsequent investigation has been, a fair and honorable acquittal. They knew what an effect a bold publication of it would have on the honest and unsuspecting yeomanry; men brought up in the simple manners of the country, unpractised in intrigue and unacquainted with the depravity of human nature.

Gardner the accomplice of Campbell in this underhanded transaction, was rewarded by being appointed consul to Demarara. Campbell attempted to take advantage of his treachery, but Gallatin was too cunning for him, and he received nothing, till threatening a disclosure of the whole affair, an ensigncy at length stopped his mouth.

A committee of the House of Representatives was afterwards appointed for the purpose of examing the account of the late secretaries; consisting of Messrs. Nicholas, Nicholson, Stone, Otis, Griswold. Waln, and Craik, the three first of whom were democrats.

This committee, after a laborious scrutiny, by their report entirely exculpated Mr. Pickering; and Gallatin himself acknowledged that "the whole of the money received by Mr.

Such folks as these are hung off hand,

Pickering, had been applied to public purposes." It likewise appeared that Mr. Pickering not only had not embezzled one single dollar of the public money, but that he had saved to the United States 14,588 dollars, by a purchase of bills of exchange on London, which, with the new school-conscience, he might very conveniently have appropriated to his own use.

Notwithstanding such was the purity of Pickering, the venal Aurora, whose unprincipled editor has done much, very much towards clamouring down every man of merit in the community, published a number of articles, with the title of "PUBLIC PLUNDER," which contributed not a little to the election of Mr. Jefferson and the establishment of Duane's importance as an editor. In one of these, Duane asserted, that on the 18th of April 1800, Mr. Pickering had drawn upon the treasury for fifty thousand dollars; and that at the time when he drew for this sum he had in his hands three hundred thousand dollars *unaccounted* for. Duane likewise declared that Mr. Pickering held in his hands, nearly double the amount of both these sums, intimating that he then was delinquent in the enormous sum of seven hundred thousand dollars.

This is one instance, among the many which might be adduced, proving the base means to which certain men have resorted, for the purpose of tarnishing the reputation of those heroes and statesmen to whose exertions we are chiefly indebted for our national prosperity. The falsehoods by which democrats have achieved the purpose of elevating themselves, and disgracing the nation, are thrown aside as soon as by their instrumentality these precious objects are attained. Thus it was said that the war office buildings were purposely set on fire by Mr. Wolcott. Thus Hamilton and M'Henry, with a number of other federal patriots, have been accused of peculation and other crimes, by their political adversaries, but not a single proof of improper conduct in office, has ever been adduced. The effect of these falsehoods, however, has been to stigmatize their characters in the opinion of many of their fellow-citizens, and to put a period to their political existence. *If such are to be the rewards of patriotism in America, it is to be feared, it will soon be a plant of rare growth.*

Yet we, *a free and happy* nation,
Reward the rogues with public station.

Now Hamilton is represented
Assaying wicked schemes invented,
By dint of which, with sudden start he
Would make himself a Buonaparte.

Not even the shelter of the grave
From democratic spite could save
This man, most worthy admiration,
An honor to his age and nation.[35]

---

35 The untimely fall of Gen. Hamilton excites emotions, which we shall not attempt in this place to express. Few writers are equal to the task of pourtraying in just colours, the character of that great man, and we cannot forbear entering our critical caveat against the style and manner of some of the eulogies which we have seen in commemoration of his untimely decease. In many of these productions we have observed a strained elevation, a redundancy of rhetorical flourishes, which appear rather to emanate from an ambition to display the talents of the orator, than from feelings of affection for the deceased, or a wish to commemorate his virtues. The expressions of grief are simply pathetic. The fancy never makes wild excursions, when the heart is wrung with anguish. The eulogies, however, of Messrs. Morris, Otis, and some few others, are pure and correct; the effusions of genius, chastened by jugdment and taste. From the latter of these performances, I am happy to present the following extract, as it is happily illustrative of that magnanimity and greatness of soul, which distinguishes the real hero, from the bold and aspiring demagogue.

> The principles professed by the first leaders of that (the French) revolution, were so congenial to those of the American people; their pretences of aiming merely at the reformation of abuses were so

plausible; the spectacle of a great people struggling tu recover their "long-lost liberties" was so imposing and august; while that of a combination of tyrants to conquer, and subjugate, was so revolting; the services received from one of the belligerent powers, and the injuries inflicted by the other, were so recent in our minds, that the sensibility of the nation was excited to the most exquisite pitch. To this disposition, so favourable to the wishes of France, every appeal was made, which intrigue, corruption, flattery, and threats could dictate. At this dangerous and dazzling crisis, there were but few men entirely exempt from the general delirium. Among the few was HAMILTON. His penetrating eye discerned, and his prophetic voice foretold, the tendency and consequence of the first revolutionary movements. He was assured that every people which should espouse the cause of France would pass under her yoke, and that the people of France, like every nation which surrenders its reason to the mercy of demagogues, would be driven by the storms of anarchy upon the shores of despotism. All this he knew was conformable to the invariable law of nature and experience of mankind. From the reach of this desolation he was anxious to save his country, and in the pursuit of his purpose, he breasted the assaults of calumny and prejudice."The torrent roared, and he did buffet it." Appreciating the advantages of a neutral position, he co-operated with WASHINGTON, ADAMS, and the other patriots of that day, in the means best adapted to maintain it. The rights and duties of neu trality proclaimed by the president, were explained and enforced by. HAMILTON in the character of Pacificus. The attempts to corrupt and intimidate were resisted. The British treaty was justified and defended as an honorable compact with our natural friends, and pregnant with advantages, which have since been realized and acknowledged by its opponents.

The blustering *old dominion* frets

By this pacific and vigorous policy, in the whole course of which the genius and activity of HAMIL-TON were conspicuous, time and information were afforded to the American nation, and correct views were acquired of our situation and interests. We beheld the republics of Europe, march in procession to the funeral of their own liberties by the lurid light of the revolutionary torch. The tumult of the passions subsided, the wisdom of the administration was perceived, and America now remains a solitary monument in the desolated plains of liberty.

Having remained at the head of the treasury several years, and filled its coffers; having developed the sources of ample revenue, and tested the advantages of his own system by his own experience; I and leaving expended his private fortune; he found it necessary to retire from public employment, and to devote his attention to the claims of a large and dear family. What brighter instance of disinterested honor has ever been exhibited to an admiring world! That a man, upon whom devolved the task of originating a system of revenue for a nation; of devising the checks in his own department; to provide for the collections of sums, the amount of which was conjectural; that a man, who anticipated the effects of a funding system, yet a secret in his own bosom, and who was thus enabled to have secured a princely fortune, consistently with principles esteemed fair by the world! That such a man by no means addicted to an expensive or extravagant style of living, should have retired from an office destitute of means adequate to the wants of mediocrity and have resorted to professional labour for the means of decent support, are facts which must instruct and astonish those, who in countries habituated to corruption and venality are more attentive to the gains than to the duties of an official station . . . . Yet HAM-ILTON was that man. It was a fact always known to

Because she has to pay her debts,

his friends, and it is now evident from his testament, made under a deep presentiment of his approaching fate. Blush then, ministers and warriors of imperial France, who have deluded your nation by pretensions to a disinterested regard for its liberties and rights! Disgorge the riches extorted from your fellow-citizens, and the spoils amassed from confiscation and blood! Restore to the impoverished nation the price paid by them for the privilege of slavery, and now appropriated to the refinement of luxury! Approach the tomb of HAMILTON, and compare the insignificance of your gorgeous palaces with the awful majesty of this tenement of clay!

We again accompany our friend in the walks of private life, and in the assiduous pursuit of his profession, until the aggressions of France compelled the nation to assume the attitude of defence. He was now invited by the great and enlightened statesman who had succeeded to the presidency, and at the express request of the Commander in Chief, to accept of the second rank in the army. Though no man had manifested a greater desire to avoid war, yet it is freely confessed that when war appeared to be inevitable, his heart exulted in "the tented field," and he loved the life and occupation of a soldier. His early habits were formed amid the fascinations of the camp. And though the pacific policy of Adams once more rescued us from war, and shortened the existence of the army establishment, yet its duration was sufficient to secure to him the love and confidence of officers and men, to enable him lo display the talents and qualities of a great general, and to justify the most favourable prognostics of his prowess in the field.

Once more this excellent man unloosed the helmet from his brow, and returned to the duties of the forum. From this lime he persristed in a firm resolution to decline all civil honors and promotion, and to

Her Nabobs join in grand committee,

live a private citizen, unless again summoned to the defence of his country. He became more than ever assiduous in his practice at the bar, and intent upon his plans of domestic happiness, until a nice and mistaken estimate of the claims of honor, impelled him to the fatal act which terminated his life.

Since quoting the above I have perused the oration of J. M. Mason, D. D. commemorative of the virtues and talents of this illustrious m.an. It is a splendid effort of genius which would have done credit to the pen of a Burke, and appears to have been inspired by a spirit akin to that of the hero it celebrates. We should think the style of the eulogy somewhat too highly encomiastic, were not the subject a Hamilton; but it is scarcely possible to employ too bold a pencil in giving characteristic scketches of such a man.

Some trails of General Hamilton, published in the *Boston Repertory*, and said to have been drawn up by the Hon. Fisher Ames, are eminently beautiful. The pencil of S. Cullen Carpenter, editor of the *Charleston Courier*, whose literary productions have acquired him a highly deserved celebrity, has pourtrayed, in letters of light, the principal features in this most distinguished character; indeed the portrait of Hamilton, as drawn by the hands of the writers we have mentioned, ought to be in the possession of every American of taste and sensibility.*

The incessant torrents of calumny, which have been poured on that truly great man, since the fatal rencontre which terminated his txistence, exhibits a lamentable proof of democratic depravity. The coaduct of a *Chronicle* scribbler in Boston in particular (said to be the late candidate for governor, Mr. Sullivan) has often called to our recollection the following lines from Churchill:

Should love of fame, in every noble mind
A brave disease, with love of virtue join'd.
Spur thee to deeds of pith, where courage try'd
In reason's court is amply justified;

101

To "kick to hell the British treaty."[36]

Or fond of knowledge, and averse to strife,
Shouldst thou prefer the calmer walks of life;
Shouldst thou by pale and sickly study led,
Pursue coy science to the fountain head;
Virtue thy guide, and public good thy end,
Should every thought to oar improvement tend,
To curb the passiohs, to enlarge the mind.
Purge the sick weal and humanize mankind;
Rage in her eye and malice in her breast,
Redoubled horror grinning on her crest,
Fiercer each snake, and sharper every dart,
Quick from her cell shall madening envy start:
Then shalt thou find, but find, alas! too late,
How vain is worth! how short is glory's date!
Then shalt thou find, when friends with foes conspire
To give more proof than virtue would desire,
Thy danger chiefly lies in acting well;
No crime's so great as daring to excell.

* We would refer our readers to *A Collection of Facts and Documentsi relative to the death of Gen. Hamilton* by the editor of the *Evening Post.*

36 We have here adorned our poetry with a very *judicious* rhetorical flourish, quoted from the declarations of the dashing nabobs of the south, who first signalized themselves by their opposition to that instrument. The virulent, and unqualified abuse, which has been heaped upon General Washington, Mr. Jay, and the whole federal party for having given origin to a treaty, which in all probability prevented our participating in the crimes and horrors of the French revolution, is scarcely to be paralleled in the annals of political contests. Nothing short of the prudence of a Washington could have stemmed the tide of democratic depravity on this occasion. None, however, of the evils anticipated from this deprecated treaty have taken place, and it is abundantly manifest on investigating the causes of Virginian virulence that *self interest* was the real motive of the *deluders* in exciting this alarm.

The funding system, tax on land,

It appears that the claims of British creditors against *Virginia, only* as exhibited by their commissioners, appointed under the 6th article of Mr. Jay's treaty, amounted to 8,500,000 dollars, but those against the whole of the New-England states were but a little rising of 100,000 dollars. These claims, although not positive evidences of debts due to their whole amount, yet furnish a clue for a proportional estimate of the debts due from Virginia, and from the New-England states.

No doubt the easiest way for Virginia to pay this debt was, to use the expressions of some of their leaders to "kick the treaty to h . . . . ll" This they might do, in the course of their proceedings without *going out of their way.*

It ought not, however, to be forgotten that this *obnoxious treaty, and the hostilities committed by England on our commerce in the year* 1793, *were the consequence of Virginia delinquency and aggression.* The legislature of Virginia, in October 1783, passed an act *to absolve British debtors from the payment of money*, even after their debts had been ascertained by judgments in courts of law. On the other hand the British refused to relinquish the possession of the northern posts. In December 1787, in consequence of an earnest requisition of congress the assembly of Virginia passed an act *apparently* to repeal all such acts of that state as had prevented, or might prevent the recovery of debts due to British subjects, according to the true intent of the treaty. But took care in a proviso to this act to *suspend the repeal*, and thereby render it entirely null, under the pretence of infractions on the part of the British, thus arrogating to themselves power, which of right belonged to the general government, and making a mere farce of their own proceedings.

The English, however, not being disposed to relish this kind of treatment, appealed to their *ultiam ratio*, commenced a war on our commerce, and thus collected their demands by virtue of the authority of their cannon. The immense losses which of consequence fell upon the merchants of the eastern and middle states in the year 1793, by British captures, will not soon be forgotten.

But this was not all. Mr. King in pursuance of instructions of the federal administration, negociated for the payment, at

Were first propos'd by Giles's band,[37]

the treasury of the United States, of 600,000*l.* sterling, nearly three millions of dollars, for losses sustained by British subjects, by legal impediments to prevent the collection of their demands chiefly against these Virginia debtors.

Thus Virginian delinquency cost the United States nearly 3,000,000 dollars, subjected us to those depredations on our commerce in 1793, by which the country sustained immense losses, and laid the foundation for Mr. Jay's treaty, which has excited so much clamour among our precious patriots against the federal administration.

37   The standing army, the funding system, and the land tax have each furnished most fruitful topics of democratic declamation, and the party in power by fully attaching to the federalists the odium, which the mere mention of these bug-bear measures, has never failed to excite, have succeeded in accomplishing their political destruction. We have already shown on what occasion the army was raised. The funding system, the theme of never ceasing clamour, from those who have uniformly opposed every public measure, which had a tendency to promote the honor and happiness of our country, met the unequivocal approbation of one of the greatest giants of the dominant faction. Gallatin in his treatise on the finances of the United States, after finding all the fault he decently could with the measures of the federal administration, has the following remarks.

Let it not be supposed that any of those reflections are intended to convey any censure on that part of the funding system, which provided for the payment of the interest of the proper debt of the United States. They are designed merely to show that the propriety of that measure must depend solely on its justice. Whether the debt had been funded on the plan of discrimination in favour of the original holders, or those who had performed the services, or, as has been the case in favour of the purchasers of certificates, the general effects would have been nearly

Who swore that duties rais'd from commerce
But slily filch our money from us.

The funds created, taxes laid,
The measures by the imps are made
A handle, plausible no doubt,
To turn the Washingtonians out.

And now the lying varlets tell us
Wolcott and Dexter were such fellows,
To carry peculation's farce on
They'd crown'd their robberies with arson.[38]

_____

the same; and unless the American government had
chosen to forfeit every claim to common honesty it
must necessarily provide for discharging the princi-
pal, or paying the interest to one or the other of two
descriptions of persons.*

It is likewise a fact that the land tax "was a measure to which
the federalists had been urged for years by their political oppo-
nents because they foresaw in it the ruin of their power." See
Bayard's speech on the Judiciary Bill.

* Here is displayed a little of this gentleman's sort of cunning.
In the name of common sense how was it possible for the
government to establish a fund in favour of some individu-
als, who might hold these securities to the prejudice of ether
individuals, who might held the same sort of securities.
Shall missory note payahle to A. or bearer, and purchased by
B. not be collected by the latter, because he paid less than its
nominal value, and run the risk of the failure of the drawer?

38 It cannot be forgotten that such was the ciy of the demagogue
papers from one end of the United States to the other. A com-
mittee, however, being appointed to enquire into the causes
of the fires, these gentlemen were honorably exculpated, and

Now swells each Jacobinic throat
With dreadful, boding, screech-owl note
And democrats are choak'd with sobbings,
Because the British hung one Robbins.[39]

To hang a murderer and a pirate
Was tyranizing at a high rate,

---

democrats were under the necessity of inventing new false-hoods to answer the purposes of the party. It happened very providentially, that all the papers which were necessary to show the perfect integrity, not only of Mr. Wolcott, but of the whole Federal administration in fiscal concerns, were saved.

39 The lie about Robbins the British pirate, so often affirmed by democrats to have been an American citizen, and born in Danbury in Connecticut, has been repeated times without number by the democratic newspapers.

This tale was propagated with an intention to throw odium on Mr. Adams for having directed the criminal to be surrendered to justice. It appears that his letter to Judge Bee, and which has been the ground of all the clamour of Robbins' sympathizing friends, merely directed him to be delivered up if proved to be a British subject and a pirate and a murderer. The man previous to his execution acknowledged himself to be a British subject, and owned that the sentence by which he suffered was just. But Mr. Carleton would not agree to this. This tender hearted gentleman, editor of the *Salem Register*, and his brethren in iniquity, declared that Robbins was a good man, and an American citizen, and Adams a tyrant, who had been instrumental in his destruction. Indeed it is not very marvellous that a good democrat should feel an interest in the sufferings of one whose life and conversation declared him to be a member of their fraternity.

> Never did trusty squire with knight
> Or knight with squire e*er jump more right,
> > HUDIBRAS.

Alarmed the gallows-dreading clan,
In love with Tom Pain's *Rights of Man.*

Poor Carleton was most sadly frighted,
Felt all his sympathies excited . . . .
Was very properly perplext
Lest his own turn might be the next.

In grade of crimes but one step higher
Had brought the vile *recorded* liar,[40]
(Were justice done in such a case)
To Robbins, alias Nash's place.

Thus theives are rarely known to toast
Their enemy the whipping post,
And felons commonly exhibit
No little spleen against a gibbet.

Hence, in these democratic times,
This hanging people for their crimes
Is thought a most obnoxious thing.
By those who know they ought to swing,

Now common decency defying,
They ply their dirty trade of lying,
Hold out such falsehoods, *in terrorem*,
That no good man can stand before 'em.

---

40 Carleton has been indicted, found guilty, and punished with
fine and imprisonment for publishing a false and malicious li-
bel on Mr. Pickering.

And many a patriot's forc'd to doff his
Old fashioned honesty for office.
Become a supple, and time serving
Rasoal, to keep himself from starving.

Each lie they tell, though ne'er so horrid a
Vile gang repeats from Maine to Florida,
And when found out and people hiss it
In sneaking silence they dismiss it

No cur can wag his tail or yelp
But what puts in his mickle help,
For every puppy in the pack
Is taught his proper scent and track.

In short *they lied, through thick and thin,*
Till Jefferson at last came in,
And made fair promises in plenty.
Provided he'd kept one in twenty.

Yes . . . . we were raptur'd when he said
We're all republicans and fed-
Ral, fellow countrymen, Americans,
And hop'd we'd done with Factions hurricanes.

With such professions all were suited
But soon his conduct all refuted,
What time his highness made a shift
To send our staunchest men adrift.

The veteran chiefs of seventy-six,

If by sad chance their politicks
Displeas'd the Carter Mountain hero,
He persecuted like a Nero;[41]

---

41   I do not mean to assert that Mr. Jefferson hung, burnt, or guil-
lotined his opponents. But perhaps the means by which the
federalists have been "oppugnated," have been but little less
destructive to the sufferers, and but little more honorable on
the part of those who have adopted such means. Starving a
man and his family, is doubtless, an effectual method of dis-
patching him.

Most of the federalists, who held offices under the Washing-
ton and Adams administrations, had devoted much time and
expense to qualify themselves for such offices, and in many
instances had relinquished lucrative professions and branches
of business, that they might the better perform the duties of
those offices. These have been displaced for young and igno-
rant persons, and in many in stances foreigners, whose sole
recommendation has been their Jeffersonian politics, while
the war-worn veteran who had fought the battles of our Inde
pendence, and grown, not only old, but fioor, in active services
for his country, is prohibited from tasting the fruits of his la-
bours, by the faction, which is now dominant, and seems will-
ing "to owe their greatness to their country's ruin."

To give a catalogue of all the worthies, who have adorned
Mr. Jefferson's Proscription list, would be to name almost
every honest man who held any office under government, at
the time Mr. Jefferson was elected.

The following is a list of a few, who were removed from of-
fice, for no other reason than their being obnoxious on account
of their political opinions:

John Wilkes Kittera, Attorney for the Eastern District,
Pennsylvania; John Hall, Marshal of the same District; Sam-
uel Hogdon, Superintendant of Public Stores at Philadelphia;
John Harris, Store Keeper at the same place; Henry Miller, Su-
pervisor of the Revenue of the District of Pennsylvania; J. M.
Lingan, Attorney for the District of Columbia; Thomas Iwan,
Attorney; John Pierce, Commissioner of Loans for the State
of Newhampshire; Thomas Martin, Collector of the District

of Portsmouth, in the same state; Jacob Sheaffe, Navy Agent at Portsmouth; Richard Harrison, Attorney for the District of New-York; Aquila Giles, Marshal of the same District; James Watson, Navy Agent for New-York; Joshua Sands, Collector of the Port of New-York; Nicholas Fish, Supervisor of the District of New-York; William Smith, Minister Plenipotentiary to Portugal; William Vans Murray, Minister Resident to the Batavian Republic; David Humphreys, Minister Pleoipotentiary to the Court of Madrid; Elizur Goodrich, Collector of New-Haven, John Chester, Supervisor of the District of Connecticut; Ray Greene, Judge of Rhode-Island District Territory; Winthrop Sargeant, Governor of the Missisippi Territory; David Hopkins, Marshal of the District of Maryland; Andrew Bell, Collector of the Port of Amboy; Aaron Dunham, Supervisor of the District of New-Jersey; James Dole, Marshal of the District of Albany; Robert Hamilton, Marshal of the District of Delaware; Harrison G. Otis, Attorney for the District of Massachusetts; Chauncey Whittlesey, Collector of Middletown, Connecticut; Amos Marsh, Attorney for the District of Vermont; Jabez Fitch, Marshal for the same District; Samuel Bradford, Marshal of the District of Massachusetts; Thomas Perkins, Commissioner of Loans for the State of Massachusetts; *cum multis aliis,* all good men and true; and we believe that their successors in office have been men, whose talents, reputation, or pretensions to public patronage, could in no way entitle them to take the precedence of the gentlemen who were displaced, had not the spirit of party turned the "world upside down."

Well might Mr. Bayard observe of such management by the party in power

> It is in this path we see the real victims of stern, uncharitable, unrelenting power. It is here, we see the soldier WHO FOUGHT THE BATTLES OF THE REVOLUTION; *who spilt his bloody and wasted his strength to establish the Indefiendence of His country; delirived of the reward of Jus services, and left to pine in penury and wretchedness. It is along this path that you may see helpless children crying for*

Humphrey and Putman, Fish, and others,
Whom Washington esteemed as brothers,
Displaced to please the vilest set
That ever plagu'd a nation yet.

But as I had from natal hour
Respect for great men, while in power
I mean right merrily to chaunt o-
Ver his praise in my next canto.

Good reader these are merely sketches
Of democratic feats and fetches,
Their tricks, to which no honest man
Has ever stoop'd nor ever can.

Thus Weishaupt erst had made no pother
His brat to poison, and its mother,
Lest crimes reveal'd should cause a schism
With founders of Illuminism.

'Twould cost whole Mexic gulphs of rhyme,
(To deal in Crusca's true sublime,)
Their deeds of darkness to display
And drag these Cacusses to day.[42]

---

breads and gray hairs sinking in sorrow to the
graive! It is here that no innocence, no merits, no
truths, no services can save the unhappy sectary,
who does not believe in the creed of those in power.

42 In order to please, if possible, those of our readers who are
fond of the "mazes of metaphorical confusion" we have here
jumbled together narrative and metaphor in a delightful
manner. The Cacus to-whom we allude was a sturdy demo-

Although, as has before been seen.
The federal hands were ever clean.
Our public money has its charms
To tickle democratic palms.

Good democrats can't live on brouse and
Take therefore now and then a thousand
Of public cash, and make amends
By being "We the People's" friends.

A hundred thousand, it is said
Was pocketed by dashing Ned,[43]

---

crat who stole some cattle and hid tlieni in a cave, (very like
Mr Jefferson's.) He was fouiul out however and destroyed by
Hercules, and

Panditur extemplo foribus domus atra revulsis;
Abstractasque boves, abjurataequc raping
Cœlo ostenduntur; pedibusque informe cadaver—
Protrahitur.———————————

Æneid Lib. viii. L. 262, &c.

43 Mr. Harrison was displaced from the office of District Attorney
for having, like Washington, Adams and other AntiJacobins.
been guilty of the heinous crime of federalism, and Ned Living-
stone appointed by virtue of his mighty merits as a democrat.
Mr. Harrison, the obnoxious federalist discharged the duties of
his office, as his political opponents acknowledge, with ability
and fidelity, and was never even suspected of having applied to
his own use the people's money. But Mr. Ned took the liberty to
appropriate to his own private purposes the trifling sum of one
hundred thousand dollars as appears by a judgment obtained
against him in the District Court of the United States, and is
now livng on the people's money, in a stile of genuine extrava-
gance at New-Orleans. If one feels a disposition to be a rogue,
what a fine affair it is to be a good democrat!

And patriot Randolph had before
With fifty thousand run a shore.[44]

Had these been Federal men no doubt
There'd been a most confounded rout,
Th' Aurora fraught with Duane's thunder
Had quick aveng'd such "PUBLIC PLUNDER."

But every democrat intends
To use some freedom with his *friends*.
And if contented with their purse
Let them be thankful 'tis no worse.

But still it seems there's something hard in 't.
When federal men, with zeal most ardent,
Have serv'd their country, every gander
Should hiss, and spatter them with slander.

Behold the play wright Barney Bidwell,[45]

---

44 It is very remarkable that with all the clamour against Messrs.
Pickering and Wolcott for pretended defalcations, misappro-
priations and other malconduct in office, that our goad dem-
ocratic committees, &c. should be so careful to forget to men-
tion the deficiency of Mr. patriot Randolph, former Secretary
of State.

45 Mr. Senator Bidwell the subject of the present eulogium, ex-
hibited the germ of those talents, which have since budded,
and blossomed and bloomed in the rankest luxuriance of de-
mocracy, in a juvenile production of most astonishing ingenu-
ity, "inlitled and called THE MERCENARY MATCH." From some
specimens of that performance with which we have been fa-
voured by the Editor of the *Boston Repertory*, we are led to
suppose that the good goddess of dullness could never boast

(And democrats declare he hid well)
Has twisted into one oration,[46]
Falsehoods enough to d—n a nation.

But this man lies to such degree I
(Forc'd, *ex necessitate rei,*)
With due civility, will strip him.
Then take and tie him up, and whip him.

And I will teach this Mr. Barney
To cheat the people with his blarney.
And I will teach him to be plying
The dirty trade of party-lying,

And first he tells us, our Great Nation
Was born slap dash, by Declaration
Of Independence, in the day time.
Most vile economy!—*in hay time!*[47]

---

of a more hopeful pupil. A small calf may make a large bull-
ock, and a stupid and conceited boy is often matured to a very
knowing demagogue.

46   We ought, perhaps, to apologise to our readers for troubling
them with remarks on such an insipid thing as the harangue in
question. But as this production of Mr. Bidwell may serve as a
specimen of the general tenor of the democratic Fourth of July
speeches which have fallen within our notice, we hope that our
remarks may be of service to such of our young gentlemen of
the New School as may be called hereafter to exhibit oratorical
talents on any similar occasion.

47   "By the Dedaration of Independence, which has just Ipeen
read, a Nation was politically born *in a day.*"
   The story of our Nation's being born on the Fourth of July,
1776, has been told us in prose and in poetry, times without

What next evinces that his knowledge is
Enough to enter some *new* Colleges,
We find him most precisely showing
How long the late war was a going.[48]

He tells us even to a minute
What time the British did begin it
And likewise, what some don't remember.
We made a peace once, in November.

After this flight, which most immense is.
Before you find your scattered senses.
Behold our orator still rising.
To matter more and more surprising.

For that in his sublime opinion,

---

number. Mr. Bidwell has added an important appendage of circumstances; and we have taken the liberty to enlarge further on the phenomena attending this birth. In the first place, we learn by Mr. B. that our nation was born very suddenly. Secondly, that in this wonderful birth, the Declaration of Independence acted as *accoucheur*. Thirdly, that this was a *political* birth Fourthly, that all this was *done in a day*. Fifthly, that this important instrument, or agent, or accoucheur, *had just been read*. Sixthly, *we* have taken the liberty to add, that in such a busy season of the year, genuine republican economy should have directed all these operations to have been performed in the *night*, which, besides a *saving* of time, would have superadded the advantages of all the silence and solemnity of a Virginian caucus.

48 "The revolutionary war," quoth Mr. Bidwell, "occupied a little more than seven years and a half, from the battle of Lexington, on the 19th of April 1775, to the sign ing provincial articles of peace on the 30th of November, 1782." Highly IMPORTANT!

GEORGE WASHINGTON was a *Virginian!*[49]
Which, since 'tis down in black and white,
"I'll bet a beaver hat" he's right.

One thing, *by accident* he miss'd
To state he was a federahst.
Possessed antipathy, most hearty
To Barney Bidwell's precious party.[50]

---

49 "The British troops commenced actual hostilities in April, 1775. An army was raised for defence, and GEORGE WASHINGTON, of Virginia was appointed commander in chief." Surprising intelligence!

50 The following extract of a letter from General Washington to Charles Carrol of Maryland, dated Mount Vernon, August 2, 1798, several months after passing all those laws, which seem so obnoxious to the party now in power, will show what right they haveto claim any advantage from the popularity of his name.

"Although," says Gen. Washington

> I highly approve of the measures taken by government, to place this country in a posture of defence, and even wish they had been more energetic, and shall be ready to obey its call under the reservations I have made, whenever it is made yet I am not without hope, *mad and intoxicated as the French are,* that they will pause, before they take the last step. That they have been deceived by their calculations on the division of the people and the powerful support they expect from their party is reduced to a certainty, though it is somewhat equivocal still, whether THAT PARTY, who have been THE CURSE OF THIS COUNTRY, and the SOURCE OF THE EXPENCES WE HAVE TO ENCOUNTER, may not be able to continue THEIR DELUSION. What pity it is the expence could not be taxed upon them.

Then full of patriotic choler,
He yells out syllables of dolour
Against your British rogues, who would
Have hung our best whigs—if they could,[51]

But carefully forgets to say
How Jefferson had run away;
How many more, in whom he glories
Had sav'd their necks by being tories.[52]

He next proceeds like ignoramus.
Or artful rogue as you could name us.

---

51   With halters about their necks, the signers of the Declaration
of Independence set their names to an instrument, which in
case of failure, they knew must be their death warrant. Yes, my
friend, had the revolution been crushed, they would have been
distinguished from common rebels, and signally executed, or
exiled.

Very true Mr. Bidwell, bat wc shall see presently where your
party will land with this kind of reasoning.

52   I would not be understood as intending to satirize the tories as
such. There were, undoubtedly, many tories, who were honest
men and true friends to their country, but who supposed that
opposition to Great Britain was, wrong in principle, and im-
possible in practice. But since our democrats are stigmatizing
the federalists, with this among other unpopular epithets, it
becomes necessary to repel the charge as often as it is made or
insinuated. I believe it will be found difficult to find any among
the native Americans, who took an active part during the rev-
olutionary war against their country, who have not since been
induced, by the same kind of time-serving policy, and want of
principle to become democrats, and who, like Talleyrand, or
the Vicar of Bray are not willing to become any thing and every
thing, which interest dictates. See note 18, p. 9.

To state the motives and intendments.
In constitutional amendments,[53]

---

53   Mr. Bidwell affirms that the amendment of the constitution, which declared a state not suable by a private citizen, and that which made it necessary to designate by electoral votes the distinct candidates for President and Vice President were *republican*. If Mr. Bidwell will give the same meaning to the term republican that Buonaparte has ever done, we shall not dispute with him. The *republicanism* of the latter is but despotism in *disguise*, and that of the former with a proper analysis will be found to be substantially the same.

    The legislature of the state of Georgia, under shelter of its inviolability has been guilty of a flagrant breach of contract— *has burnt its records* and shaken the pillars of society by striking at the right ofproperty. Similar cases may again happen, and according to Mr. Bidwell's *republican* amendment, there can no responsibility attach to the violation of a principle, which forms the basis of civilized society. The other republican amendment opens a wide door for intrigue and corruption, takes away a powerful check which the smaller states possessed over the larger, and flies directly in the face of the constitutionble; as it originally stood.

    The reasoning of Mr. Tracy respecting this *amendment*, (falsely so called) one would suppose was irresistible and indeed we do not pretend to so much charity as not to be induced to *impeach the motives* of those State cobblers, who by this and other similar proceedings, have frittered away our Constitution, and broken down those barriers which, by the wisdom of its framers, were designed to give stability to society.

    The following extract, quoted from Mr. Tracy's speech in the Senate of the United Stales upon this subject, contains arguments and facts, which ought to have been conclusive against this mischievous innovation.

       The constitution, is nicely balanced with the Federative and the popular principles; the Senate are the guardians of the former, and any pretence to destroy this balance, under whatever specious

Through labyrinths of nonsense trudges,
To fib about the federal judges,[54]

---

names or pretences they may be mentioned should be watched with a jealous eye. Perhaps a fair definition of the constitutional power of amending is that you may, upon experiment, so modify the constitution, in its practice and operation *as to give it in its own principles a more complete effect.* But this is an attack upon a fundamental principle, established after long deliberation, and by material concession: a principle of essential importance to the instrument itself, and an attempt to wrest from the small states a vested right and by it to increase the power and influence of the large States.

Nothing can be more obvious than the intention of the plan, adopted by our constitution for choosing a President. The Electors are to nominate two persons, of whom they cannot know which will be the President. This circumstance not only induces them to select both from the best men; but gives a direct advantage into the hands of the small states, even in the Electoral choice; for they can always elect from the two candidates, set up by the Electors of large states, by throwing their votes upon their favorite; and of course giving hira a majority, or if the Electors of the large stales should prevent this effect they can scatter their votes for one candidate, then the Electors of the small states would have it in their power to elect a Vice President. So that in any event the small states will have a considerable agency in the election. But if the discriminating or designating principle is carried, as contained in this resolution, the whole agency of the small states, in the Electoral choice of Chief Magistrate is destroyed, and their chance of obtaining a federative choice, by states, if not destroyed is very much diminished.

54 Among the sophisms and misrepresentations with which this

Proceeds, adroitly to abridge

harrangue is teeming, those respecting our federal judges are not the least mischievous. Mr. Bidwell informs us that "the office of an English judge is and always has been repealable by an act of the Legislature." To this we shall oppose the conclusive reasoning of General Hamilton, taken from his *Examination of the President's Message abthe opening of Cogress December 7. 1801.* than which a more able political tract never fed from the pen of a statesman.

"One more defence of this *formidable claim*" (to wit, of abolishing the offices of the Federal Judges)

> is attempted to be drawn from the example of the Judiciary establishment of Great Britain. It is observed, that this establishment, the theme of copious eulogy on account of the Independence of the Judges, places these officers on a footing far less firm than will be that of the Judges of the United States, even admitting the right of Congress to abolish their offices, by abolishing the Courts of which they are members: and as one proof of the assertion, it is mentioned that the English Judges are removable by the King, on the address of the two houses of Parliament.
>
> All this might be very true, and yet would prove nothing as to what is, or ought to be the construction of our Constitution on this point. It is plain from the provision respecting compensation that the framers of that Constitution intended to prop the independence of the Judges beyond the precautions which have been adopted in England in respect to the Judges of that country; and the intention apparent in this particular, is an argument, that the same spirit may have governed other provisions. Cogent reasons have been assigned, applicable to our system, and not applicable to the British system, for securng the independence of our Judges against the Legislature, as well as against the Executive power.

The subtle speech of Breckenridge.

It is alleged that the statute of Great Britain of the 13 of William III. was the model from which the framers of our constitution copied the provisions for the independence of the Judiciary. It is certainly true, that the idea of the tenure of office during good behaviour, found in several of our constitutions, is borrowed from that source. But it is evident that the framers of our federal system did not mean to confine themselves to that model.—Hence the restraint of the legislative discretion, as to compensation hence the omission ofthe provision for the removal of the judges by the executive, on the application of the two branches of the legislature; a provision, which has been imitated in some of the state governments.

See No. 17 of a series of essays with the signature of Lucius Crassus, originally published in the *Evening Post*, and afterwards printed in a pamphlet.

Again, says the learned orator Bidwell, "The very act erecting the circuit courts expressly abolished pre-existing courts.* Yet it was afterwards contended that the courts created by that act could not be constitutionally abolished."

The *truth*, however, is, that that act did not abolish pre-existing courts in such a way as to affect the dignity or emoluments of the judges who held offices under the first establishment. The number of the judges of the supreme court was to have been reduced from six to five, and the acreduction was deferred to the happening of a vacancy. But an extract from Mr. Morris' speech will exhibit the fallacy of Mr. Bidwell's reasoning in a point of view which cannot but be conclusive against him.

It is said, that by this law, the district judges in Tennessee and Kentucky are removed from office, by making them circuit judges. And again, that you have by law appointed two new offices, those of the circuit judges, and filled them by law, instead of

Then prates about each federal tax.
And dealing out his thumps and thwacks,
Hits Madison, a clever joke,[55]

---

pursuing the modes of appointment prescribed by the constitution. It does indeed put down the district courts, but is so far from destroying the *offices* of district judges, that it declares the persons filling *those offices* shall perform the duty of holding *circuit courts*; and so far is it from appointing *circuit judges*, that it declares the circuit courts shall be held by the district judges.

Mr. Bidwell in the next place is pleased to inform us that judges are annually elected in Connecticut. But he does not say that such annual election is brought about by violating the constitution; neither does he say that an independent judiciary would not be a desideratum in that state.

* "The act now under consideration is a legislative construction of this clause in the constitution, that congress may abolish as well as create these judicial officers; because it does expressly, in the 27th section, abolish the then existing courts for the purpose of making way for the present."— Breckenridge's speech.

55 Mr. Bidwell rails at the federalists for levying direct taxes, complains of the permanent offices (contingent he should say) thereby created; and among others, the land tax is an object of his particular animadversion. The act, however, which imposed this terrible tax, was not altogether of federal origin; and if there is any odium to be attached to that measure, (which I deny) our democrats ought, in due degree, to suffer. This will appear from the following statement, every word of which can be abundantly proved from public documents:

A committee of wajs and means, consisting of one member of each state, were appointed for the purpose of dt vising the best method of raising a tax. The democratic gentlemen, with Mr. Maddison at

Right o'er the sconce, a knock down stroke!

The stamp act rails at, as a horrid
Thing with the beast's mark in its forehead,
Although 'tis known to all but asses.
It did not touch the lower classes.[56]

---

their head, proposed, and (this having become the opinion of the majority) reported in favour of a land tax, and in consequence Mr. Wolcott was directed to frame a report for that purpose, and present it at the next session of congress, when a report was accepted in favour of the land tax. Mr. Maddison, whose measure it was considered to be, was the man who particularly appeared on the floor as its defender and supporter. It is likewise a fact, that Mr. Gallatin, in his book of finances, has expressly recommended a land tax to the administration.

New-York Evening Post, July 15. 1803.

56 Nothing can prove more effectually the influence of names, abstracted from the things which they represent, than the circumstance of the federal stamp act having been obnoxious to the middling, and lower classes of the American people. Farmers and mechanics, who perhaps would not be liable to pay a cent a year, were prevailed upon by demagogues to be very much alarmed at the idea of this tax being something dreadful in its nature and tendency,—something like the old British stamp act, in which, not the *tax itself*, but the right to *impose* it was the object of dispute. Too many well meaning men were prodigiously frighted at the idea of the stamp act being the harbinger of Federal Monarchy, or some other sort of incomprehensible tyranny. They therefore opposed this terrible measure, and were *indulged* with taxes on brown sugar, salt and bohea tea, in its stead, by which a revenue is derived altogether from the middling and lower classes. This looks as if it might be possible for the people to be "their own worst enemies."

Then heaps upon the honest heads
Of independent upright Feds,
Whatever measure could be found.
With something dreadful in its sound.

At length winds up with such a series
Of wicked and deceptive queries.[57]
That all must own this son of slander
Well fitted for his party's pander.

Honestus joins in dismal tone,[58]
And howls about a dreadful loan,
In which the Fed'ral Government

---

57 We shall not fatigue our readers, with a repetition of those que-
ries. They are in substance merely inquiries whether the peo-
ple of the United States would be pleased with the re-adoption
of the same measures which formerly charactet ised the feder-
al administration? Whether a land tax, excise law, a standing
army, &c. &c. would be again submitted to by the citizens of
the United States?

    To this we might answer in a word: Similar circumstances
might render similar measures not only advisable, but indis-
pensable to preserve our independence as a nation. If a Galla-
tin should organize an insurrection; if Gallo-American faction
should form a league with Buonaparte, or a French ambas-
sador, aided by wrong-headed and treacherous Americans,
should attempt to prostrate our country at the foot of France;
if Great-Britain or France should find leisure from their own
disputes to commit depredations on our commerce, we shall
be under the necessity of again recurring to federal men, and
federal measures, *or resign our honour, our respectability,
and probably, our independence as a nation.*

58 One of the proprietors, and the principal writer in the *Boston
Chronicle*, assumes the signature of Honestus.

Gave no less sum than eight per cent.[59]

Though well the said Honestus knows
From what necessity it rose.
And had foundation, in reality.
From his dear party's own rascality.

He knows peculiar exigencies
Led to great national expences.
And that this loan at its creation
Received our best men's approbation.

He knows that Washington declared
Those great expences should be shared
Among such fellows as Honestus
And others like him, who infest us.[60]

Yet still this creature's always carping.
The self same tune for ever harping
And has a deal of mischief done.
As drops perpetual wear a stone.

---

59 This loan which has occasioned so much clamour among our
    demagogues, was rendered necessary by the dangers which
    threatened us from France, and from the expences of Gallatin's
    insurrection. A committee of congress, who were, no doubt,
    nearly as competent to judge of this business as Mr. Honestus,
    with the concurrence of Mr. Nicholson, and other democrats,
    unanimously reported that they saw "no reason to doubt that
    these loans were negociated on the best terms which could be
    procured, and with a laudable view to the public interest."

60 In proof of this assertion, we would refer to General Washing-
    ton's letter to Mr. Carrol. See page 116.

Thus have our Federal men been branded
By artful modes, and underhanded.
And slander'd in a way surpassing
The cruelty of an assassin.

By vile imported convicts goaded,
Harrass'd, with ignominy loaded.
By imputation, oftentimes
With weight of their opponent's crimes.[61]

But look at ev'ry Federal measure
Which has incurred such high displeasure,
And there's not one which you can mention,
But pleads at least a good intention,

Have they their private interests further'd
That now their reputation's murther'd?

---

61 Pre-eminently hard is the fate of federalism, and sad is the
destiny of the followers of Washington, in being stigmatized
with the crimes of their opponents, and criminated tor the
misfortunes and expenses which were the necessary result
of the conduct of their political adversaries, Virginian delin-
quency caused great depredations on our commerce, and this
was imputed to federalism. Democrats organized a whiskey
insurrection, which caused great national expenses, these
too were said to be the consequence of federalism. The dom-
ineering views of France, aided by the French faclioii in tliis
country, in the opinion of Wasiiin^lon, Adams, and the oiii-
er sages and patriots who at that time directed our councils,
rendered a provisional army necessary. This too was the sin
of federalism. But

Troy yet may wake, atone avenging blow.
Crush the dire authors of their country's woe.

And have they not 'mid party-war
Made public good their polar star?

It must be own'd that their political
Career was not a little critical;
Such times our land would overwhelm,
If democrats had been at helm.

It must be own'd whate'er they've done
Was sanction'd by our Washington,
And be allow'd as no less true
He had no *private ends* in view.

Though many a rogue belonging unto
The hireling Jeffersonian junto.
Has boldly said, but saying lied,
Our Washington was *on their side!*—

Yet he abhorr'd them, and what worse is,
Denounced them as our nation's curses,
But gave his strongest approbation
To Adams's administration.

And each and all the accusations
Of Federal crimes and peculations.
Their adversaries knew full well
Were lies malicious, false as h-ll.

If such must be the modes that our
Great men must *wriggle* into pow'r,
Our government will prove a curse

Than that of Algiers ten times worse:—

Until a tyrant of a king,
An emperor, or some such thing,
And he the essence of the devil
Become a necessary evil.[62]

---

62 It is well known that the faction, which has built itself up on
the ruins of the Washington and Adams' administrations, have
been clamorous in their complaints against the federalisls, for
their pretended prdlilection to monarchy. Treatises written
expressly in favour of the American government, and of the re-
publican constitutions of the several stales have been tortured
into meanings quite foreign from the ideas of their authors,
in order to suit the nefarious purposes of unprincipled parti-
sans. Private conversation, uttered in moments of conviviality,
has been reported and misrepresented, with all the artifice of
the most malicious ingenuity. Still we are not informed of any
thing more having escaped the lips of any of the leading federal
characters than general expressions of *apprehension*, lest this
government should degenerate through anarchy to despotism;
and the hon. Fisher Ames, who staiub among the most promi-
nent of these pretended monarchy-loving men, has declared in
substance, that *if monarchy should ever he established in this
country, it will be the work of the Jacobins.*

The Jeffersoniad

ARGUMENT

With deference due, and huge humility,
Approaching Don Perfectibility,
We laud the man, by Demo's reckon'd
A sort of Jupiter the second,[1]
Whose most correct administration
In annals of *Illumination*,
Will ever shine superbly splendid,
A long *time* after time is ended.

ith awe, scarce short of adoration.[1]
Before the glory of our nation,
With scrape submissive, cap in hand.
We, Doctor Caustic trembling stand;

---

1   A very judicious encomiast on the "greatest man in America," in an *elegant puff*, published, and republished in almost every democratic Newspaper in the United States, has amoug other *dashing matters*, drawn a flaming comparison between Messrs. Jefferson and Jupiter. These two deities seem to share the universe between them, and to hurl about their thunder and lightning at an astonishing rate. Perhaps there never was a comparison, which, as rhetoricians express themselves, went more completely *on all fours*, than this to which we allude. We think, however, that our Mr. Jupiter jun. whenever he condescends to put on the terrible, is muck, the most august of these two personages.

And offer with all veneration
Due to his Highness's high station,
Our services to daub and gloss over
A philanthropical philosopher.

The mighty Chief of Carter's Mountain,
Of democratic power the fountain,
We would extol, his favour buying
By most profound and solid lying.[2]

Sure never lucky man of rhyme
Was blest with subject more sublime,
And ere his virtues we've reported,
We shall or ought to be—*transported!*

Touched by our pencil, every fault
Shall fade away like mount of salt,
Which late, 'tis said, in weather rainy,
Was melted in Louisiana.[3]

---

2   By most profound and solid lying.

Butler, speaking, doubtless of a demagogue, says that he was,

————————for profound
And solid lying much renown'd.

A man may lie not only with impunity but with applause, provided his falshoods have a tendency to further the views of the hypocritical demagogues of the day. See note 12, p. 6.

3   Although we have not yet received *official intelligence* of this most extraordinary phenomenon, yet, the silence which Mr. Jefferson has of late observed on the subject of this stupendous curiosity, warrants the conclusion which we here take the

Posterity shall puff the Statesman,
Whom we will prove is our first rate's man,
Nor Gaffer Time shall dare to tarnish
The character we mean to varnish.

But shall we not, as poets use
First set about to seek a muse,
One of Apollo's fiddling lasses,
Who runs to grass on Mount Parnassus?

Dost think we had not better choose
Some mad cap Delia Cruscan Muse,
To teach us featly to combine
A world of nonsense in a line?

Or call on some frail worldly wench,
As did the revolutionary French,
When th' impious monkies bent their knees on
Before their strumpet-goddess Reason?[4]

Or shall we undertake to hire
Some democratic muse, a liar,
Who would, for pelf, in lays most civil,
Sing Hallelujahs to the devil?

---

liberty to draw, of its absolute fusion.

4   It is a fact well known to every one in the least conversant in
the history of the French Revolution, that religious homage,
with a great number of blasphemous ceremonies was rendered
by the chief actors in that scene of desolation to a common
harlot. The object of their adoration was tricked out with char-
acteristic tawdriness, and personated REASON at that time the
idol of those atrocious infidels.

Or seek in dark and dirty alley
A Mr. Jefferson's Miss Sally,
In our *Free Government* no matter
Whether coal black, or swart mulatto?

No—but with Gallatin's best whisky
OURSELF will get a little frisky,
Then, either foot a poet's stilt on,
We'll strut away sublime as Milton.

Some say our chief regards religion
No more than wild goose, or a pigeon,
But I'll maintain, what seems an oddity,
He's overstock'd with that commodity.

The man must have religion plenty
To soar from "no god" up to "*twenty*,"
No doubt of common folks the odds
As no God is to twenty Gods.[5]

---

5   We have ever greatly admired the wonderful political pliancy
    of some of our clerical characters, in supporting with so much
    ardour, a man wiio has ever been hostile to the christian reli-
    gion. But these gentlemen no doubt suppose, that the reports
    of Mr. Jefferson's infidelity are all federal lies. We will how-
    ever furnish them with a few facts and arguments with which
    the federalists fortify their assertions, not doubting in the least
    that these candid and learned divines will contrive to muster
    arguments to prove, that Mr. Jefferson is a very pious and or-
    thodox sort of a man; and though perhaps they would not go
    so far as to assert with a certain itinerant holder-forth in Mas-
    sachusetts, that Mr. Jefferson is the sixth angel mentioned in
    the revelation, yet, they will probably maintain, that he has as
    much political piety as Oliver Cromwell, of genuine republican
    memory.

Though his high mightiness was skittish.

Mr. Jefferson's invitation to Tom Paine, has somewhat the appearance of no great regard to religion. But doubtless it was supposed, that the claims of the latter as a politician were such, as to entitle him to the very extraordinary attention of the former, especially, as Paine had written a letter against General Washington, an opponent to Mr. Jefferson's party, which teemed with the most unqualified abuse.

Mr. Jefferson says, in his *Notes on Virginia*,

> It does me no injury for my neighbour to say, there are twenty Gods, or *no God*; it neitber picks my pocket, nor breaks my leg; if it be said, his testimony in a court of justice cannot be relied on, reject it then, and be the stigma on him;

and speaking ofthe state of religion in Pennsylvania and New-York, he says, "religion there is well supported, of different kinds indeed, *but all good enough*; all sufficient to preserve peace and order."

Now, although federal clergymen might be induced to adopt the language of Mr. Smith, and exclaim, "which ought we to be most shocked at, the *levity* or *impiety* of these remarks?" yet, democratic clergymen will, if they would be consistent, declare all this to be a federal lie, and that those passages in the *Notes on Virginia* which we have quoted, are federal interpolations, intended to traduce the fair fame of the "greatest man in America."

But there is an astonishing charge lately made by a writer in the *United States Gazette*, that demands a refutation, which we, although the professed eulogist of Mr. Jefferson, are sorry to confess, are unable to furnish; but we hope our fellow-labourers in the vineyard of democracy will supply us weapons, wherewith to knock down this impudent adversary of our immortal chieftain.

"The most gentle temper," says this anti-Jeffersonian scribbler,

> may be urged until it becomes impatient, and this, I confess, was the case with myself, when on the

When menaced by the bullying British
The Feds are wrong to make a clatter
About the Carter-Mountain matter.[6]

---

road between Baltimore and Philadelphia, I heard a
minister of the gospel declare, that the report of Mr.
Jefferson's infidelity was "*a Federal lie.*" To coun-
teract an imputation so ungenerous and unjust, and
for the information of those, who are not so entirely
hoodwinked as not to see anything, however obvious
and palpable it may appear, I have thought proper to
subjoin the following statement, and if Mr. Jefferson
will deny its truth, he shall be immediately informed
of the name of the person who made it.

B. Hawkins Esq. (don't start Mr. Jefferson) once
a member of congress, and now high in trust and
presidential favour, wrote a pamphlet in vindication
of the doctrines of the Illuminati, and among others,
of the doctrines of *chance* and *materialism.* He sent
one copy of this pamphlet, yet in manuscript, to Mr.
Jefferson, and another copy to Mr. Macon, speaker
of the house of representatives. I say he sent those
copies, and I ask Mr. Jefferson to deny it.

Mr. Jefferson, in order to elude the curiosity
of the Post-Office, sent him an answer in latin, in
which he has recourse to that unintelligible slang
which marks his public messages, but in which he
does unequivocally express his approbation of every
sentiment contained in the work, and does request
Mr. Hawkins to cause it to be published, in order to
enlighten the minds of the people of America. I say
he did send this letter, and I beseech the President
to deny it. The answer of Mr. Macon was not in latin;
Mr. Macon does not write latin.

This impudent federalist, who thus slanders the chief mag-
istrate of a christian country, certainly deserves to be indicted,
and not allowed to give the truth in evidence.

6   Some of our good democrats, as it behoveth them have stren-

uously denied the fact of Mr. Jefferson's masterly retreat from Charlottesville to Carter's Mountain. Now, although we propose to proceed at least to the end of the Canto, stating "false facts" in favour of the subject of our present eulogy, yet we propose to *lie* with somewhat more caution than Mr. Jefferson's advocates have generally done. We therefore will state what some of the wicked federalists have asserted, and leave it to some of our fellow-labourers in the vineyard of democracy, to *lie down* such opposition.

Mr. Smith of South Carolina, in his impudent pamphlet, to which we have referred before (see pages 105 and 110, vol. 1.) has the following allegations against Mr. Jefferson:

"Mr. Jefferson has generally sacrificed the civil rights of his countrymen to his own personal safety." We are told in a public address, by Mr. Charles Simms, of Virginia, who must have been well acquainted with the circumstances,

> that Mr. Jefferson, when *governor* of Virginia, *abandoned the trust* with which he was charged, at the moment of an invasion by the enemy, by which, great confusion, *loss and distress, accrued to the state*, in the destruction of public records and vouchers for general expenditures.*
>
> Now, here was a period of public danger, when Mr. Jefferson's attachment to the civil rights of his countrymen, might have shone very conspicuously, by facing and averting the danger; here would have been a fine opportunity for him to have displayed his public spirit, in bravely rallying round the standard of liberty and civil rights; but, though in times of safety, he could *rally* round the standard of his friend, Tom Paine, yet, when real danger appeared, the governor of the ancient dominion dwindled into the poor, *timid philosopher*; and instead of rallying his brave countrymen, he lied for safety from a few lighthorsemen, and shamefully abandoned his trust.†

'Twas better far to make excursion.

There is likewise one Thomas Turner, Esq. of Virginia, a gentleman of very respectable character, &c. &c. but we are somewhat apprehensive that he is a federalist, and as such, *in our capacity of Eulogist to Mr. Jefferson*, we shall most assuredly take the liberty to be very severe upon him, for stating the following most abominable truths (for, the greater the truth, the greater the liber) against Mr. Jefferson.

At the time Petersburgh was occupied by the British troops, under command of Generals Philips and Arnold, Mr. Jefferson, who was then governor of the state, did participate in the partial consternation excited by the situation of the British army, and *did abandon* the seat of government, at a period, and with an awkward precipitation, indicative of timidity, unwarranted by any immediate movement of the enemy, and forbidden by a regard to those duties, which belong to the station he held. This fact is well recollected, and can be proved by many of the oldest and most respectable inhabitants of the city of Richmond, and I belicve would not be denied by the candid supporters of Mr. Jefferson himself.

The sequel of his conduct, after the assembly returned to Charlottesville, and on the approach of Colonel Tarleton, to that place, stands attested by thousands of witnesses, and can never be forgotten by those of his countrymen, whorespect the character of a firm and virtuous public officer, and wlio abhor that ofthe dastardly traitor to the trust reposed in him. His retreat, or rather hhjiight from Monticello, on the information that Tarleton had penetrated the country, and was advancing to Charlottesville, was ctfecied with such hurried abruptness, as to produce a fall from his horse, and a dislocation of the shoulder. In this situation he proceeded about sixty miles souths to th€ county of Bedford, whence he for"warded his resignation to the assembly (who had in the niean time removed to Staunton, and)

By way of something like diversion,

who theretfpon elected General Nelson governor. The circumstances are substantidly and literally true; nay, the abdicatioa of the government must be a matter of record.

* Mr.Leven Powell, of Virginia, also states, in his public address,

That when Tarleton, with a few lighthorte, pursued the assembly to Charlottesville, Mr. Jefferson discovered such a want of firmness, as shewed he was not fit to fill the *first executive office*; for, instead of using hit talents, in directing the necessary operations of defence, he quitted his government by resigning HIS OFFICE; this too, at a tittle which tried men's souls; at atiitie ivlien the affairs *of America stood in doubtful suspense, and required the exertions of all.*

The Governor of Virginia, during the *invasion* of the state, by a small British force, instead of *defending* the commonwealth at that alarming juncture, voluntarily and suddenly *surrendered his office*, and at that crisis, his country teas required to choose anotlier Governor! Is there any security he ivould not act in like manner again, in like circumstances?

† This charge has been attetnpted to be got rid of, by producing a vote ofthe assembly of Virginia, after an inquiry into his conduct, acknowledging his ability and integrity, are altogether silent on his want of firmness, which had been the cause of his flight.

It was natural for his friends in the assembly to varnish over this business- as well as they could; and the danger being past, there being no prospect of his being again exposed in that station, and his fiight proceeding not from any criminality, but from a constitutional weakness of nerves, it was no

Than like *un*-philosophic hot-head
To run the risk of being shot dead.

Such saving prudence mark'd a sage
A *great man* of a former age,—
One Falstaff, famous as our head man.
Thought *honour* nothing in a dead man.

But being Governor of the State,
(Some carping folks presume to say't,)
He ought t' have stood some little fray,
Smelt powder ere he ran away.

Modern philosophers know better
Than their most noble minds to fetter,—
Their new-school principles disparage
With *honour*, *honesty* and *courage*.

Besides, 'tis said by other some
That charity begins at home,
That each man should take care of one.
Nor fight when there is room to run.

It is moreover my desire
That Turner be esteemed a liar,
Convict, by Duane's Declaration,

---

difficult matter to get such a vote from the assembly; more especially, as the character of the state was no less implicated in the business than that of the governor.

And hung for *theft* and *defamation*.[7]

And I'll make plain as College Thesis,
Our Chief as bold as Hercules is,
By proofs which must confound at once,
Each carping, scurrilous Federal dunce.

A Chief who stands not shilly shally,
But is notorious for—a *Sally*[8]

---

7   The very *respectable* editor of the Aurora, as well as his com-
peers; Mr. Richie of the *Richmond Enquirer*, Mr. Paine and
other democratic writers, have shown wonderful adroitness in
parrying the thrusts which have been made at Mr. Jefferson's
character. Some have said that the accuations, provided they
were all *true*, amounted to *nothing*. Others have undertaken
to prove the whole a parcel of federal lies. But the Aurora-man
has attacked the character of Mr. Turner, in order to invalidate
his testimony with so much vigour, that the same Mr. Turner
will never be able to show his head among *honest men*. He has
told a comical, and, what is wonderful, in part, a true story,
how one Tom Turner stole a cloak from a member of congress
from Virginia. But the editor of the *Evening Post* has spoiled
the whole, by the following explanation.

> The truth is, the cloak in question belonged to
> Mr. William Hillhouse, member of congress from
> Connecticut, and it was taken from him by one Mr.
> Thomas Turner, or as Duane has it, *Tom Turner*;
> but Tom Turner, instead of the respectable Virginia
> planter, who wrote the letter to Dr. Park, was a man
> of the same name, who belonged to the Philosoph-
> ical Society of Philadelphia, of which Mr. Jefferson
> was President; and what is more, he was like pillo-
> ry-Nichols, of Boston, and Callender, one of Mr. Jef-
> ferson's confidential CORRESPONDENTS.

8   This line contains, we think, what Edmund Burke would call

Might Mars defy, in war's dire tug,
Or Satan to an Indian hug.

Therefore ye Feds, if ye should now hard
Things mutter of a nerveless coward,
'Twill prove your characters, ye quizzes.
Black as an Empress's black phiz is.

'Tis true some wicked wags there are,
Who laugh about this dark affair,
But I can tell this shameles faction
Theyought t'admire the same transaction;

And did they rightly comprehend
How *means* are sanction'd by the *end*,
They'd change their grumbling tones sarcastic
To eulogies encomiastic.

'Tis our right-worshipful belief,
This fine example of our Chief,
Of *commerce* join'd to *manufactures*
Makes in his character no fractures:

And we will prove, sans disputation.

"high matter." Indeed, we are far from being positive, that we are not in this place somewhat beyond our own comprehension; an error of which, we are the more apprehensive, as we have observed it to be a common fault among those writers who advocate democratic politics. We think, therefore, that it will be most judicious for us to leave it to our commentators to decide, whether, by the term *Sally*, we mean an attack upon an enemy, or dalliance with a *friend*.

Our Chief has wondrous calculation;
In politics nine times as able
As Mazarine or Machiavel.

For where's a readier resource
For that sweet "social intercourse,"
Which at a grand inauguration
Was promis'd this our happy nation?

And if, by his example, he goes
To recommend the raising negroes,
The chance is surely in his favour
Of being President forever.

A southern negro is you see, man,
Already three-fifths of a freeman,
And when Virginia gets the staff.
He'll be a freeman and a half.[9]

Great men can never lack supporters,
Who manufacture their own voters;
Besides 'tis plain as yonder steeple,
They will he *fathers* to the people.

And 'tis a decent, clever, comical,
New mode of being economical

---

9   The preponderance which Virginia has already obtained in the
     scale of representation, will enable her to proceed to increase
     the privileges of her black population. In this she will be gov-
     erned by the strict rules of Republican propriety, which always
     consults the greatest good of the greatest number.

For when, a black is rais'd, it follows
It saves a duty of ten dollars,[10]

Besides, sir opposition-prater.
That foul reproach to human nature.
The most nefarious guinea trade
May fall by presidential aid.

And he's a wayward blockhead, who says
This making negroes or pappooses
Is not accordant with the plan
Of Tom Paine's precious *Rights of Man.*

Therefore, your best and and wisest course is
With Antifeds to join your forces,
And all combine to daub and gloss over
Our philanthropical Philosopher.

I know it has been urged by some,
That he who has a wife at home
Flesh of his flesh, bone of his bone,
Might let mulatto girls alone.

---

10   This is a duty, which has been proposed, and probably will
     at some future period, be adopted in the southern states, to
     prevent the importation of slaves. It is surprising, that, among
     all the calculations which have distinguished our penny-sav-
     ing administration, this pleasant scheme has not been adopt-
     ed more generally. But a word to the wise will not be thrown
     away. Our southern nabobs will improve on this hint: sable
     nabobbesses will be all the rage; and establishments for the
     manufacturing of slaves, will be as common as those for gin or
     whiskey.

But they who say it must be fools
In doctrines of th' illumin'd schools;
Not one can cobble human nature,
Or make a modern Legislator:—

Indeed, they show in this respect
So small a reach of intellect,
They must have shallow pates, commanding
Scarce one inch depth of understanding.

One whose philanthropy's embrace
Incloses all the human race;
Is forced full many schemes to try,
Where more is meant than meets the eye.

All kinds of cattle, 'tis agreed,
Improve whene'er you cross the breed,
With sheep and hogs it is the case,
And eke the Jacobinic race.

We therefore' think it best to tether
Your blacks and democrats together;
For in this pleasant way 'tis said
The lustiest patriots may be bred.

And we've no doubt this making brats
Between your blacks and Democrats,
Will serve like varnish or japan
For perfecting the race of man.

Fine scheme! the more we turn it over,

The more its beauties we discover;
This intercourse ofblacks and whites
Will set the wicked world to rights.

Behold the Hartford Mercury-man
Adopts with ardour this new plan,[11]

---

11 In the *Mercury*, a democratic newspaper, was republished
from the *National Intelligencer*, a paper, under the immedi-
ate patronage of Mr. Jefferson, a precious paragraph, prettily
prefaced as follows:

THOUGHTS ON THE TRUE
PATH TO NATIONAL GLORY

The course of events will likewise inevitably lead to a
mixlure of the *whites* and *blacks*; and as the former are
about five times as numerous as the latter, the blacks
will ultimately be merged in the whites. This, indeed,
appears to be the great provison made by nature, and,
viewing the subject in its political aspects, we cannot
feel too much satisfaction at there being an ultimate
issue, however remote, independent of the exertions of
statesmen, which, *notwithstanding* its *repugnance to
our reason*, as well as prejudice, will arrive,

No doubt, Mr. Mercury-man!—a most happy expedient
truly!—"notwithstanding its repugnance to our reason"!—And
what mortal can sufficiently admire thy wonderful magnanim-
ity, O thou! the GREAT MAN, whom we are humbly attempting
to eulogize, in the being-one of the first to *put in practice* this
philanthropic plan; by virtue of which, "the blacks will ulti-
mately be merged in the whites."!
    What say you, O ye fair daughters of Columbia! (we mean
the *white ones*) will ye be pleased with a hymeneal jottery, for
the purposes aforesaid, in which every fifth lady-adventurer
shall draw the delectable prize of a black paramour?
    But as this notable scheme is of democratic origin, it would

Will doubtless aid us in his station,
To bring it into operation.

And other ministerial prints,
(No doubt from Presidential hints)
Are all alive upon this topic.
So pleasant, and so philanthropic.

The more the thing we look at, true 'tis.
The more we see its myriad beauties,
For this most precious plan discovers
A new and charmingfield for lovers.

Each flaxen-headed swain will trill his
Love song to vvoollen-pated Phillis!
And pining Corydons will bilk
Their Mistresses of buttermilk!

Each flaunting buckish tippy bobby.
Will take a black wench for his hobby,
And Belles keep fashionable honeys,
Crow-colour'd loves, like Desdemona's.

And none but fools and arrant asses
Will care for "pale unripened" lasses.
Who can succeed to storm the trenches

---

be the heighth of impudence for your *old-fashioned*, *un*-philosophical federalists, to interfere in the least. No—the benefits which may result from ths motley mixture, and scheme aforesaid, ought to be shared exclusively among *genuine* democrats. Those alone will be found worthy to walk in
"THE TRUE PATH TO NATIONAL GLORY."

Of blooming beautiful black wenches!!

And whenin billing kisses sweet
Pasteboard and blubber lips shall meet,
'Twill be allowed such love surpasses
E'en nectar sweetened with *molasses!*

Besides our *daughters* and our *wives.*
If happily this project thrives.
Will strengthen Jefferson's resource*
By Sambo's social intercourses.

And pray friend Babcock send your wife,
(Now while your theory is rife)
Or bid your daughter sans a fee, go
And practice on it with a negro.

The uglier monster too the better,
But should you hesitate to let her,
'Twill prove the scandalous hypocrisy,
Of your pretensions to democracy.

All hail Columbia's transmutation
To one great grand mulatto nation!
And may success attend each dally,
Of Mr. Jefferson and Sally!

But left this subject so adorable.
To future bards who may be more able;
In lays supernal and amazing,
To set it absolutely blazing.

We will pass on and find out whether,
We cannot find another feather,
Or sprig of laurel, which may hap
To fit his Mightinesses cap.

Our noble Chieftain is, I wist,
The most renovvn'd philanthropist,
That ever yet has hatch'd a plan
That went to meliorating man:

Has formed a scheme, which we delight in.
To stop the horrid trade of fighting;[12]

---

12 To prove what a prodigiously benevolent sort of a gentleman
    we have taken the liberty to eulogize; and to furnish our read-
    ers with a most delightful specimen of close, accurate and in-
    vincible logic, we will oblige them with some extracts of a letter
    from Mr. Jefferson to Sir John Sinclair, President of the Board
    of Agriculture at London, dated March 23, 1798, but lately re-
    published in the democratic papers, by way of applauding the
    passive obedience and non-resistance measures of our *creep-
    ing* andministration.

    I am fixed with awe (says our Chieftair,) at the
    mighty conflict, in which two great nations are ad-
    vancing, and recoil with horror at the ferociousness
    of man.* Will nations never devise a more rational
    umpire of differences than that of force? Are there
    no means of coercing injustice, more gratifying to
    our nature, than a waste of the blood of thousands,
    and the labour of millions of our fellow creatures?
    We see numerous societies of men (the aboriginals
    of this country) living together without the acknowl-
    edgment of either laws or magistracy, yet they live in
    peace among themselves, and acts of violence and in-
    jury are as rare in their societies as in nations which

Bid England cease from war's alarms,

keep the sword of the law in perpetual activity. Public reproach, a refusal of common offices, interdiction of the commerce and comforts of society are found as essential as the coarser instrument of force. Nations like these individuals stand towards each other only in the relations of natural right. Might they not like them he *peaceably punished* for violence and wrong? &c. &c.

Now let us look at, and of course, as in duty bound, *admire* this stream of humanity issuing from the fountain of philanthropy. What a sublime idea is that of providing a "rational umpire of differences" between warring nations who shall "coerce injustice" by " means gratifying to our nature," and teach them to

————feel "the halter draw.
With good opinion of the law."

And because a parcel of American savages, sparsely scattered over immense wilds, "live without the acknowledgment of either laws or magistracy, in peace among themselves," &c. how very logically follows the ergo the populous, ambitious, and powerful nations of the old world may be ruled by Mr. Jefferson's notions of "the relations of right" and warring empires, as well as hostile individuals be peaceably punished by "public reproach, a refusal of common offices," &c.†

Now were we not absolutely and bonafide determined to be Mr. Jefferson's advocate, we should first pick a quarrel with his premises, and then proceed to knock down his conclusions. We should say that the aboriginals of this country have their Chiefs, who have the authority of magistrates, that they are far from always living at peace among themselves, but murder is among others, a common crime, and sometimes a whole tribe is extinguished in cold blooded revenge of accidental homicide; that their wars are as bloody as those of civilized nations, and that they generally torture and put their prisoners to death, with fiend-like malice and ingenuity.

148

And Buonaparte lay down his arms.

That is to pacify all nations,
By fine palavering proclamations,
Stating in lieu of cannon's thunder,
'Tis *unpolite* to rob and plunder.

The only obstacle I see to't.
Is, that some rascals won't agree to't
For spite of all our Chief can say,
They will go on and fight away!

But then he sbows the good he would do,
Provided, what he would he could do;
And when a man's a good intention,
He ought said good intent to mention.

And I'd rely with all my heart,
On his persuading Buonapart'
To give us liberty, as much

---

* We cannot but observe, that Mr. Jefferson's being so terribly
terrified at the thoughts of shedding human blood, even in a
"mighty conflict," is a total departure from the principles of
his sect of philosophers. The illuminati in general, and Mr.
Godwin in particular, have no scruples af that sort. See Note
33. p. 49.

† This mode of subduing the refractory was probably invented
by Mr. Gallatin, who in his whiskey insurrection concern,
tuas chairman of a committee of insurgents, who resolved to
have no intercourse nor dealings with the officers of govern-
ment, "withdraw from them every assistancet and withhold
all the comforts of life," &c.

As France has done the Swiss and Dutch.

Then don't let fed'ralists provoke him,
And Mr. Jefferson will stroke him.
Till he will condescend, I trow,
Our commonwealth to take in tow.

No doubt our bright affairs with Spain,
Are in their present happy train,
In consequence of our sweet temper,
And President *eadem semper*.

But should we chance to think that our
Security consists in power,
Negociate with our arms in hand,
The Lord knows only where we'll land.

Most of our democrats know fully,
That *lying down* disarms a bully;
That *nothing* ever is a stranger
To *every thing* that looks like danger.

And doubtless French and Algerines,
Will be persuaded by such means,
'Tis best to let alone our commerce,
Not take our hard-earn'd money from us.

Therefore I say, and will maintain,
The man must be a rogue in grain,
Who won't acknowledge our good President,
The greatest man on this earth resident.

Though Gossip Fame has been a talker,
Of some attempts at Mrs. Walker;[13]

---

13   Here we shall be obliged, once more, to be severe on the be-
fore-mentioned Thomas Turner, Esq. for having the temerity
to tattle slander against the man, whom good democrats de-
light to honour.

> The father of Colonel John Walker (says this
> man, who thinks he can "tell truth and shame the
> devil") was the guardian of Mr. Jefferson, and ad-
> vanced a part of those funds, which were applied to
> the education of the latter; an education affjrding
> those talents, which have been so strangely per-
> verted, which have been insidiously employed in
> the conception ofschemes, foul, ungrateful, homble.
> At a very early period of their lives. Colonel Walker
> and Mr. Jefferson contracted an attachment which
> grew up with their years aiid ripened into the clos-
> est intimacy.—Their professions were mutual; their
> confidence unbounded. While things were in this
> situation, Mr. Jefferson was meditating the unnat-
> ural purpose of seducing the wife of his best friend,
> and to this end (taking advan tage of the confidence
> of Colonel Walker, and availing himself ofthe timid-
> ity of the lady, whose affection for her husband pre-
> venteil the disclosure ofa transaction, which might
> lead to an exposure of his life, devoted himself for
> ten years, repeatedly and assiduously making at-
> tempts, which were as repeatedly, and with horror
> repelled. For ten years was this purpose pursued,
> and at last abandoned (as he himself acknowledges)
> from the inflexible virtue of the lady, and followed
> (as .he also acknowledges) by the deepest and most
> heart-wounding remorse.*

All this I HAVE SEEN: NOT in newspapers;not in extracts; not
in copies of letters.—I HAVE SEEN IT in the ORIGINAL CORRE-
SPONDENCE BETWEEN MESSRS. WALKER AND JEFFERSON, every

Yet this is silly, slanderous stuff,

letter of whicn bears the signature of the writer, or has been since acknowledged by him, under his own hand. In this correspondence Mr. Jefferson repeatedly and fervently confesses that the guilt is all his own; the innocence all Mrs. Walker's; and that he shall never cease to revere, and attest the purity of her character, and deprecate his unpardonable and unsuccessful artempt to destroy her. His contrition, his misery, are asserted in the warmest terms, and his acquittal of Mrs. Walker pronounced in the strongest language of his pen. Among other concessions he owns, that in order to cover the real cause of the separation between Colonel Walker and himself, he did FABRICATE a note respecting an unsettled account which he said had produced the schism, and which he expressly acknowledges had no FOUNDATION IN TRUTH. Let it not be forgotten that the attempts against the honour of Mrs. Walker were carried on DURING THE LIFE-TIME OF MRS. JEFFERSON, than whom a better woman and better wife never existed."

And must the head of a great nation, the idol of a *free* people, and the patron of Tom Paine, be lacerated and scarified in this manner? Surely not with impunity, for lo, Tom Paine hath taken up the gauntlet in his defence! and now it behoveth all who would not choose to be buried alive in the filth of obloquy, to sneak out of the scrape of opposition to Mr. Jefferson, with all possible celerity. The letter of Mr. Turner, says the author of the *Age of Reason*, and the enemy of Washinton, and the friend of Mr. Jefferson, is a "*putrid production*" but "having nothing else to do" he has "thrown, away an hour or two," in "examining its component parts." Mr. Turner and Mr. Hurlburt, (the latter is the gentleman, who distinguished himself by a famous speech in the Legislature of Massachusetts, in the laudable attack made by the minority of that body on the liberty tof the press) he politely stiles "*two skunks who stink in concert.*" This is succeeded by other arguments at least as convincing, and as delicately expressed, but somewhat too "*lengthy*" for insertion.

---

*   The reader will please to observe, that this remorse of Mr. Jefferson, so unworthy a philosophist, took place before his

Or if 'twere true 'tis *right enough*.

Your pure professors of perfection,
In morals can have no defection;
Like *upright* people, so particular,
They stand up *more* than perpendicular.

Now I've no doubt but what this scandal,
Is nothing but a federal handle,
To blast our Emperor's fame, who's not less
Than Scipio or Joseph spotless.

But protest enter'd first I may,
Just mention what some people say,
Who ought to suffer bastinading,
For crime of President-degrading.

Some say 'twas vile ingratitude,
In Mr. Jefferson, so rude,
To attack his benefactor's wife,
The pride, the solace of his life;—

The virtuous woman to annoy,
By siege as long as that of Troy,
And bring bad principles to aid[14]
His systematical blockade.

---

illumination. C. C.

14 We have heard it reported by some vilitier of Mr. Jefferson,
that he endeavoured to induce Mrs. Walker to compliance
with his wishes, by putting in hef way certain *sentimental* trea-
tises, said to be proper on such occasions.

But I'll maintain he is consistent,
His conduct hasn't a single twist in't;
If having *twenty Gods*, he drives
To have at least as many wives.

Among your new-school rights and duties,
There's no monopoly of beauties,[15]
And he's a churl, who will not lend
His pretty wife t' oblige a friend.

No man, who is not old and frigid,
Be most unconscionably rigid,
Will e'er "oppugnate" this morality
Of such a pretty genteel quality.

And were all true which is related
About a note once fabricated,
By which his highness did intend
To ruin one he cali'd his friend;

'Twas right to set himself a brewing
This cross-grain'd lady's husband's ruin,
Who, had he been polite, had chuckled
At chance to be a great man's cuckold.

From such examples husbands may chance
To learn a little French complaisance,
And married prudes to put no cross over
The wishes of a great philosopher.

---

15   For some further illustration of this delectable doctrine, we
would refer our reader to p. 61, Note 25.

Though he imported Thomas Paine,
(For Chronicleers have lied in vain,)[16]
T' oppose with acrimonious vanity,
Law, order, morals, and Christianity.

'Twas right, for aught I can discover,
To send and fetch the fellow over,
For Freedom, by his aid may chance

---

16 The *Boston Chronicle*, and we believe many other de mocrat-
ic papers, delclared that the report of Mr. Jefferson's having
invited Paine to return to this country, was a falsehood of fed-
eral fabrication, invented on purpose to slander Mr. Jefferson.
But, when Paine published the letter, with that accommodat-
ing versatility, which is no doubt absolutely necessary for the
support of their party, they applauded the President for that
very measure. The letter itself is couched in terms so highly
respectful, and is highly lionorary to both parties in the corre-
spondence. The following arc extracts:

> DEAR SIR,
> Your letters of Oct. 1st, 4th, 6th, 16th, came duly
> to hand, and the papers which they covered were,
> according to your permission, published in the
> newspapers, and under your own name. These pa-
> pers contain precisely our principles, and I hope
> they will be generally recognised here.
> You expressed a wish to get a passage to this
> country in a public vessel. Mr. Dawson is charged
> with orders to the captain of the *Maryland* to re-
> ceive and accommodate you back, if you can be
> ready to depart at such a short warning.
> That you may long live to continue your *useful* la-
> bours, and to reap the reward in the thankfulness of
> nations, is my sincere prayer. Accept assurances of
> my high esteem and affectionate attachment.

With us to flourish as in France.[17]
The man who has such service done.
By neat abuse of Washington,[18]

---

17   Paine has given us a specimen, in one of his letters to the cit-
      izens of the United States, of the success of his labours in the
      cause of liberty in that genuine republican Robespierre seized
      him, together with many other proninent patriots, and impris-
      oned him eleven months, proposed to requite his revolutionary
      services with the guillotine. The downfall of the tyrant, however,
      prevented this termination to Paine's political labour and the
      arch Infidel has come, not to infect this country with the poison
      of his seditious and blasphemous publication, but, as Mr Jeffer-
      son says, to "continue his useful labours among us."
         But it somehow unfortunately happens, that Tom Paine's
      merits are not fully appreciated by certain of Mr. Jefferson's
      admirers. In a newspaper entitled the *Freeman's Journal*, es-
      tablished under the auspices of Governor M'Kean & Co. at Phil-
      adelphia, we find Mr. Tom Paine's quondam friends attacking
      him in a most merciless manner. We will give a short paragraph
      as a specimen of the unmerited abuse which is lavished on this
      almost a martyr, in the cause of licentiousness and infidelity.

         Had this polluted monster remained in France,
         he would have conferred a particular favour on this
         country. Infamous and execrated, he might have
         'gone to his own place,' unheeded and unregarded,
         like any other outcast from society. But, as if the
         measure of his iniquity was not yet full, this foe to
         God and man has come hither to plague us.

         But let Mr. Tom Paine never seem to mind a little *quid*
      abuse, for he has received "assurances of" Mr. Jefferson's
      "high esteem and affectionate attachment."

18   A specimen or two of delicate invective, taken from Paine's let-
      ter to George Washington, President of the United States, dat-
      ed Paris, July 30th, 1796, and printed by Benjamin Franklin
      Bache, the worthy predecessor of William Duane, the present
      editor of the *Aurora*, will doubtless very much oblige our good

Deserves the highest approbation
From our great *tip-end* of the nation.

Moreover 'tis a proper season
To burnish up the "Age of Reason,"
Lest, peradventure, too much piety
Sap the foundations of society.

And we moreover understand, he
Supports the state—by drinking brandy,
And if he lives, will free the nation
From debt, without direct taxation.

But though our Chief to all intents is
A paragon of excellencies,
The wicked Feds are always prating
Matter the most calumniating.

---

democratic readers and show what a well qualified champion
Mr. Jefferson has enlisted in his defence.

I declare myself opposed to almost the whole of
your administration; for I know it to be deceitful, if
not even perfidious.

Injustice was acted under pretence of faith; and
the Chief of the army became the patron of the fraud.

Meanness and ingratitude have nothing equivo-
cal in their character. There is not a trait in them
that renders them doubtful. They are so original vic-
es, that they are generated in the dung of other vic-
es, and crawl into existence with the filth upon their
back. The fugitives have found protection in you,
and the levee room is the place of their rendezvous.

For I've heard many a crabbed Fed,
While things like these he muttering said,
Though I stood tortur'd all the while in
A state which set my blood a boiling:

A fine man he to head our nation,
The very soul of fluctuation
'Twould take the stamina of two men
Like him, to make out one old woman.

What though the democratic host
His wisdom and his talents boast,
For pelf or office, I would lay all
I'm worth, the rogues would worship Baal:

But they may white-wash all they can,
They cannot quite disguise their man,
For something of his native hue,
With all their daubing, will peep through.

Wisdom, in him descends to cunning;
Talents—a knack at danger shunning;
Morality—to be complete in
What some old-fashioned folks call cheating.

In literature, his reputation
A fabric is, without foundation.
What serves to please his party, some say
Is quite exuberant and clumsy.

What though he writes with some facility

What fascinates our wise mobility,
Who ever find out something grand in
Whate'er is past all understanding;

With all his sophimore's rotundity,
With all his semblance of profundity,
Pore pages over, you'll scarce see a
Novel, or well-express'd idea.

His stile is tinsel, glare and whimsey,
No lady's novel half so flimsey;
As full of glaring contradictions
As Ovid's works are full of fictions.[19]

19　Mr. Jefferson's writings, both political and philosophical, have been so often the subject of the very just encomiums of his party, and have on the contrary been so often bandied to and fro as the footballs of federal raillery, that it would be difficult to excite public attention to a critical canvass of their merits. His pretensions to meritorious authorship appear to be founded, principally on his *Notes on Virginia*, a work which few village schoolmasters could not have executed better.

　　We will however compare some of his tenets as displayed in that work, with some later productions of the distinguished author, for the purpose of showing his consistency as a politician.

　　Speaking of the population of America, Mr. Jefferson remarks, that

> the present desire of America is to produce rapid population, by as great importation of foreigners as possible. But is this founded in good policy? Are there no inconveniences to be thrown into the scale against the advantage to be expected from a multiplication of numbers, by the importation of foreigners? It is for the happiness of those united in society

And what, indeed, we might expect,

to harmonize as much as possible in matters which they must of necessity transact together. Civil government being the sole object of forming societies, its administration must be conducted by common consent. Every species of government has its specific principles: Ours, perhaps, are more peculiar than those of any other in the universe. It is a composition of the first principles of the English Constitution with others, derived from natural right and reason. To these nothing can be more opposed than the maxims of absolute monarchies. Yet from such we are to expect the greatest number of emigrants. They will bring with them the principles of the government they leave, imbibed in their early youth; or if able to throw them off, it will be an exchange for an unbounded licentiousness, passing as usual from one extreme to another. It would be a miracle were they to stop precisely at the point of temperate liberty. Their principles with their language they will transmit to their children. In proportion to their numbers, they will share with us in the legislation. They will infuse into it their spirit, warp and bias its direction, and render it a heterogeneous, incoherent, distracted mass, I may appeal to experience, during the present contest, for a verification of these conjectures; but if they be not certain in the event, are they not possible, are they not probable? Is it not safer to wait with patience for the attainment of any degree of population desired or expected? May not our government be more homogeneous, more peaceable, more durable? Suppose twenty millions of republican Americans, thrown all of a sudden into France, what would be the condition of that kingdom? If it would be more turbulent, less happy, less strong; we may believe that the addition of half a million of foreigners, to our present number, would produce a similar effect here.

His morals are as incorrect

Now for the display of that convenient versatility, which is one of the most essential characteristics of a great statesman. In the President's message of December, 1801, we are told that

> a denial of citizenship under a residence of 14 years, is a denial to a great proportion of those who ask it, and controls a policy pursued from the first settlement, by many of these states, and still believed of consequence to their prosperity. And shall we refuse to the unhappy fugitives from distress that hospitality, which the savages of the wilderness extended to our fathers arriving in this land? Shall oppressed humanity find no assylum on this globe? Might not the general character and capabilities of a citizen be safely communicated to *every one* manifesting a *bona fide* purpose of embarking his life and fortune permanently with us?

In the *Notes on Virginia* we also learn,

> That the political economists of Europe have established it as a principle, that every state should manufacture for itself: and the principle like many others we transfer to America, without calculating the different circumstances, which should often produce a different result. In Europe, the lands are either cultivated, or locked up against the cultivation. Manufacture must, therefore, be resorted to of necessity, not of choice, to support the surplus of their people. But we have an immensity of land, courting the industry of the husbandman. Is it best, then, that *all our citizens* should be employed in its improvement, or, that one half should be called off from that, to exercise manufacture and handicrafts for the other? Those who labour in the earth are the chosen people of God, *if ever he had a chosen people*; whose breasts he has made the peculiar deposit for substantial and genuine virtue.—It is the focus

As are his writings—froth and flummery

in which he keeps alive that sacred fire, which otherwise might escape from the earth. Corruption of morals in the mass of cultivators is a phenomenon of which no age nor nation has furnished an example. It is the mark set on those who, not looking up toheaven, to their own soil and to industry, as does the husbandman, for their subsistence, depend for it on the casualties and caprice of customers. Dependence begets subservience and venality; suffocates the germ of virtue, and prepares fit tools for the designs of ambition. This, the natural progress and consequence of the arts has sometimes perhaps been retarded by accidental circumstances: but generally speaking, the proportion which the aggregate of the other classes of the citizens bears, in any state, to that of its husbandmen, is the proportion of its unsound to its healthy parts, and is a good enough barometer, whereby to measure its degree of corruption. While we have land to labour let us never wish to see our citizens occupied at a work-bench or twirling a distaff. Carpenters and smiths are wanting in husbandry: but for the general operation of manufacture, let our workshops remain in Europe. It is better to carry provisions and materials to workmen there, than bring them to the provisions and materials, and with them their manners and principles. The loss, by the transportation of commodities across the atlantic will be made up in happiness and permanence of government. The mobs of great cities add just so much to the support of pure government, as sores do to the strength ofthe human body.

The above was written in 1782. In the year 1793, Mr. Jeffersjon, then Secretary of State, having occasion to fall out with Great Britain, in a report relative to commercial restrictions of other nations, and the measures which the United States ought to pursue to counteract them, recommends the imposition of heavy duties, or excluding such foreign manufactures

Express them both in manner summary.

as we take in Greatest quantities, for

> Such duties (he observes) having the effect of in-
> direct encouragement to domestic manufactures
> of the same kind may, *induce the manufacturer to
> come himself* into these States; and here it would
> be in the power of the State governments to cooper-
> ate essentially, by opening the resources of encour-
> agement which are under their controul, extending
> them liberally to artists in those particular branches
> of manufactures for which their soil, climate, popu-
> lation, and other circumstances have matured them,
> and fostering the precious efforts and progress of
> household manufacture, by some patronage suited
> to the nature of its objects, guided by the local in-
> formation they possess, and guarded against abuse
> by their presence and attention. The oppressions on
> our agriculture in foreign parts would thus be made
> the occasion of relieving it from a dependence on the
> councils and conduct of others, and *promoting arts,
> manufactures* and *population* at home.

Mr. Jefferson's Message contained the first proposition for
an attack on the judiciary, and he is well known to have gone
hand in hand with his estimable party, in the courageous and
successful inroad made on the aristocratic constitution of the
United States, by putting down the federal judges by the doz-
en. That in this respect he has made great improvements in
the theory of liberty, since writing his *Notes on Virginia*, will
abundantly appear from the following quotation from that
work, so highly celebrated by the admirers of genuine freedom.
Speaking of the government of Virginia, he remarks, that

> All the powers of government, legislative, executive
> and judiciary, result to the legislative body. The con-
> centrating these in the same hands is precisely the
> definition of *despotic government*. It will be no alle-
> viation that these powets will be exercised by a plu-

rality of hands, and not by a single one. One hundred and twenty-three despots would surely be as oppressive as one. Let those who doubt it turn their eyes to the republic of Venice. As little will it avail us that they are chosen by ourselves. An elective despotism was not the government we fought for; but one which should not only be founded on free principles, but in which the powers of government should be so divided and balanced among several bodies of magistracy, as that no one should transcend their legal limits without being effectually checked and restrained by the others. For this reason, that convention which passed the ordinance of government, laid its foundation on this basis, that the legislative, executive and judiciary departments should be separate and distinct, so that no person should exercise the powers of more than one of them at the same time. But no barrier was provided between these several powers. The judiciary and executive members were left dependent on the legislative for their subsistence in office, and some of them for their continuance in it. If therefore, the legislature assumes executive and judiciary powers, no opposition is likely to be made, nor if made, can be effectual; because in that case they may put their proceedings into the form of an act of assembly, which will render them obligatory on the other branches. They have accordingly, in many instances, decided rights which should have been left to judiciary controversy; and the direction of the executive, during the whole time of their session, is becoming habitual and familiar.

See *Notes on Virginia*, Query xii.

One more specimen of Mr. Jefferson's openness to conviction, and the facility with which he relinquishes an error of opinion the moment he discovers it, we shall furnish from his philosophical disquisition on the colour and other properties of negroes. Our philosopher, after stating certain modes by

With great pretence to Mathematics,

which the evil of slavery in Virginia might be annihilated, such as that the black slaves

> should continue with their parents to a certain age, then be brought up, at the public expense, to tillage, arts or sciences, according to their geniusses, till the females should be eighteen, and the males twenty-one years of age, when they should be colonized to such place, as the circumstances of the time should render most proper sending vessels at the same time to the other parts of the world for an equal numberof white inhabitants,

proceeds with the following profound observation:

> It will probably be asked, why not retain and incorporate the blacks in this state? I answer, deep-rooted prejudices entertained by the whites, ten thousand recollections by the blacks of the injuries they have sustained, new provocations, *the real distinction which nature has made*, and many other circumstances, will divide us into parties, and produce convulsions, which will never end but in the extermination of the *one or the other race*. To these objections, which are political, may be added others, which are *physical and moral*. The first difference which strikes us, is that of colour; whether the black of the negro resides in the reticular membrane, between the skin and the scarfskin, or in the skin itself; whether it proceeds from the colour of the blood, or the colour of the bile, or from that of some other secretion, *the difference is fixed in nalure*, and is as *real* as if its seat and cause were better known to us. And is this difference of no importance? Is it not the foundation of a greater or less share of beauty in the two races? Are not the fine mixture of red and white, the expressions of every passion, by the greater or less suffusion of colour in theone, preferable to the

I'd ask, is his report on Staticks,

eternal monotony, which reigns inthe countenances of the other race? Add to these, flowing hair, a more elegant symmetry of form, their own judgment in favour of the whites, declared by their preference of them, as uniformly as is the preference of the ourang-outang for the black women over those of his own species. Besides those of colour, figure and hair, there are other physical distinctions proving a different race; they have less hair on the face and body they secrete less by the kidnies, and more by the glands of the skin, which gives them a very strong and disagreeable odour.

They are in reason much inferior to the whites. It is not against experience to suppose, that different species of the same genus, or varieties of the same species may possess different qualifications. Will not a lover of natural history, then, one who views the gradations in all the races of animals, with the eye of philosophy, *excuse an effort to keep those in the department of man as distinct as nature has formed them.*

He afterwards observes,

that the improvement of the blacks in body and mind, in the first instance of their mixture with the whites, is observed by every one, and proves that their inferiority is not the effect merely of their condition in life. Among the Romans, their slaves were often their rarest artists; they excelled too in science, insomuch as to be employed as tutors to their masters' children. Epictetus, Terence and Phoedrus, were slaves; but they were of the race of whites. *It is not their condition, then, but* NATURE, which has produced the distinction.

Mr. Jefferson doubtless wrote these observations previ-

And Standard Measures worth a fig?[20]

ous to his having obtained an intimate acquaintance with the good qualities of the blacks. But some subsequent investigations, could not but lead a man of his penetration, to reject any pre-conceived opinion, unfavorable to this "race of animals." And instead of keeping those in the department of man as distinct as possible, he now not only maintains, that the *"true path to national glory"* leads to a mixture of the *whites* and *blacks*, (See note 11, p, 166) but has condescended to add *example* to precept, to teach us by his own experiments the soundness of his philosophy.

It is probable that the new light, which he obtained by the only true mode of philosophising, led him to the candid confessions contained in a congratulatory letter to his worthy and learned brother, Benjamin Banneker, said to be, the author of an almanack, &c. In this last production, he declared in the teeth of his former theory, that

> he rejoiced to find that *Nature* had given to his *black brethren* talents equal to those of other colours, and that the *appearance* of a want of them, was owing *merely* to the *degraded condition* of their existence, both in Africa and America.

There is a philosopher of pliability for you! none of your rigid personages who will remain obstinate in error, against the light of reason, and his own and other men's experiments. This whirling to the left about, in consequence of the wonderful phenomenon of a Negro Almanack, (probably enough made by a white man) wasas masterly a manoeuvre, in a political, as the retreat to Carter's mountain, in a military point of view.

20   Mr. Jefferson's report on weights and measures has been highly celebrated by his party, but the mischief making Federalists have made many unmercifuj strictures on its defects. To show with what kind of logick Mr. Jefferson, has been assailed we shall again have recourse to the pamphlet of Mr. Smith, in which Mr. Jefferson and his pretensions are so roughly handled.

No; 'twould disgrace the learned pig.

Mr. Jefferson was required "to report to the House a proper plan for establishing uniformity in the currency of weights and measures of the United States."

The object of a plain, sensible man, more anxious to render solid services to the country, than to acquire reputation by a *pedantick* display of science, would naturally have been, to ascertain the existing currency, weights and measures in the United States, and to establish such *standard*, as would be most conformable to the *general* use, and attended with the least innovation and distress.

In respect to uniformity in *measures*, nothing more would have been requisite than to have proposed that some determined standard should be made and lodged in some public depository, to which access might be had, when necessary.

Instead of this, Mr. Jefferson proposes a system, which professes *extreme minuteness, precision and accuracy*, and yet, when examined, is found to leave *everything to the skill and accuracy of a Watchmaker;** a system, depending on *criteria*, which he considered as *important* and yet, which are not *defined* in such manner as to admit of an application of them.

He begins the report with observing, "that there exists not in nature a single subject, or species of subject accessible to man, which permits one constant and uniform dimension." The causes of this variation of dimension are stated to be *expansion* and *contraction*, occasioned by change of *temperature. Iron* is stated to be the *least expansible of metals*, and the degree of expansion of a pendulum of 58. 7, inches is said to be from 200 to 300 parts of an inch.

Mr. Jefferson, however, says, "that the globe of the earth might be considered as *invariable in all its dimensions*, and that its *circumference* would furnish an *invariable measure.*" But if a small portion of the least expansible metal, *iron*, is so affected by *temperature*, how can it be true, that the globe would furnish an *invariable measure?* Is not the whole earth, composed as it is of various elements, all *more* expansible than iron, liable to be affected by changes of temperature? Are not different sides of the earth presented to the sun, at different Seasons of the year? Is not the whole globe nearer to the sun in some parts of its orbit, than at others? Is it not, of course, more susceptible of *heat*, and more affected by *attraction*, both of which operate to affect the dimensions of our globe? Is it likely that earth, water, and other elements, are so equally distributed through our globe, as that the degrees of expansion and contraction, occasioned by changes of seasons, exactly counter balance each other? Was it not known to Mr. Jefferson, that no two of the great circles of our globe are of equal circumference, and that this rendered his position, at *least doubtful?*

Mr. Jetferson says, "that no one circle of the globe is accessible to admeasurement in all its parts, and that the trials to measure portions have been of such various result, as to shew that there is no dependence on that operation for certainty." If this be true, what were the *data* upon which it was asserted, that the whole *circumference* would furnish an *invariable measure?* The Frencli philosophers now say the conirary, and they have lately *actually* taken a *section* of the earth for their standard. Who is to decide between these doctors, or are they all aiming to puzzle plain-people, by an *affectation* of accuracy, which is unattainable?

Mr. Jeiferson's standard is "a uniform cylindrical rod of iron, of such length, as in latitude 45 degrees, in the level of the ocean, and in a cellar or other place, the temperature of which does not vary throughout the year, shall perform its vibrations, in small aiid equal arcs, in one second of mean time."

The degree of 45 degrees is assumed, because it was proposed by France, and because it was the northern boundary of the United States. He says, "let the completion of the 45 degrees then give the standard for *our union*, with the hope," he *facetiously* adds, "that it may become a *line of union*, with the rest ofthe world;" a pleasant conceit! it was kind in this profound philosopher to emerge from the depth of his experimental cellar, to enliven this scientific and *abstruse* subject with a pun.

But our philosopher's hope of a *line of union* with the rest of the world is already defeated; the French, have, since his report, taken a section of a meridional line for their standard*. Their pendulum for 45 degrees is to vibrate 100,000 seconds, while Mr. Jefferson's is vibrating 86,400.

The French have outdone even Mr. Jefferson in innovation; thus illusory has the expectation proved, that the hobby-horse of one philosopher will be respected by another.

But why *this attempt* at absolute accuracy? He admits that the pendulum of 45 degrees differs from the pendulum of 31 degrees, only 1-679 part of its whole length, and that this difference is so minute that it might be *neglected, as insensible for the common purposes of life*. There was some reason for the attempt beyond a display of learning, or there was not; if *perfect exactness* was desirable, why where the following *causes* of *uncertainty* and *error* unnoticed?

1st. The experinient, he says, must be made in the *level of the ocean*, to prevent that *increment to the radius of the earth and consequent diminution of the length of the pendulum*, which a higher situation would produce: what is the *level of the ocean?* the tide rises in 45 degrees about fifteen feet, and there are levels of the ocean at *high-water, low-water,* and at *all points* between these extremes. *Perfect exactness* required that the expression, *level of the ocean,* should have been defined: this *omission* has since been rectified in a bill which passed the House of Representatives last session.*

2d. The experiment, says the report, must be made in a cellar or other place, the temperature of which does not vary throughout the year. This is important, or it is not: if *important,* why not *define* the *temperature,* that it might be ascertained by a thermometer. There are few or no natural caves or cellars, in which the temperature does not vary: variations are frequently noticed in the deepest caves and mines: various causes may affect the temperature: Mr. Jefferson admits this, in his Notes, p. 21, where he allows that " *chymical agents* may protluce in subterraneous cavities, a *factitious heat;*" and these may more or less, affect the temperature inmost caves or cellars.

The *pendulum,* however, admitted by Mr. Jefferson, to be liable to *uncertainties,* for which he offers no *remedies:* how does it appear that these uncertainties are not more important than the causes of error, to which his attention has been directed?

3d. "Machinery" (says the report, page 8,) "and a power are necessary, which may exert a small but constant effort to renew the waste of motion, but so that they shall *neitlier retard nor accelerate* the vibrations."

But it adds, in the next page, "to estimate and *obviate this difficulty* is the *artist's province.*" What is this, but to say, that the standard of the United States shall be the pendulum of some clock, made by Mr. Leslie, or some other artist, thus *discarding* at once *all reliance* upon the principles before advanced. The *difficulty* of ascertaining the centre of oscillation, (which he admits to be impossible,

Some *borrowed* things are well enough,[21]

unless in a rod, of which the diameter is *"infinite-ly small,"* he thinks however *can be obtated by* Mr. Leslie, the watchmaker.

Mr. Jefferson then proceeds to apply his standard, 1st. To *measures of capacity.* These he propos-es should be *four-sided,* with rectangular sides and bottom, for which he gives the following reasons: *"cylindrical* measures have the advantage of *supe-rior strength*; but square ones have the *greater ad-vantage of enabling* every one, who has a rule in his pocket, to *verify their contents,* by measuring them." Did it notoccur to this profound mathematician, that a man with a *rule* in his pocket, could *as easily* meas-ure the *diameter* and *depth* of a cylindrical half bush-el as the sides and depth of a square box?

2d. To *weights.* The standard of weights is pro-posed to be a definite portion of *rain water,* weighed always in the *same temperature.* "It will be neces-sary," says he, "to refer these weights to a deter-minate mass of substance, the specifick gravity of which is invariable; *rain water* is *such* a substance, and may be referred to every where, and through all time". But the temperature is *not defined*; rain wa-ter is variedby several causes dust, insects, &c. will create a difference in its weight. The French, in their late plan, have outdone Mr. Jefferson; their stand-ard is distilled water, ascertained by a defined tem-perature."

Such is the cruel manner in which the federal rogues cut up a genuine philosopher.

* Report, p. 3. "In order to avoid the uncertainties which re-spect the centre of oscillation, it has been proposed by Mr. Leslie, an ingenious artist of Philadelphia, to substitute for the pendulum, an uniform cylindrical rod, without a bob."

21 A part of Mr. Jefferson's report on weights and measures, was

But all his *own* is stupid stuff,
And goes with fifty proofs beside
To prove his *head* and *heart* allied[22]

Who's vile enough to be defender
Of his base paper money tender,

---

founded on ideas taken from a volume of the society of Arts and Agriculture, published in Europe. The fluxional calculations are the work of a Professor in Columbia College. See *The Minerva*, a newspaper printed in New-York, of July, 1796.

22 There is a great affinity between that obliquity of intellect, which leads a man to *think* incorrectly, and that depravity of heart, which tends to immoral conduct. A wrong-headed enthusiast, who is addicted to an incorrect and whimsical mode of reasoning and thinking, may easily allay the qualms of conscience by the opiate of sophism, and even become what Godwin calls an *"honest assassin."* Perhaps there have been but few crimes of magnitude committed, in which the perpetrators have not been able to persuade themselves, that they were justifiable, if not commendable. Religious, political and philosophical enthusiasm have, each in their turn, impelled mankind to deeds of horror, from which the most abandoned would revolt with abhorrence, if they did not believe that they were actuated by motives which are praiseworthy.

The dexterity with which our knight-errants in sedition reconcile their conduct to the dictates of their reason, is well exemplified by Butler, in the character of Hudibras, who thus justifies the breaking of his oath:

He that imposes an oath makes it,
Not he that for convenience takes it;
Then how can any man be said
To break an oath whenever made."

But these being grave old-school reflections, it would be very improper to indulge them in a canto, set apart like this, for celebrating an illuminatus.

In which he would defraud, forsooth,
The friend and patron of his youth.

Ingratitude, of crimes the worst,
In none but serpent-bosoms nurst,
It seems but qualifies a man
To head the democratick clan.

Was it not scandalous hypocrisy,
To please the looking-on mobocracy,
For him to sob, and sigh and groan
O'er the green grave of Washington.[23]

When this same gentleman had paid

---

23   It is well known that Mr. Jefferson made a very pretty and suit-
able parade of grief at the tomb of General Washington. And
asr emarked by a poet in the *Utica Patriot*,

> A genuine tear from a genuine chief
> Is a genuine proof of a genuine grief!

The federal editor of the *New-York Erening Post*, in his
aristocratical way thus remarks upon this subject:

> Will the reader once accompany us to the sad-
> dened groves of Mount-Vernon. Behold this same
> Thomas Jefferson at the tomb of Washington! See
> him approach the hallowed spot, surrounded by spec-
> tators!—he kneels before the sacred dust!—he weeps
> outright at the irreparable loss of this greatest, best,
> and most beloved of men!—sobs choak his utterance!
> he clasps his hands in token of pious resignation to
> the will of heaven, and retires in silence amidst the
> blessings of those whose sympathy he had beguiled
> by presenting his "profession of sorrow."

One who set up the lying trade,
A scoundrel from a foreign nation
To stab that hero's reputation?[24]

---

24 Though the circumstance of Mr. Jefferson's having paid Callender foe his services iu abuse of the *Federal Constitution, Washington, Adams,* and many others of our revolutionary patriots, is proved by letters written with his own hand, yet democrats, with that laudable pertinacity, which is the soul of their party, would never believe a word about the matter.

Convince some men against their will,
They're of the same opinion still.

The intelligent and indefatigable editor of the *Boston Repertory*, makes the following plaint on the occasion

How often have we been stigmatised as infamous slanderers, for asserting that Mr. Jetferson patronised Callender in his virulent abuse of the *Federal Constitution*, Washington and Adams. It was a federal lie, and no democrat would yield credit to a circumstance, which, if true, would exhibit Mr. Jefferson in the blackest colours of political hypocrisy, and allied to that demon of slander, for the purpose of *lying* down his betters. We now offer irresistible proof—Mr. Jeiferson's letters to Callender, in his own hand writing. ONE DEMOCRAt, and one only, has called to satisfy himself!

Now this is as it should be. Stick to your party, genuine republicans! right or wrong.

Our good democrats, with the greatest propriety, as it adds to their popularity, are always fond of uniting the names of Washington and Jefferson. That Mr. Jefferson was friendly to General Washington, and his administration, will appear from the following *elegant extracts*, taken from the *Prospect before Us*, at that time patronised and its specimen sheets inspected by *Mr Jefferson*:

What think you of his double shuffle,

Speaking of General Washington, Mr. Jefferson's editor says,

He could not have committed a more pure and *net violation of his oath* to preserve the constitution, and of his official trust; or a grosser personal insult on the representatives.

By his own account, Mr. Washington was twice a TRAITOR. He first renounced the king of England, and thereafter the old confederation. His farewell paper contains a variety of mischievous sentiments.

Under the old confederation matters never were nor could hare been conducted so wretchedly, as they actually are under the successive *monarchs* of *Braintree* and *Mount Vernon*.

Mr. Adams has only completed the scene of ignominy, which Mr. Washington had begun.

The republicans were extremely well satisfied at the demise of the general. They felt and feared his weight in the scale of aristocracy; but they found it necessary to save appearances with the multitude by presenting a profession of sorrow. It is a real farce to see the manner in which the citizens at large were treated, in this instance, by both parties. *The second burial!* But it is impossible to proceed with gravity; or to comprehend by what means Adams and congress kept from laughing in each other's faces, when they past their *unanimous* resolution to recommend the delivery of *suitable orations*, discourses and public prayers.

Callender having thus handsomely handled Gen. Washington, attacks Mr. Adams in a manner equally masterly. But by further quotations we may perhaps, by the weight of our notes, break the peg of our poetry, and fall into the merciless fangs of

When he and Genet had a scuffle,[25]

the criticks. Good democrats, however, with their usual ingenuity, have attempted to wipe away every stain from Mr. Jefferson's immaculate character.

In the first place they contended that the report of Mr. Jefferson's having been concerned in the Prospect before us was a "federal lie." Mr. Jefferson's letters however put them down on that point.

They then affirmed that Mr. Jefferson paid Callender one hundred dollars after having read the specimen sheets of the *Prospect out of charity*. Finding this ground untenable they pretend that Mr. Jefferson knew nothing of the contents. But it appeared that Mr. Jefferson paid Callender fifty dollars, in part, after Callender had been convicted of sedition for publishing the *Prospect*, and of course Mr. Jefferson must have been acquainted with the contents of the work, and that Mr. Jefferson moreover remitted Callender's fine of 200 dollars, when the contents of the *Prospect* had long been known.

The editor of the *Boston Repertory* declared that he was possessed of a paragraph in Mr. Jefferson's handwriting, which was incorporated with Mr. Jefferson's own slander in the body of the *Prospect* "without marks of quotation." The Enquirer (a man lured to vindicate Mr. Jefferson) admits that Mr. Jefferson wrote a short and harmless paragraph and *but one*, in the whole book. Unfortunately, however, for Mr. Jefferson's advocate the paragraph which he acknowledges was written by Mr. Jefferson is totally different from that mentioned by the editor of the *Repertory*. But this *Enquirer*-man is doubtless well versed in what Cheetham calls the "*arts of able editors*."

25 Genet was *privately* encouraged by Mr. Jefferson in his projects to prostrate America at the feet of France, but opposed *officially* in his capacity of Secretary of State. Genet complained that Mr. Jefferson had treacherously become the instrument of his recall, after having persuaded him that he was his friend, and initiated him into the mysteries of state. And declared "if I have shown my firmness (in opposing the President,) it is because it is not in my character to *speak* as many people do in *one way* and act in *another*, to have an official language and a

Did it become one in his station
To show so much prevarication?

Will any democrat declare
That was a very pious prayer,
Which he for Adams, whom he hated,
So solemnly ejaculated?[26]

Has he paid nothing to maintain
The press of demagogue Duane,
Teeming with foulest defamation
Of Washington's administration.[27]

---

language *confidential*."

26   When Mr. Jefferson entered on the daties of his office as
Vice-President he eulogised Mr. Adams, then President, in the
following terms,

> No man more sincerely prays that no accident may
> call me to the higher and more important functions;
> (the presidency) they have been justly confided to
> the eminent character, which has preceded me here,
> whose talents and integrity have been known and
> revered by me through a long course of years, and I
> *devoutly pray* he may be long preserved for the gov-
> ernment, the happiness, and the prosperity of our
> common country.

This was a masterly stroke of policy, more especially, when
it is considered that Mr. Jeiferson, at the time of uttering this
solemn petition was employing his purse, pen and influence,
in ruining the reputation, and destroy ing the influence of Mr.
Adams.

27   Mr. Jefferson is one of the principal patrons of the *Aurora*, and
was the *institutor* and patron of the *National Gazette*, which
abounded with abuse against the federal administration, with

Pray plaster over, if you can, sir,
The foolish and sophistic answer
Which his sublimity did dish up
About th'appointment of old Bishop.

Have not his partisans so senseless
Stripped our great nation quite defenceless?[28]
While Europe rings with war's alarms,
And half the world is up in arms?

Our native rigour paralys'd,
That now our character's despised,
And sunk in foreign estimation
To lowest point of degradation?

Plundered by every rascal pirate,
Who thinks us mark enough to fire at,
And forced to suffer with humility
Insults from Spanish imbecility.[29]
Though democratick impudences,

Washington at its head.

28 Of thirty-four armed ships, our administration have sacrificed, at the shrine of economy (sold for one-fourth part of their cost) all but thirteen, and some of those which remain are rotting in *philosophical* dry docks. But *economy* is the order of the day, and a *wasteful economy*, is a contradiction in terms.

29 Depredations on our commerce are committed daily, by the Spaniards and other nations of Europe (Sept. 1805.) Mr. Jefferson however, has said, that "history bears witness to the fact, that a just nation is trusted at its bare word, when recourse is had to armaments and wars to bridle others." It is to be lamented that these depredators should spoil the president's *fine theory.*

179

To merit making false pretences,
Proclaim us prosperous and happy,
Like Stingo with his jug of nappy.

Yet this prosperity they boast,
The theme of many a July toast,
Is all the fruit of Federal toils,
Though Demo's *riot* in their spoils.

What though they boast their knack at saving,
'Gainst Federal waste forever raving,
Still decency should keep them dumb,
For what they say is all a hum.

In Africk, lo, what triumphs won
Have told the world what might be done,
Did not a weak administration
Contrive to paralyse the nation!

The *Federal* navy overawes
Fell hordes of murderous Bashaws,
From whence each democrat assumes
To deck his sconce with borrow'd plumes.[30]

---

30   *Mareat cnrnicula visum*
      Fuvtivis nudata coloribus,
                         HOR.

    Stripped of their borrow'd plumes, these crows forlon
    Shall stand the laughter of the public scorn.

    The federalists are accused by their political opponents of
having been sparing of their eulogies on the heroes who dis-

Thus Duane's Turner cut a figure,
And felt, no doubt, as big, or bigger
In cloak he'd stolen, as if the same
Had been his own by rightful claim.

Why don't our Carter-hill commander,
Who's so beset with Federal slander,
Pursue the rogues who "dare devise"
Against his Majesty such lies;[31]

---

tinguished themselves at Tripoli. This, if true, evinces the folly and stupidly of that party; for those men, who have been most distinguished by their exploits against those pirates, were *federalists*, and most of them commissioned by Washington and Adams.

31 To show to what an amount the impudence of some federal newspaper editors will carry them, we will make one or two extracts from remarks of the editor ofthe *New York Evening Post*, on Mr. Jefferson's inaugural speech No. 2. Mr. Jefferson, having reference to some tough libellous *truths*, which have appeared in the federal newspapers agauist him, observed in his speech, that "the artillery of the press has been levelled against us, charged with whatsoever its licentiousness could devise or dare," and that "he who has time, renders a service to public morals and public tranquillity, in reforming these abuses by the salutary coercions of law." Coleman, supposing, no doubt, that nobody could ever find "time" for attending to these "salutary coercions," makes perhaps very true, but very *libellous* remarks.

Mr. Jefferson in his speech had observed, "I fear not that motives of interest may lead me astray; I am sensible of no passion which could seduce me knowingly from the path of justice." Mr. Coleman comments as follows: "He, who with the *bribery of office* has corrupted the integrity of the nation, has demoralized the American people for the purpose of personal aggrandizement, now boasts that no motives of interest can lead him astray. He, who in a publick address to the senateof

Because in spite of his renown

the United States, solemnly declared that Mr. John Adams was an eminent character, whose talents and integrity had been long known and revered by him (Mr. Jefferson) through a long courie of years, and had been the foundation of a cordial and uninterrupted friendship between them; and concluded with "devoutly (his own word) devoutly praying," that the same Mr. Adams "might be long preserved for the government, the happiness, and prosperity of our common country," went away and hired a mercenary rascal to make it his business to traduce this very Mr. Adanis in the most violent language that his invention could supply. Yes, he feasted his eyes with the perusal of the manuscript, in which the man vith whom he had so long, as he told the senate, "maintained a cordial and uninterrupted friendship," was spoken of as the lowest of wretches, where he was denominated the most execrable of SCOUNDRELS, the scourge, the scorn, the outcast of America, without abilities, and without virtue, and then returned it with the most unqualified approbation, saying, that "*such papers could not fail to produce the best effect*," and as a part recompence, sent him an order for fifty dollars on account of previous work. Need any thing mure be added? yes, one tale shall be added, and in very explicit language, so that if the Attorney General of the United States can "find time," and Mr. Jefferson should still remain of opinion, after seeing the article, (and I know he honours the *Evening Post* with his perusai) that it will be rendering a "service to pubiick morals and publick tranquillity," to resort to the "salutary coercion of law," and prosecute the editor for a libel, matter may not be wanting on which to found the indictment. I only stipulate for the pritilege of giving the truth in evidence. Then be it known, that he who now holds himself up to the world as a man incapable of being seduced by passion from the path of rectitude, stole to the chamber of his absent friend by night, and attempted to violate his bed. * * *

As it generally happens, that when once the devil gets hold of a man he seldom lets him go with a single crime on his head, so this man, to the baseness of his first attempt, added a second. As a cover to the

He knows the truth would put him down,
Nor has he hardihood to sport
His rotten character in court.

Thus spake this mattering son of slander,
And made it plain to each bye-stander
He was a rogue belonging unto
The most nefarious Essex junto.[32]

---

abrupt disconnection of intercourse that followed the disclosure of the secret to the husband, he told abase and slanderous lie, and said, that his intimacy with Mr. Walker had been broken off by Mr. Walker's unhandsome conduct in the settlement of an estate, which he had in charge; all which now stands on record, being very handsomely engrossed with his own hand. Now let Mr. Jefferson, if he pleases, call this a "false and defamatory publication," and recommend a prosecution accordingly.

What a daring fellow this, but nobody can "find time" to prosecute him. Moreover, Mr. Jefferson's vindicator in the *Richmond Enquirer*, has made this appear to be a very trivial affair, for he says,

IF THE TALE OF MRS. WALKER WAS REHEARSED TO A NATION OF ANCHORITES, THE WOULD SMILE AT ITS ABSURDITY; THAT AN INDIVIDUAL SHOULD BE ABUSED, CENSURED, AND THREATENED WITH EXPOSURE IN THE PUBLIC PRINTS, FOR HAVING, FORTY YEARS SINCE, FELT AN IMPROPER PASSION: AT A TIME WHEN YOUTH, EXEMPTION FROM MATRIMONIAL OBLIGATIONS, AND THE FORCE OF FEELING MIGHT BE PLEADED WITH JUSTICE!!!

32   The Essex Junto is one of the bugbears, with which the *Boston Chronicle* scribblers frighten the babes and old women of democracy. But this, like many other gun-powder plots against the peace and dignity of the *sovereign people*, is a phantom which they have conjured up for the purpose of deception. The men whom they would designate as an Essex Junto, are as

But should I ever hear again
A scoundrel mutter such a strain,
I'll teach the knave by dint of banging,
A prettier method of haranguing.

For know ye stubborn Feds, that I
Am very nearly six feet high,
Stout in proportion, own a cudgel
For those of Jefferson who judge ill.

With plenipotent paw a club in,
I'll give each Fed'rai rogue a drubbing
Who wont *humillime* succumb,
At beat of our poetick drum.

And kneel before the mighty man,
Who leads the democratick van,
The glorious Chief of Carter's mountain
Of democratick power the fountain;—

The theme of demi-adoration,
The very right-hand of our nation,
Compared with whom, all heroes must rate
As gun-boat liken'd to a first-rate.[33]

---

much interested in the preservation of a Republican government, as any men in the community, and would, by the introduction of a Monarchical government, dig a pit for their own destruction.

So say the Federalists, but they are Monarchy-men notwithstanding, and wish to make John Adams king.

33 The curious system of Mr. Jefferson, for creating a naval force adequate to the defence of our commerce, by gun-boats, No's.

And though I shan't have much to say t'ye,

1, 2, &c. up, perhaps, to 5 or 6, is thus described in the New
Year's Message, from the carriers of the *Boston Palladium*. Al-
though gun-boat number one, as there exhibited, may appear
to be somewhat too consequential to be introduced by way of
comment on our *political text*, yet, as it appears to have some
connection with our simile, we give it a place.

Have not our wise administration
Done certain wonders for the nation?
O yes—they've built us more than one boat.
In modern jargon call'd a Gun Boat.
Yes;—they have built us—let me see,
Enough to make out *nearly* THREE,
But one of those, O what a rare go,
March'd to a cornfield for a scare-crow!
Which show'd Miss Gun-Boats calculation,
And that *she knew her proper station!*
O *did her masters* but know *theirs,*
L—d, how 'twould brighten our affairs.
  Our Gun-Boats! themes of adimiration
To every seaman in the nation,
The very essence, in reality,
Of vast *philosophisticality!*
One round half dozen, I've a notion,
Would carry terror through the ocean,
And eight or ten, in my opinion,
Would give us Neptune's whole dominion!
  Should Britain come, with all her shipping,
Good L—d, we'd give her such a whipping,
She'd wish the navy of her island
Had been just nineteen leagues on dry land
Before she'd impudence to enter
On such a perilous adventure;
For Number One will sink her navy,
In half a second, to old Davy,
Then, as we wish her nothing but ill.
Her petty, paltry isle we'll scuttle,
And since 'tis time th' Old Nick had got 'em,

You'll find my arguments are weighty,

Send the whole nation to the bottom!
What mighty matters might be done,
For instance, Gun-Boat Number One,
From Washington descends in might,
With head and tail "chock full of fight!"
Abash'd, potowmack hides his head
Neptune, half petrifi'd with dread,
And awe, and admiration rapt in,
Resigns his chariot to the Captain.
Great Captain Buckskin; please to ride in't,
Terrific Sir, and here's my trident
You cut a dash so big and mighty,
You've sadly frighten'd Amphitrite!
My sea-nymphs sure have lost their wits,
There's Thetis in hysteritk fits
Take mydominions, every foot,
O L—d! O L—d! but pray don't shoot
Now gallant Number One, by chance,
Meets England's fleet combin'd with France,
Is soon prepared at bolh her ends,
Stand clear all rogues, except our Friends!
Now comes the fleet in line of battle.
The heaven's rebellowing cannons rattle,
Each smoke envelop'd grand first-rater,
Looks like the mouth of Ætna's crater.—
goes our gun, like Pluto's mortar,
Splash!—*there they are—all under water!!!*
Not quicker, struck by Jove's own thunder,
Did earth-born Titans erst knock under,
Than these when hit by their superiors,
From Gun-Boat, Number One's posteriors.
But were it true, as has heen said.
By many a wicked muttering Fed,
That every Gun-Boat is a wherry,
Which might disgrace old Charon's ferry;
Still, when Sir Johnny Randolph's taught her,
She'll *keep the peace in shallow water,*
Strike rampant porpoises with awe,

Withal, so manfully propounded,
If not convinced, you'll be confounded.

By knocking down each Federal prater,
I'll e'en surpass our Legislature,
In bold display of sheer authority,
In *dumb* and *dignifi'd* majority.[34]

But now my modest little Muse,
Who drips with Hybla's honey dews,
Her court'sy makes to curry favour,
With Federal gentlefolks, who waver.
Good Messrs. *almost* Democrats,
If you were not as blind as bats,

And govern mackerel by law;
Dog-fishes, dolphins, if they've wit,
To our Sea-Mammoth will submit,
No grampus dare to stand a scratch,
And even a shark would find his match!

34 The wisdom of our democratick members of Congress was
never more abundantly manifested, than in the affair of their
condescending to remain silent, when they had nothing to say
for themselves. There is, unquestionably, no small share of
prudence and self-denial necessary, for an individual to curb
that unruly member, the tongue. How great then must have
been the prudence and resolution of our good democrats, in
congress assembled, who, for the sake of expediting publick
business, could sit mute, and endure to be pelted by argu-
ments which they could not answer.

Mr. Dana's eulogy* upon the "dumb legislature," will re-
main a monumentum cevi of the wonderful wisdom which was
manifested by the majority on that occasion.

* See debates of congress, 1802.

Before our Chief, your trembling knees on,
You'd deprecate his wrath in season.

No more at Jefferson be railing,
Nor scout the party now prevailing,
Although the tail "has got the upper
Hand ofthe head, for want of crupper."[35]

The character of this our nation,
'Tis time to place on some foundation,
Which may without deceit declare
To all mankind just what we are.

And IF Americans are jockies,
If public virtue but a mock is,
Then—"Hail Columbia! happy land!"
Where scoundrels have the upper hand!

But let Columbia be contented,
As she's at present represented,
Nor at our democrats be vext,

---

35 This beautiful simile we have borrowed from Butler. That au-
thor applies it as descriptive of the democracy of the body nat-
ural of his hero, Hudibras; but we think it happily illustrative
of the present organization of the body politick of our country.
If the reader, however, better likes the following simile, from
the same author, Butler, it is much at his service.

> For as a fly that goes to bed,
> Sleeps with his tail above his head.
> So in this mongrel state of ours.
> The rabble are the supreme powers.

Lest their great prototype come next.

Now I'm a man, who would not keep ill
Terms, with my sovereign friends, the people,
Have therefore strove with main and might
To wash their Ethiopian white.

That I might suit them to a tittle,
Have stretch'd the truth—and lied a little,
For which, my complaisance, I beg,
They'll hoist my bardship up a peg

Or two or so, for I've a notion
That none can better bear promotion,
And I'll accept of any thing
From petty juryman to king.

Besides, I fancy that his highness
Wont treat his eulogist with shyness,
But compliment me with a pension,
 And fine things which I need not mention;

For Canto Fourth, of this my poem,
Read by his Mightiness, will show him,
He has a friend expert enough in
The democratick art of puffing.

But please his Righness-ship, I wont
Be Deputy to Mr. Hunt—[36]

---

36 The appointment of a Mr. Hunt to be governor of a district in
    Louisiana, exhibits wonderfal proof of Mr. Jefferson's solici-

No, were it offered 'twould be vain, he
Wont catch me in Louisiana.

---

tude to reward merit, and long tried and faithful services. It is
true, that this gentleman is yet a boy in years, to say nothing of
his intellect; but his exertions iu favor of Mr. Jefferson, have
been to the full amount of his abilities. Only those who are best
acquainted with his excellency, governor Hunt, can appreciate
the stupendous degree of discernment, which Mr. Jefferson
has displayed in his appointment.

The Gibbet of Satire

ARGUMENT

The Bard proceeds in an ungrateful
Task, which is, hangman-like, and hateful,
A gang of hypocrites t'expose.
And deeds ot intamy disclose;
And on the rack of satire, stretches
A set of weak and wicked wretches,
Whose inauspicious domination
Portends destruction to the nation.

YE Tories, Demos, Antifeds,
Of hollow hearts, and wooden heads,
In Washington's own estimation,
The curses of our Age and Nation.[1]

Who and what are ye, Patriots stout.
For Freedom, who make such a rout?
Ye are, or should be, men, I'm sure,
Whose hands are clean, whose hearts are pure.

O yes! your purity so nice is,

---

1 General Washington expressed this idea in his letter to Mr.
Carrol, See note 145, p. 168, Vol. I.

The best among you have their prices;[2]
Flour-Merchants, public defalcators,[3]
Horse-Jockies, swindling Speculators.—

The scum—the scandal of the age,
A blot on human nature's page;
In these two epithets included.
Deluding knaves, and fools deluded.[4]

---

2   Citizen Fauchet of glorious memory, in his intercepted letter, (which caused the dismission of citizen Randolph, also of glorious memory, the virtuous author of "Precious Confessions") has the following passage:

> Mr. Randolph came to see me with an air of great eagerness, and made the overtures of which I gave you an account in my No. 6.—Thus, with some thousands of dollars, the Republic of France could have decided on civil WAR, or on peace! Thus the consciences of the pretended patriots of America, have already their prices! What will be the old age of this government, if it is thus early decrepid!

See Phocion's Pamphlet.

3   The "Precious Confessions" of Pseudo-Patriot Randolph, are too well known to require any elucidation in this place. Mr. Randolph, however, is not the only pretended good republican, who has been a public defalcator.

4   We speak of the leaders of the Faction. There are, undoubtedly, a great number of honest Democrats, who have been led away by the Faction, to whom this line is not applicable. If a man has no better means of political information, than the Jacobin Newspapers throughout the union, he can be no other than a Democrat, although he may be deficient neither in integrity nor disceniment.

Step forward now, and "hear affrighted.
The crimes of which ye stand indicted;—
Now elevate your culprit paws,
While "We the People," try your cause.

Step forth, Honestus, lank and lean,[5]
With lantern jaws and haggard mien,
A wight, Lavater would decide,
Was Envy's self personified.

Sir, have you any thing to say
Of scrape fraternal with Genet?
And did you, if the truth were told,
E'er pocket any of his gold?

Does the arch Democrat inherit
A greater spleen against true merit?[6]

---

5   This Honestus is a well known scribbler in the *Boston Chron-icle*, one of the most mischievous and malignant democratic Newspapers in the United Slates. We should say nothing of the man's phiz, did we not believe it to be indicative of the quali-ties of his mind.

6   By adverting to Mr. Honestus's writings, with the signature of "OLD SOUTH," &c. we shall perceive that his demagogue-ship has spirted his venom at many of the most distinguished char-acters in the union. He has attacked the clergy in a most in-sidious manner, and some oF his essays are *better calculated* to do mischief with certain class in society, than if they were *better written*; as they are addressed to the *prejudices* and *weaknesses* of the *lowest classes* in the community.

    He is constantly criminating the clergy for interfering in politics. The "People (he says, p. '21%, of his volume of Chron-icle Essays) are willing to hear *gospel truths*, though, they may be displeased with *political heresy*." And pray what is this

And though Democracy he founded,
Is he by viler gangs surrounded?[7]

---

political heresy? Opposing the man with "no God or twenty Gods." Again, p. 220 of the same volume: "If the apostles had acted as some of our modern clergy do, *they would have ruined, in the first outset, the whole system of revelation!*" Mr. Jefferson has here an advocate worthy of himself!

I think lean in no way express the reasons why the clergy ought to exert themselves in opposition to Mr. Jefferson, more forcibly than by presenting my readers with the following extract from remarks on the Thanksgiving Sermon of Mr. Parish, by the Editor of the *Boston Repertory.*

> It is true, the President of the United States, and the clergy of our country are at variance; but.the controversy is not on subjects of politics, on forms of government, or measures of administration. The clergy have "not quit their proper character, to asume what does not belong to them." It is their mislfortune to live in an age, when a man is promoted to the chief magistracy of the nation, who has wantonly assaulted the religion of our fathers, and treated those doctrines with contempt, which Christianity teaches us are essential to human felicity. It is Mr. Jefferson, who has left the character of the civilian, who has sported with the principles of our religion, and no alternative is left for the watchmen of the christian faith, but to retreat before his baleful influence, and apostatize from the injunctions of their divine teacher, or to step forth like faithful soldiers, and repel the scoffs, the sneers, and sophistry of the assailant The elevated station of Mr. Jefferson, so far from imposing an obligation of silence, calls on the clergy for a more zealous exertion of their powers in defence of reiigicn, in proportion as his writings are like to possess greater weight from his political ascendance.

7   We do not pretend to give a history of Honé's private Jock-

Hast thou supported thy life long,
One measure not precisely wrong,
One single thing, when you your best did,
Whose usefulness by *time* is tested?[8]

When did the tyrant Bonaparte,
E'er find an advocate more hearty?
Or one more ready to advance
The wildest whims of frantick France?[9]

Are you the Jacobin of spirit,
Who first *found out* your own great merits
And in political careering,

---

ey-club. Suffice it to say, that the nefarious renegade, Pasquin,
is one of his privy counsellors, and he alone is a gang.

Since writing the above, Pasquin has relinquished the ser-
vice of the *Boston Chronicle,* in which he and Honestus were
Co-editors. [Oct. 1805]

8   This observation does not apply, exdusively, to the demagogue
now under consideration. None of those measures, of which
democrats have been such strenuous advocates, have been
found of practical utility; and since they have been in power,
they have copied the example of the federalists, except in cer-
tain measures, which are calculated to oppress the poorer peo-
ple; such as repealing taxes on carriages, loaf-sugar, and other
luxuries, and increasing them on salt, and other necessaries of
life.

9   A review of the scrawl of this, and other Chronicle patriots, on
the subject of the French revolution, ever rccalls to memory,
the following lines from Cowper:

Yon roaring boys, who rave and fight,
    On t'other side the Atlantick,
I always thought were in the right,
    But most so, when most frantick.

First practis'd *self-electioneering?*[10]

How came you, modest Sir, to hit on
This horrid practice of Great Britain,
When you, as every body knows,
Are one of her determin'd foes?

Are you indeed the very man,
Who *seem'd* t'oppose the Funding Plan,
An hypocritical pretence
To pocket its emoluments?[11]

Has it not been your constant aim,
The passions of the mob t' inflame
Their jealousy and pride exciting
By flattery, falsehood, and backbiting?[12]

---

10 We believe Honestus is the personage who introduced in Mas-
    sachusetts that appendage of British corruption, self-election-
    eering. He first mounted the hustings, Westminster-like, and
    told all the world *what nobody knew before*, that he was *himself*
    a very proper candidate for office, a friend to the people, &c.

11 Honestus was once a very strenuous opponent to the funding
    system. Now, forsooth, as Commissioner of Loans, he is pock-
    eting the people's money, in consequence of holding an office,
    which is an appendage of the same owe obnoxious system.
    What a pure patriot!

12 We have but one simple apology to make for taking notice of
    "OLD SOUTH," alias "Honeslus." In this apology we beg leave to
    repeat a sentiment which we have before expressed, that the
    bite of an asp may be as fatal as the *paw of a lion*. Old South's
    writings would be esteemed by us as too insipid for animad-
    version, were they not calculated, by virtue of that same insi-
    pidity, to be very mischievous. He never soars above the level
    of the understanding of the lowest class of the community, and

Pray Sir, if one may be so bold,

---

like a fanatical preacher, his essays are always addressed to the passions and the feelings of those men, whose passions and feelings are *strong*, but whose intellects are *weak*, and who are the soul of all these violent revolutions, which leave society worse than they found it.

"OLD SOUTH" is ever harping on the subject of the "BENEVO-LENCE AND THE DIGNITY OF THE PEOPLE." It would be very well to recommend those virtues, and to suppose that they do exist in a high degree in America, as this supposition may do something to wards forming a NATIONAL CHARACTER among Americans, and lead to a high sense of honor and honesty, without which there can be no real freedom, or long continued national prosperity. But what conclusions does Mr. OLD SOUTH draw from his premises under that head? That if the people were left destitute of restraints, by enjoying liberty without law, all would be "BENEVOLENCE AND DIGNITY." But the experience of all ages!5 against him. A purely democratick government would soon be a *savage state.**

"OLD SOUTH," in a long essay on the subject of "the benevolence and dignity of the people," produces one extraordinary instance of *democratick* insanity, in proof of his assertions: "As soon," says he,

> as peace was proclaimed between the two nations, (France and England) the people exercised their *natural benevolence*, and rushed forth like a torrent, to receive with open arms, the messenger of this joyful intelligence; the city of London resounded with "long live Bonaparte! long live the French nation!" the horses were dismissed from the carriages, as being too slow in their progress, and the people became the promulgators of the glad tidings, by conducting the herald to the metropolis.

Here is Bone's specimen of "BENEVOLENCE AND DIGNITY." These *biped coach-horses* of Mr. Lauriston, exhibited much *democraitick* dignity in their silly manoeuvre of dragging this "herald of peace" to St. James' palace. But what said those who

How many lies may you have told,
Since you, and certain other knowing
Knaves, set the Chronicle a going?

Now, ere too late, begin repentance.
Before the people pass their sentence,
That they no longer will be bit
By such a shallow hypocrite.[13]

---

knew something of this subject? That the peace was hollow, insincere on the side of Bonaparte, and that England must arm, and beon the alert, or submit to the domination of that unprincipled usurper.

This is an instance among a thousand, of Honé's inconsistencies. The man is wrong-headed; he has furnished his noddle with a jumble of facts and principles, but has not sufficient strength of intellect to digest, and draw proper conclusions from the things which come within the sphere of his knowledge. A "*little learmng*," with a *great deficit* of common sense, makes a man very mischievous in society.

* See note 29. p, 21, Vol I.

13 We are not fond of calling names, but it somelimes becomes necessary for a right uiulerstanding of things. That Mr. Honestus has endeavoured to make his patriotism a stepping-stone to power, is evident from his conduct, which has not been quite so equivocal as his professions.

Mr. Honestus pretends to rank himself with the patriots of 1775, and anathematizes all those who will not pronounce his Shibboleth, as old tories. But unless we are wrongly informed, this gentleman, during our revolutionary war, although perhaps not in a cave, sought an asylum in obscurity. He began, however, to fish in the troubled waters, which succeeded the revolution, about the time of Shays' insurrection, and has been ever since constant in his efforts to arm the passions against the intellect of the community, and set the physical, in battle array against the intellectual powers of society.

For though you stride, without remorse,
Fell faction's hobbling hobby horse,
The jade may toss, by sudden flirt,
Your demagogue-ship in the dirt.[14]

For freedom you may make a pother,
But 'twill be known, one time or other,
How oft the People's good is lost in
The greater good of Mr.————[15]

Step forward, "simple" Tony Pasquin,[16]

The motives of Honestus in such proceedings, are probably, similar to those of all other demagogues. Pride and ambition impel him to strive to be a great man. But nature having been somewhat niggardly with regard to those endowments, which, in regular governments, are thought necessary to qualify a man for office, Honestus has no other way of gratifying his leading propensity, than to excite confusion, in order to rise in the tumult. But, notwithstanding all his canting about his friendship to the people, we have never heard of his hesitating to pocket their money, even for services in those offices which he had stigmatised as burthensome and expensive. And for such a friend to the people!

14   So have I seen with armed heel,
      A wight bestride a common-weal.
      While still the more he kick'd and spurr'd.
      The less the sullen jade has stirr'd."

HUDIBRAS, Canto I.

15   Austin—as in Benjamin Austin, Jr (1752 - 1820), a Massachusetts politician, writer, and pamphleteer, who was an advocate of republican principles and a critic of Federalist policies. —Ed.

16   This reptile, who is the right hand *Chronicle*-mart, has been so pre-eminently infamous, that it appears there was put one step which the creature could take to complete the degradation of

his character, to the lowest pitch of which human nature is capable. This step he has taken, by enlisting into the *Chronicle* service, and exerting himself to diffuse the poison of his principles among the poor deluded beings, who are so simple as to reap the effusions of his "jobbernowl."

We shall not here attempt, what we once intended, a sketch of his biography, but merply state a few particulars, which will be evincive of the kind of talents, which are necessary to qualify a man for the eminent station of Editor of a democratic Newspaper.

In Tony's celebrated law-suit against Faulder and others, which has been published in the *Repertory* in this town, and which we remember to have seen in England, there appears such adevelopement of the infamy of this most detestable of all wretches, that one would not think it possible, that a human being, who possessed the least pretensions to respectability in society would be his associate.

I will not trouble the reader with any minute strictures on the character of this pitiful vagrant, but merely conclude this note with the concluding remark of Mr. Garrow, in the trial to which I have above referred, together with a statement of the result of the trial, in which this pure-hearted patriot sought recompense for having been *calumniated.*

> I see by your countenances, gentlemen, that it is unnecessary to proceed any further with this man's infamous and abominable productions. I will not, therefore, harrass your feelings; let them rest for the present—but I will appeal to your sense of propriety, to that of all who hear me, and ask, whether this common libeller, this vile traducer of honour and integrity, this hireling blaster of youth and innocence, should be suffered to come into this court, and ask satisfaction for being described under the character he has voluntarily and ostentatiously assumed? Should he, who has been proved before you to be the author of works, of which every line is calumny, sue for your protection, under the pretence that

he is calumniated? Shall he say to you, gentlemen, I have been, from my youth up, earning a scandalous subsistence by vilifying my sovereign, insulting his august family, belying his ministers, traducing his courts of justice and subjects, from the highest to the lowest; give therefore, ample damages, because this dirty occupation is not sufficiently profitable?

Shall he say, I have violated the ear of modesty in my writings, I HAVE RIDICULED THE ORDINANCES OF OUR HOLY RELIGION, I HAVE BLASPHEMED——

Here some of the jury got up, and Lord Kenyon desired Mr. Garrow to stop, that more was evidently unnecessary.

He then said, that it was tlieir duly to consider whether the author of such works aj Ihey he:ii\I read and describ--cd, Iiad a right to call for damages.

With whatface (ccmtinued his lordship) can this fellow find fault with the publication of the defendant, when it appears that the passage here libelled, attaches to him merely as Anthony Pasquin, a name which he has prefixed to writings of the most *infamous nature?** It appears to me that the author of the Baviad, has acted a very meritorious part in exposing this man; and I most earnestly wish and hope that some method will, ere long, be fallen upon to prevent *all such unprincipled and mercenary wretches* from going about, unbridled in society to the great annoyance and disquietude of the public.

The jury, without a moment's hesitation, nonsuited the plaintiff, and the audience "hissed Jiim out of Court."

* Amongother stupid productions of Tony, which Here read on this occasion, was his *Pin-Basket for the Children of Thespis.* In this he thus speaks of the celebrated Edmund Burke:
——"And—Mun, with his mouthful of Christ!!"
Horrid wretch!

In Presidential favour basking,[17]
A very proper sort of crony,
For such a wight as Mr. Hone

I'm free to own, that I'm amaz'd,
Your heart deprav'd, your noddle craz'd,[18]
That even our leaders of sedition,
Should use you for a politician.

Our Yankey-Statesmen put to school,
To such a sorry sort of tool,
Who can't write English if he dies,[19]
Will, doubtless, turn out wondrous wise!

---

17 We have good authority for asserting, that this *fine writer*, received a very handsome douceur from Mr. Jefferson, for his services in puffing the *Notes on Virginia*.

18 We have seen sundry specimens of Tony's "admired performances," as he calls them, which were so stupidly wild, unmeaning, and unintelligible, that we have thought with Mr. Gifford, in a similar case, that nothing could match them short of a "transcript from the darkened walls of Bedlam."

19 Mr. Garrow has justly said of Tony, that his English was as incorrect as his conduct.

This paltry scribbler, since the above was written, has quitted the *Chronicle* service, after grumbling a few anathema respecting the small encouragement afforded him in his labours in the cause of republicanism. What we have written, however, will serve to show what sort of <u>beings</u> constitute the best of democratick newspaper editors and stand as a monument of infamy against the party in whose service such a rotable advocate was retained; and in whose service he would, probably, have continued his *meritorious* exertions, had not the voice of publick contempt fairly booted him from the scene of action.

With such a dirty wretch as Tony,
Who but Honestus would be crony?
And what vile renegade but Tony,
Would be the intimate of Hone?

Your friends, the Feds, are much delighted
To see such noble souls united,
And when death threatens *squally weather*
They hope e'en thenyou'll, *hung together!*

Come forward, *spitting* Mathew Lyon,
Thy flaming wooden sword pray tie on,[20]
Hold up thy head, man, don't be frighted,
Abolder warrior ne'er was knighted.

Great Hero of Ticonderogue,
So long as valour is in vogue,
Thy name and merits shall be shouted,[21]

---

20   A wooden sword is said to have been presented to this warri-
or, who is alike renowned in the cabinet and in the fieid, as a
tribute of respect for having *prudently* retreated from a post,
where it is not impossible he might have been killed or taken
by the enemy, had he remained. General Gates, however, like
an old aristocrat, ordered our Irish Fabius to be drummed out
of camp for cowardice.

21   We are extremely solicitous to eulogise this wonderful war-
rior, and have even gone so far as to hammer out a song, in
the prettiest stile imaginable, for no other purpose than to
celebrate, and, if possible, to perpetuate the achievements of
our Hibernian hero. Although we are not addicted to be very
vociferous on the theme of our own praises, still we must beg
leave to observe, that in our opinion, the following song has
more delicacy, sweetness, sense, sensibility, &c. &c. than all
the sonnets of Miss Charlotte Smith put together, and we rec-

Nor once by infamy be scouted.

---

ommend it to be sung by way of catch, glee, sonata, &c. &c. at all the meetings of good democrats, assembled in self-created constitutional societies, or midnight electioneering caucusses, ox-roasting junkets, &c. &c. &c.

THE DAGON OF DEMOCRACY,
A BRAN NEW SONG.
[TUNE—"O Cupid Forever."]

O COME let us praise
In beautiful lays,
 A wonderful idol of party,
And each Democrat,
Shall laud Mister Pat,
 The Wooden Sword hero so hearty.

CHORUS

O then ye are lucky.
Good men of Kentucky,
 To choose spitting Matt, for your idol;
Come frolic and caper,
By the blaze of his taper,*
 And sing, fol de rol,, diddled! dol.

No Commandment you break,
Though an Idol you make,
 Of the ugly, old Democrat, seeing
That nothing at all, Sirs,
Flies, walks, swims or crawls, Sirs,
 In the likeness of such an odd being,

Othen ye are lucky, &c.

'Tis said that he brags
How one pair of stags.
 Erst paid for his passage from Europe;
But the price of a score,

Thou shalt be held in more repute
Than fam'd Calig'la's Consul brute;
Or mighty Mammoth, prairte dog,
Or the best educated hog.

Duane and thou at loggerheads,[22]

Would scarce send hint o'er,
And pay for his hangman a new rope!*
O then ye are lucky, &c.

When our Independence
He strove to defeiid once,
Great Britain look'd blue at his wrath, Sirs!
But Gun-powder's smell,
Didn't suit him so well,
So he's knightof the dagger of Lath, Sirs.
O then ye are lucky, &c.

Good L—d, what of that?
He's a fine Democrat;
And health to the brute shall go round, Sirs!
And O ye are lucky,
Good men of Kentucky,
To choose such a brute for your idol,
Come froliek and caper,
By the blaze of his taper,
And sing, fol de rol, diddle di dol.

* We mention this circumstance to shew that the price ttf the
beast has risen. When he first landed in this country, he to as
sold to a Mr. Hugh Hanna, of Litchfield, in Connecticut, for
a pair of steers.

22 This pair of paddies have lately attacked each other with no
small degree of virulence. Lyon, (the less ferocious beast of the
two) by turning Stages' evidence, has *brought out* his friend
Duane, and given some characteristick sketches of *himself* and
party, which cannot fail to amuse all those who can contem-

Make fine amusement for the Feds,

plate the *backside* of human nature with complacency. Had not the tail of the body politick in America, got the upperhand, and as Butler says, "sergeant bum invaded shoulders," we would turn with disgust from such exhibitions of enormity as are presented to view by the fallingout of these rogues among themselves. But as they have a more intimate acquaintance with each other's projects than honest men can have, it may not be bad policy to attend to their criminations, set a thief to take a thief, and pardon a few who will be active in convicting the rest.

Lyon has lately addressed a letter to Duane, which perfectly betrays the character of both these turbulent demagogues; and if Americans will hereafter be duped by such unprincipled wretches, they will deserve to be doomed to slavery. A short extract or two from Lyon's letter, will show what sort of a tool Duane is supposed to be, by his own party, and what honest means those in power have employed, in order to aggrandize themselves at the expense of the country.

After comparing Duane to a "*skunk*" and declaring him to be a "*would-be tyrant*" he proceeds as follows:

> A wretch (to wit, Duane) hunted tor his crimes, from Asia to Africa, from Africa to Europe, from Europe to America, landed on the Atlantick shore of the United States, seven or eight years ago, incapable of earning his bread, by common honest laborious industry, poor and pennyless, driven for his petulence from the station which first offered him subsistence in America, when a ragged vagabond, with a downcast guilty look like Cain, expecting every man's hand to be raised against him; bemired with filth, and shunned as a spectre; with no other distingnishing property than that of ability to write with severity; *to givefalsehood and lies some semblance of truth, and to give truth the appearance of falsehood.* The democrats of this country were taken in by him; by their countenance and indulgence, he became the conductor of a press, which had been

And all good men are overjoy'd,

distinguished for its correct course: they enabled him to put on a clean shirt, to fill his belly, to look a little sleek and hold up his head. * * *

I told the members (of Congress) to give the man money, all you can atford—let us support him through the crisis, and if our party succeeds in obtaining the reins of the government, the paper will support itself; if we fall, it must fall.

I foresaw, his charges would be made up, something like those made for printing for the house of representatives of the United States, which the committee of that house, with all their vigilance, have not been able tore duce, nearer than 30 per cent, to what other people will now do it for, when the lowest bidder has the work.

I often told my republican friends, in those days, that the lies of this man would injure our cause, if the conflict *lasted long enough to have them exposed.* A thousand times has he brought a blush on the face of the honest men of our party, when they read his unfounded attacks against their opponents; with regret, the most discerning foresaw, that themselves would be subject to the same insults and indignities, whenever they happened to displease this unprincipled scaramouch of their own architecture.

This person is suspected by some, to be at this time favourable to the views of a foreign potentate, [Buonaparte] who wishes to see *democracy* and *republicanism*, (very distinct things by the way) wrote down and brought into disgrace in this country,

&c. &c.

Thus spake the valorous knight of the wooden sword; but he still remains the very good friend of this "*unprincipled scaramouch*" and, tells Duane "although a provoked monitor,

To see such patriots thus employ'd.

And thou hast well contriv'd to win.
The heart of Goodman Gallatin,
And I've no doubt, but he would pleasure ye,
With all the money in the treasury.[23]

---

still your old friend is not your enemy," That "his republican friends think highly of Duane's services." &c.

One would suppose, that if Lyon had the least symptoms of returning honesty, he would not continue to support a man, whom he declares to "be a wretch hunted for his crimes from Europe to Africa," &c. and whose claims for patronage, consist altogether "in ability to write with severity; *to give falsehood and lies sonic semblance of truth, and to give truth the appearance of falsehood,*" one that he suspects to be "favourable to the views of a foreign potentate," &c. &c. And that his party would not feel proud in having employed, and continuing to employ, an "unprincipled wretch, whose LIES, they were told, would injure their cause." But like masters like man. They are all democrats, thev are all shuffling demagogues.

23   The Genevan evinced his partiality to the paddy, as follows:

The Knight of the Wooden Sword, was, in 1803, agent to the United States, for furnishing supplies to the army. He drew a bill on the treasury of the United States, for money which would not be due for a number of months. The bill, however, was presented, and immediately paid.

Mr. Steele, late secretary for the Missisippi territory, drew on the treasury of the United States, for money which was then due to him, under an act of congress, for services performed in collecting the direct tax. The bill was presented, and Gallatin acknowledged it to be due, but would not pay it until all the returns under the direct tax had come in, and the accounts were settled. The bill remained unpaid fourteen months, till the accounts were settled, when the holder called again on Mr. Gallatin. But the cunning Genevan would not then pay the bill, because all the money due for these services was-not drawn for at the same time.

'Tis said by some, O far fam'd Matt,
Although a noted Democrat,
Thou dost design to turn about,
And join the fallen Federal rout.

And wouldst thou condescend, my hearty,
To head the *tertium-quid* third party?[24]

The *Washington Federalist* makes the following remarks
on this scandalous procedure:

> The baseness of this transaction is only to be fully
> underslood, by comparing it with the one first de-
> tailed. In the first, we see a man despised by every
> person of character in the United States, made the
> agent of Government, and such anxiety shown to
> render him services, and to honour his drafts, that
> they are paid many months before they are due. On
> the other hand, we see a faithful and good officer,
> universally respected and esteemed, draw'ing upon
> the treasury for money acknowledged to be due to
> him. The secretary, instead of paying it, puts it off
> on frivolous pretexts, for more than a year, and then
> subjects the drawer to very great expense, trouble,
> and delay, which might have been avoided, by stat-
> ing the objections at first. The damages occasioned
> by the protest, are regulated by the different states.
> In few are they less, and some more than 15 per cen-
> tum on the whole amount, besides interest, cost,
> and charges. A pretty little sum for an American to
> pay, for the whim or caprice of an insolent foreigner!

24 Many of our formerly violent democrats, have become dis-
    gusted with their party, and have learned in the dear school
    of experience, what was foreseen by the federalists from the
    time in which our government was first organized, that the
    kind of liberty and equality, for which they have been conten-
    tious, would not be practicable in society. These gentlemen

Demo's and Feds would all be merry,
Fell Discord's tomahawk to bury.

Thy dagger, formed of toughest lath.
Would quell the rage of party wrath;
And, wav'd by thee like conjurer's wand,
Chase Discord's demon from the land.

Next on our list is Tony Haswell,
But he's so small a thing, that as well
Might giant bold assail musquitoe,
As we attack the puny creature.

Still as his party set him high.
For once, we'll condescend to try,
If we, by any possibility,
Can hit this essence of nihility.

But lest the reader think the topic

---

talk about forming a third party, of what they are pleased to call true Americans, which is to comprise all the *moderates* of both parties. This may be well enough, but these true Americans, must become in effect Federalists, whatever they may be pleased to denominate themselves, if they purpose to pursue the real interests of their country. But if their intention is to introduce a new order of things, a system of measures different in principle from those of the Washington and Adams administration, their leaders should be chosen from among the Democrats who distinguished themselves by thwarting the views of those men who laid the foundation for whatsoever of national prosperity we now enjoy. Among these we can think of no person whose courage and conduct so well entitle him to that superb station, as the Knight of the wooden Sword.

On which we treat, too microscopic.
We'll merely undertake to show,
Our gnat-ling in a note below.[25]

---

25   This petty dealer in sedition, has, a number of years past, ed-
ited a Newspaper, printed at Bennington, Vermont, which has
been as virulent and mischievous, as the limited talents of the
particle, which conducted it, would permit.

    We once endeavourcd to give the public an idea of the *thing*,
and *its* Newspaper, in the following lines:

> At Bennington, a set of fellows,
> Of Tony made a pair of bellows,
> Then plied their tool, with skill amazing,
> To set sedition's coals a blazing;
> And hope by dint of perseverance,
> To make all smoke within a year hence.
> In other words, the crooked set,
> Hir'd him to print a dull Gazette;
> A viler and a dirtier thing,
> Ne'er caus'd its editor to swing.
> His papers, take them as they rise,
> Have fewer paragraphs than lies;
> E'en Virgil's Fame, with all her tongues,
> And many ahundred pair of lungs,
> And who with ease, as Poet's say,
> Can forge ten-thousand lies a day,
> Has brok'n her brazen trump, and sighing;,
> To Tony yields the palm of lying!
>
> But quoth the reader, tell me why
> You thus would cannonade a fly!
> Would not a warrior simple be,
> At tilt and tourn'ment with a flea!
> We own our error, gentle reader,
> And stand rebuk'd for our procedure.
> Then, Tony, thou may'st creep along,
> Unnotic'd in our future song,
> From satire's arrows still exempt,

The next great man that I can think on,

Because thou art *beneath contempt!*

Tony, however, continuing to swell like the frog in the fable, we were under the disagreeable necessity of making a second attempt to hit him, and in our opinion, made a very good shot, in the following sketched of

THE ORIGIN AND FORMATION
Of the SOUL *of a noted little* DEMOCRAT.

Certain sages, learn'd and *twistical*,
By reasoning not one whit sophistical,
Have prov'd what's wonderful, to wit,
The smallest atom may be split,
Then split again, *ad infinitum*,
And diagrams, which much delight 'm,
By Mr. Martin, make it out,
Beyond the shadow of a doubt.

Matter thus splittable, I ween,
With half an eye it may be seen,
That *spirit*, being much diviner,
May be proportionably finer,
Nor is this merely *postulatum*,
'Tis prov'd by facts, and thus we state 'em.

Dame Nature, once, in mood of merriment,
Perform'd the following droll experiment,
She took a most diminish'd sprite,
Smaller than microsopic mite,
An hundred thousand such might lie,
Wedg'd in a cambric needle's eye;—
And then by dint of her divinity,
Divided it *one whole* Infinity,
Next cull'd the very smallest particle,
And shaped the Democratic article,
That little, d-l-sh, dirty dole,
Which serves for Tony Haswell's soul!

Is no less man than Lawyer L——n.
With whom compared, your Mansfields, Holts,
Are but a set of asses' colts.

Lord how my Muse and I should glory
To paint his matchless oratory,
For benefit of future times,
In *ævi-monumentum* rhymes.

But poets, critics, each a million.
And each a Homer or Quintillian,
With each apen can't set forth fully,
The merits ofour modern Tully.[26]

Not e'en the facund Mr. Bangs[27]
Can equal his sublime harangues.
When all his eloquence unmuzzling.

But, *mirabile dictu!* notwithstanding we thus impaled this insect on the point of the needle of Satire, the puny, cat-lived animalcule is still in existence, and *dashes* m the character of a leading Democrat in Vermont.

26   The idea expressed in this stanza, we have borrowed, with some little alteration, from *The Battle of the Kegs*.

> A hundred men, with each a pen,
> Or mure, upon my word, Sir,
> It is most true, would be too few,
> Their valor to record. Sir.

27   A notorious Counsellor at Law, who displayed much of the art of turning and twisting, in the Legislature, in the famous case of Young and Minns, alias the Common-wealth of Massachusetts, vs. Mr. Jefferson.

He untwists Jury cause so puzzling.

By help of statute, tome and code,
A pretty decent waggon load,
When Sugar Cause he had in hand, he
Had almost made it sugar candy.[28]

---

28 Perhaps some of our readers would prefer to have the story
of this famous cause told in prose, and as we are solicitous to
gratify the palates of all those who expect entertainment from
our Parnassian Restaurateur, we beg leave to present them,
together with the flummery of our poetry, a relish of roast beef
from the *Fredcrickstown Herald*, of September 29, 1804.

The editor of that excellent Newspaper, thus expresses him-
self of the personage whose case is now under consideriation:

In the National Intelligence of the 19th inst. the
following compliment is paid to Mr. Lincoln, by a
writer under the signature of Curtius. "The short
period during which he held his seal [in Congress]
had not admitted of a *development of his talents*,
but he entered the body with the reputation of em-
inent talents."—We should be glad to know with
what reputation he *left* it? The truth is, that he en-
tered the body with the reputation of being one of
the writers of a "Worcester paper called the *Ægis*,
and was supposed to be one of the authors of a series
of *essays*, (if a mass of slander, personal, vindictive
and unjust, deserves the name) called the "FARMER'S
LETTERS;" this was the only evidence which the pub-
lic had received of his talents, and with this reputa-
tion he entered the house, and with this reputation
only he left it. It is true, that a farther "*development
of his talents*" did not take place during his stay in
Congress; but it is not true that it was owing to "the
short period" to which it was confined. He remained
sufficiently long to have developed his talents on
the many important and interesting topics which

With Common and *un*-Common Law,

were each day the subject of discussion. Awed by the splendor which surrounded him, he dared not expose his prate to the keen animadversion of his contemporary opponents. Having just sense enough to practise the maxim of *"vir sapit qui pauca loquitur,"* he shielded himself in a stupid silence, and sat scowling at the eminence which he had not the power to resist. he therefore went out of Congress as he came in, with the reputation of being a weak spoke in the wheel of government.

Mr. Lincoln was now appointed Attorney General of the United States, and during the long period in which he has held, we will not say discharged, that office, he has permitted a farther *developement of his talents*, by making one speech and an half in the Supreme Court.

The first speech was a sufficient developement of his talents, to induce Administration to believe that in any future developement, it might be necessary for the interests of the country, that he should be assisted by other counsel, and therefore, in the celebrated case of the *Sugar Refiners*, Mr. Dallas was employed, at the expense of several hundred dollars, to render this assistance. The cause was tried at the capitol, in Washington, during he sitting of Congress, before chief Justice Marshal, and Judges Chase and Washington. The hall of the court was crouded with spectators, among whom were observed many foreigners of distinction, and members of Congress. The honourable Levi Lincoln arose—one hand was rested on a large pile of law books, which it would seem he intended to use, the other contained a roll of manuscript notes of the case, to which it would seem he intended to refer. He neither used the one nor referred to the other. He was on the floor about ten minutes, when having concluded his prefatory remarks, he said, "I will now inform this honourable Court, of the first point which I have taken in this

In which no man could pick a flaw,

case."—He paused, "I say, may it please your honours," (continued he, after a little hesitation) and paused again.—The Court listened with the utmost attention; the spectators who were at a little distance from the bar, anxious to witness the event which this illustrious instance of the *"montes parturiunt"* seemed to promise, closed up in a semicircle around the balustrade of the forum. "And I was saying, (said Mr. Lincoln) I have made a point."—He had so. He had reached one which he could not surmount. He told the Court that he begged their kind indulgence; that he felt Exceedingly embarrassed, and wished a few minutes for recollection. The Court bowed assent, and Mr. Lincoln sat down.

After a pause of fifteen minutes, during which there was the most solemn stillness, Mr. Lincoln rose again. He continued to speak about ten minutes more. His manner was wild, incoherent, and unargumentative, and seemed to be an unconnected, promiscuous, and irregular assemblage of words, without the smallest attention to an *ordo verborum*. "I have now come, (said he) may it please your honours, to the second point proposed—the second point which I have taken is this—I have got (said he) to the second point."—He, however, was never able to get any farther, and the Court remain yet to be informed what that second point was. Mr. Lincoln was obliged once more to apologize to the Court for being unable to proceed. He said, he felt an embarrassment which he could not conquer, and that Mr. Dallas would go on with the cause. A confused murmur was heard throughout the hall; it was the hum of vexation, disappointment, and keen remark. Some bf the auditory felt chagrined at this debasement of our national dignity; some felt disappointed and astonished that this exertion of forensic eloquence, should have terminated in such a mortifying *developement of the talents* of the Attorney General; and others laughed

He did so learnedly begin,
'Twas thought his head was Lincoln's Inn.

First he advanced with hems! and hahs!
May't please your honours, in this cause,
"With your good leave, I say, as how,
"My point the first, I'll open now:

"May't please the Court—I would say—hem,
"Fore Gad I'min a fine dilemm'!—
May't please the Court—your honours please,
My arguments are *simply* these:

"Let my opponents do their worst,
"Still my first point is—point the first—
"Which fully proves my case, because
"All statute laws are—statute laws!!!

"That is to say—the matter's here,
"Since I have made this point so clear,
"In favour of my cause and client,
"Then our side's right, you may rely on't.

"I think this argument is pat
"In point, it therefore follows—that—;
"Good Lord, I wish I were a mile hence!"

---

at tue impotency which they had predicted—whilst
the poor Mr. Lincoln sat down at the bar, and cov-
ered his face with his hands. It would be vain to deny
the truth of this statement; the hundreds who were
present can testify to its truth.

Quoth Lincoln—but quoth Sheriff—"silence!"

Our Lawyer having found, I trow,
That point the first would hardly go,
Now stopp'd to cogitate a little,
To hit point second to a tittle.

Point first delivered, as you see, his
Head was not *pregnant* with ideas.
Therefore to put things in a train,
lie sat down to *conceive* again.

For our great elocution's model.
Having discharged his loaded noddle.
Found that he must, let who would scoff,
E'en load again or not go off:

Now having charg'd, he rose and fir'd—
A word or two, which all admir'd.
Then for truce put in petition.
As he was out of amunition.

And after many a tug, he found
That point the second kept his ground,
With most provoking "oppugnation"
To our great Lawyer's grand oration.

But tho he suffered sad defeat,
Friend Dallas cover'd his retreat,
And, luckily, by his assistance,
The enemy was kept at distance.

But I by no means would pronounce ill,
Of our great man, as chamber counsel,
Although some say he did not shine
In Callender's remitted fine.[29]

Still his opinion's always good,
Provided this be understood,
That when you have it stated, nicely,
'Tis what it *should not be*, precisely.[30]

---

29 The following account of the leading features of the case to
which we here allude, is extracted from the *New York Evening
Post*; "On the 28th of May, 1800. James Thompson Callender,
was legally convicted of a misdemeanor, and sentenced to pay
a fine of two hundred dollars, to be imprisoned nine months,
and find security for his good behaviour for a certain term, be-
yond the expiration of his imprisonment." Shortly after Cal-
lender had paid the fine into the hands of the Marshal, and
after the term of his imprisonment had expired, a general par-
don of the misdemeanor, *remitting and releasing all penalties
incurred, or to be incurred, by reason thereof*, was granted,
and sent to the Marshal. Doubts were suggested, whether, hav-
ing once received the money from Callender, the officer could
legally pay it back to him. These doubts were communicated
to the acting Secretary of State; [to wit, the Hon. L. L. Esquire]
who, after a delay of nearly a month, replied, that the question
had been considered, and that "before a fine is paid into the
Treasury, a pardon remits and restores it to the party conclud-
ing with a direction to 'restore the money to Mr. Callender,'
which was accordingly done."

The arguments which are adduced in the able discussion
of the subject, a part of which we have here quoted proving
that when a fine is paid, it becomes property vested, and that
a charter of pardon does not imply restitution, are too long to
be here inserted.

30 I hare often thought Pope's sentiment, expressed in the follow-
ing lines, peculiarly applicable to the profession of law.

In fine, I think his honour's law-mill,
Should go by water, like a saw-mill,
For that his only chance, I trust, is
To *chance* to do his clients justice.

But surely never man shone brighter,
Than our said lawyer as a writer,
Not even Honestus can write better
Than I've seen many a "Farmer's" letter.[31]

A little learning is a dangerous thing.
Drink deep, or taste not the Pierian spring;
For shallow draughts intoxicate the brain
But drinking largely, sobers us again.

A man who has but a smattering of law knowledge, is sure to steer wide of justice and common sense, and attempt to make mischievous distinctions between law and right.

31   The acute, sagacious and subtle essays, which are supposed to have been written by our American Junius, with the title of *A Farmer's Letter to the People*, will ever remain a stupendous monunient of the astute, penetrating and profound genius of *Democracy's "Demosthenes"** Such ductility of fancy, such malleability and intertexture of simple nonsense, into complicated and unintelligible rhapsody, was never, perhaps, exceeded by the mad cap French revolutionary declaimers of liberty and equality. We did intend to have favoured our readers with our critical remarks on these wonderful productions, pointing out some of those passages which seem possessed of Colossean merit. But as we do not wish to inundate our readers with a flood of *verbiage*, whhout so much as a tinkling rill of *meaning*, we carinot do ourselves the high honour of making copious quotations. We will, however, mention two sentences from Letter No. X. the one a little involved, and the other not *quite true*.

IF there is no sense of decency remaining, none inculcated by public teachers; IF no beauties are seen in propriety or consistency of couduct; IF principles of enmity to public authority are disseminated and nurtured; IF the precepts of the wisest, and the experience of the greatest men of ancient and modern times, are held in contempt and rejected, because they are embraced by the officers of government; IF their unexamined, and untried measures should continue to be rudely, suddenly, prematurely and wickedly anathematised by vulgar rashness and sacerdotal prejudice, merely because they are theirs; vain will be our retrospect on past exertions, or revolutionary acquisitions; delusive our hopes of the future, and miserable the condition of the present and after generations.

"IF a body meet a body"—&c. or to rise to the "pinnacle of the foundation" of this subject,
IF a man be like a man, who

Sometimes to sense, sometimes to nonsense leaning,
Is always *blundering* round about his meaning.

pray who else is he like? The next paragraph which we shall select for our readers "negative instruction," is an absolute falsehood. Speaking of a Note addressed to the public by the Editors of the *Mercury*, proposing to enlarge its size, and entitle it the *New-England Palladium*, our author says, that "for less, infinitely less, was Lyon convicted, Callender and Cooper punished." To those who have read the note and the libels to which it was compared, any comments on this round assertion, would be perfectly frivolous.

* The merit of this figure, we confess, consists entirely in its application, for we borrowed it from one of the Farmer's Letters (we forget which) wherein the prophet Habakkuk is styled "Prophecy's Demosthenes."

'Tis true, he has not much pretence
To grammar, reason, common sense;
What then? his language is sonorous,
And,"We the People," forms the chorus.

What though he flirts about and flounces,
From falsehood into nonsense bounces,
He works for our good like a dray horse,
Or satan journeying through Chaos.

Sure such an Ovid in a Murray,
Wont be forgotten in a hurry,[32]
Whose every word contains an adage,
Meant to reform a bold and bad age.

We next will stretch on satire's rack,
A callous wretch in faded black,
A nuisance in our "happy land,"
A sort of junior Talleyrand.

Democracy has not a rogue.
Amongst her dashers now in vogue,
A single Jacobin, or scarce one
More mischievous than this said Parson.

---

32   How sweet an Ovid in a Murray lost,

said the Poet; but had he been so fortunate as to have heard
the Sugar Cause argued, and have perused the *Farmer's Let-
ters*, he would have ejaculated something very like the above
happy couplet, on perceiving the fine-writer, and profound
lawyer, happily blended in the person of the Attorney General.

'Twere well had he been hung, before he Began to print th' Observatory,[33]

---

33   The following sketch, from the *Boston Gazette* of July, 1804, is somewhat declarative of the demerits of this renegado Parson:

> The *Walpole Observatory* is understood to be edited by a broken Parson, who, we are told, was drummed out of a parish in Connecticut. There is no want of candor in remarking, and we leave it to others, to apply the remark, if they think it applicable, that there is no worse man in society than he who is a renegade from his own profession. When a black coat is too tight for a man's linabs he seldom gets any decent one that will fit them. When the virulence of a man's politics or temper, or the high bribes that a party offers for his profligacy, have induced a person to strip off the clergyman, he is generally found to be more deeply corrupt than if he had never endured the restraints of a good character. Tired of being a hypocrite, he spits, like Matthew Lyon, in the "world's face, and says, Shame, I defy you—Faclion pay me and I will lie for you.
>
> In the most Federal part of Newhampshire, there was, and still is, a verv respectable and useful Newspaper,. called the *Farmer's Museum*. The old revolutionary patriot, so well known, Isaiah Thomas, whom Mr. Jefferson has dismissed for his good services from the Post office, is the principal proprietor. To attack Federalism in its strong holds, and to carry the party war into the enemy's country, like Scipio when he invaded Africa, this Parson, who had never seen a Printer's type, was sent every one will believe, *by the Administration*, to print an Opposition Paper, at Walpole, where it was not wanted for information, as there was an excellent paper printed there before. There must be something found to encourage this poor Parson to set up a press, where it is manifest there was so little room for his busi-

Which would have sav'd an inundation

ness. What could be done for him belter than resort
to the Administration for a good fat offering, that
this Priest of Jacobinism might live upon it, till he
could revolutionize the slate of New-Hampshire,
and bring in Mr. Langdon to be governor. For that
end no doubt he was sent, and to cover up from the
eyes of the people the intermeddling of our rulers in
the politics of the state, this new comer was appoint-
ed Printer of the Laws of the United states. But the
office, it is understood, was erected for the man, and
for the occasion; for the Laws were printed before in
Portsmouth, and one printer to a State is as much
as has been heretofore deemed necessary, especially
when wc consider that New-Hampshire is a small
state.

A needy tool for our great men wvas, however,
wanted, and must be providsd for, and in such a way
as to hide or seem to hide the business—for in truth,
saving appearances was all that was regarded.

Now we beg to know, how much is allowed to
the *Observatory* for printing the Laws of the Unit-
ed States! Enough, we believe, to support a Jacobin
press. If we are right in this conjecture, then the
people's money is taken by the friends of reform and
economy, and squandered on a worthless tool of of-
fice, a profligate minion, in reward for deceiving and
inflaming the people of New Hampshire. We hope
the accounts of the Department of State for pub-
lishing the Laws, will be scrutinized, and though the
Federal members cannot hinder the work of corrup-
tion, they may be able publicly to expose it. Instead
of the press being free to combat error, as a great
man chooses to say we make no doubt the Jacobin
press is supported by the people's money, to deceive
them. It is a servile, base, wicked tool of a Jacobin
faction. It is a bell that never ceased ringing for fire,
when there was none; and now the Brissotiness and
Robespierrists are in power, and have set the coun-

Of lies, which overspread the nation.

try and constitution in a blaze, at the four corners, the bell is muffled.

No sooner did this man come into New-Hampshire, than he began to know more than any body else about the affairs of the state; and very busily spread jealousies and suspicions about the honesty and correctness of the State Treasurer's accounts. In this he followed the example of the *Committee of Caluntnies* in Congress, who reported against WOLCOT, PICKERING and MC. HENRY, a number of charges, that even a Democratic majority in congress did not dare to support. In like mnnner there was a Democratic majority in the New Hampshire legislature; but they, more candid than the Nicholson and Randolphs, did examine the charges and found them *false*.

The same *Observatory* man has stated in his paper, that the votes for Governor Gilman were a minority. In this he has been solidly confuted; still, however, a lie well stood to, he thinks, as good as the truth, and he stands to it. He stands to it, that Mr. Jefferson is *chaste*—no poacher in Mr. Walker's family—is a brave man never hid from Tarlton—is a good christian—as good as Condorcet or Pain—and breaks out into the most outrageous exclamations against the Federal slanderers, who can dare to publish that such a Joseph for virtue, such a Joseph Surface for talking about it—such a Solomon in council—such a Sampson in combat—who so abhors to council shed blood, and so delights to shed ink—such an Old Testament saint, as his Notes on Virginia attest, can be nothing less than an American Bonaparte, a Dieu donnè—heaven sent to be our Consul for life, and our Emperor by inheritance—with renjainder over to Mr. Eppes and his issue.

A good salary for printing the laws, requires, that tough stories by Col. Walker, or Callender, or any body else, should be resolutely *brow beaten*. A thou-

For this same Jacobin high flyer,
Is such a Satan of a liar,
He lies through habit, strange to tell,[34]

---

sand dollars a year will greatly assist a man to stand strong in his faith. This reverend Vicar of Bray will not believe, nor allow the people of New-Hampshire to believe a word to the prejudice of his patron, as long as he holds his office.

The post riders make their contracts with the Post Master General, and it is easy to see that Jacobin zealots wilt be preferred. See then how completely the press is 'made subject to the new administration; how the *Obseratory* can be almost forced upon readers, and how the *Museum* can be obstructed. The French is not more subject to his Imperial Majesty, the Citizen Consul, than the Jacobin press to Mr. Jefferson.

We are told that for weeks before election in this state, the Federal papers did not circulate in some parts of the district of Maine. Every one can conjecture why it happened, though no one can precisely unravel the circumstances, and tell how.

Is it the opinion of the Administration, that the people of New-Hampshire are more easily deluded than those of Connecticut? This *Observatory* man was known in Connecticut, and there he had no influence. Was it necessary to send him away from home, to enable him to do misclnef; or is New-Hampshire thought to be stupid enough to give success to a baffled and disgraced Connecticut. Jacobin? For our parts, we believe better things of the Citizens of New-Hampshire; and as the attempt to influence them is bareface, and truely insulting to their independence, they will, we trust, evince at the next election, that they are as Federal as Connecticut.

34 This stupid fib-teller hammered out half a dozen falsehoods about a single toast, drank on the 4th of July, 1804. What made the thing the more ridiculous, and would have silenced

Even when the truth would do as well:

His every paragraph's invented
To make the people discontented,
To raise the restless mob, and shove 'em.
To pull down all that seems above 'em.

And he has been at work to plaster
His grand illuminated master,[35]
But time would fail to set forth how well
He daubs it on, as with a trowel.

At length the rogue has drawn a prize,
An *office*, earn'd by peddling lies,[36]
But this said office is at most,
An *exile* to a western post.

We have the honor next to pin
On Satire's Gibbet, Gallatin,
(Our Gibbet not his only one,

---

him for ever, had he not been a Democrat, and ergo, a friend to
the people, was, the circumstance of there being a number of
respectable persons in the neighbourhood, sho were witnesses
to his falsehoods on that occasion.

35 This man, with matchless effrontery, has repeatedly affirmed
in his lying vehicle, in substance, that a purer and more spot-
less character than that of Mr. Jefferson never was enjoyed by
any mere man; aad even goes so far in his blasphemous im-
pudence, as to compare this man, with "*twenty* Gods, or NO
God," with our Saviour!!!

36 Mr. G. is appointed Secretary to his Excellency Gen. Hull, who
is also appointed Governor of Michigan.

If Justice always had been done.)[37]

37   That Mr. Gallatin was active in the Pittsburgh insurrection, will not, we presume, be disputed by Democrats, if we present them with vouchers, extracted from a Newspaper under the direction of their own party.

In Bache's paper of Sept. 1, 1792, appeared the following account of the proceedings of the insurgents, at the commencement of an insurrection, which cost the United States above a million of dollars.

At ameeting of sundry inhabitants of the Western Counties of Pennsylvania, at Pittsburgh, on the 21st day of August, 1792:

Col. *Jolrn Gannon* was placed in the chair.

ALBERT GALLATIN, appointed Clerk.

The Excise Law of Congress being taken into consideration, a committee was appointed to prepare a draught of resolutions, expressing the sense of the meeting on the subject of said law.

Adjourned to 10 o'clock to-morrow.

The committee appointed yesterday, made repost, which being *twice* read, was unanimously adopted:

"And whereas some men *be* found amongst us so far lost to every sense of virtue and feeling for the distresses of this country as to accept offices for the collection of the duty;

"*Resolved therefore.* That in future vre will consider such persons as unworthy of our friendship: *Have no intercourse or dealings with them*, WITHDRAW FROM THEM EVERY ASSISTANCE, *and* WITHHOLD ALL THE COMFORTS OF LIFE, which depend upon those duties, that as men and fellow-citizens, we owe to eack other, and upon all occasions treat them with that contempt they deserve, and that it be, and it is humbly, and most earnestly reconimended to the people at large, to follow the same kind of conduct towards them."

(Signed)   JOHN CANNON, *Chairman.*

ALBERT GALLATIN, *Clerk.*

Mr. GALLATIN, afterwards, perceiving the insurrection would fail, sought and obtained pardon of General Washington. But that he retained his political rancour, is evident from the dismission of General Miller from the office of Supervi-

For that th' imported Financier,
Deserves such destiny, is clear
Nor shall the rogue, by any fetch.
Escape us, as he did Jack Ketch.

But no! our moderate Feds say "tut!
"The man deserves some notice—but
"The *truth*, though quoted from the Bible,
"Against such great men, *is a libel.*"[38]

You, Gentlemen, may think, perhaps,
That you are mighty *prudent* chaps,
But know, good Sirs, as these times are,
The heighth of *prudence*, is—*to dare.*

Go, timid Lilliputian souls,
Whom such a vile old saw controuls,
Go, hide your carcases in caves,
Or sit ye down, contented slaves.

But I'll make, with your worship's leave,

---

sor, immediately after Mr. Gallatin's coming to the Treasury,
whose offence consisted in his having commanded a body of
troops who were actite in quelling Mr. Gallatia's insurrection.

38   We find many of our moderate Federalists somewhat squeam-
ish in this particular. They urge, that the exposition of the
crimes of great men chosen into office by the people, is a
disgrace to our national character. But there so very candid
gentlemen should inform us, whether our national character
would not be more disgraced by suffering such characters and
such conduct as enter into the composition of our men and
measures to pass without animadversion?

Slap at this great man from Geneva,
Who wormed his way to elevation,
And holds the purse-strings of the nation!

'Tis true, this gaunt Genevan, whilome,
Found this our land, a rogue's "asylum,"
Since which, in public matters, his chief
Delight has been in making mischief.

Was soon an imp of insurrection,
A very Jack Cade to perfection,
And seized the horns of Mercy's altar,
To save his gullet from a halter!

In faction's cause alert and brisk, he
Was once a champion in the whiskey
Rebellion . . . . therefore was among
The rogues whom Justice might have hung.

And had her Ladyship foreseen
His future management, I ween,
In her strong noose she'd made his neck fast,
As cheerfully as eat'n her breakfast.

By Washington, this rebel, pardon'd,
In wickedness grew still more hardened,
His industry and cunning bent
To overturn the government.

To Congress sent, in evil hour,
To head the party now in power;

When mischief was a-foot, 'twas certain
This arch rogue was behind the curtain.

And oft he would the Feds surprise,
By artful, well, digested lies,
Wire-drawn, thro' many along harangue,
With all the art of all the gang.

But, whereas, in these happy times,
A wretch is qualified by crimes
And scoundrel cunning for high station,
HE HOLDS THE PURSE-STRINGS OF THE NATION!!!

Well, if no sages of our own
Can give our Government a tone,
Let us submissively receive a
Set, fresh from Ireland, France, Geneva.

Let us in Congress hear with patience,
The worthless scum of foreign nations,
Threaten in vile outlandish squeal,
To stop of Government "*de veel!*"

Though many a foolish Demo, fancies,
This man's the soul of our finances;
That we have not a single native
Can rival this imported caitiff.

Pray, tell me, what the wight has done
But simply copy Hamilton;
Such plodding imitative work

Might be performed by any Clerk.

Thus a poor wretch, with scarcely brains
Enough to walk in when it rains,
May whirl an organ handle round,
And make it all so sweetly sound.

But should the lubber of a Vandal
Pretend he had the skill of Handel,
The very mob would find him out,
And hoot him for a lying lout.[39]

But let us grant, in mere civility,
That Gallatin has vast ability,
And in finance, yields not a whit,
To Sully, Hamilton, or Pitt,

'Tis neither politic nor just,
A foreign runaway to trust,
A treacherous and intriguing pest
As keeper of the public chest.

Indeed I'll bet you ten to one, he,
(His fortune made with Yankies' money)
Without a drawback, will *reship*,
And give his silly gulls the slip.

---

39 The idea pourtrayed in this simile we borrowed from the *Bal-ance*, an excellent federal paper, printed at Hudson, (see an editorial article of Jan. 1st, 1805) Mr. Croswell will be good enough to help himself to an equivalent from any of our best rhetorical flourishes, and accept four acknowledgments into the bargain.

Then, should we sink in Anarch's sea,
AVould this Genevan care? Not he,
Provided he can save himself,
Together with his ill got pelf.

Step forward. Demagogue Duane,
Than whom, a viler rogue in grain
Ne'er, fortified by mob alliance,
Durst bid the powers which be, defiance.[40]

Law, Order, Talents, and Civility,
To thy right worshipful *mobility*
Must bow, whilst thou, their knowing man,
Lead'st by the nose, thy kindred clan.[41]

Thou art, indeed, a rogue as sly,
As ever coin'd the ready lie,[42]

---

40   This vile renegado, by virtue of his influence with the mob, is one of the most powerful personages in the United States. He is said to have remarked, that Mr. J——a dare as well be d—d as affront him.

41   The efforts of Duane, and of his designing and wrong-headed scribblers who labour for the *Aurora*, are ever directed to the purpose of destroying all kinds of distinction in society, except merely such as a cunning man may establish as leader of a mob. The learned professions are the constant objects of his abuse, and that of the advocates for levelling systems who dash in the *Aurora*. Should his plans succeed, brutal strength, and savage cunnings will be the only foundation for eminence. Indeed he has laid the axe at the root of civilization, and unless graat exertions are made to counteract the influence of that vile vehicle of poison, which he publishes, its deleterious effects will, for ages, be felt in America.

42   The man who cannot otherwise be convinced of the turpitude

And, on emergence, art not loth
Thy lies to sanction with an oath.[43]
Few good or great men can be nam'd

---

of this and certain other artful Pseudo-Patriots, is request-
ed to peruse certain statements made by a Mr. John Wood,
a foreigner, printed at New-York, 1802, relative to a history
which he had undertaken to write of the *Administration of
John Adams.* This history was compiled, as the author states,
from materials collected from the *Aurora*, Duane's private
letters, and Callender's works, and was suppressed by the in-
fluence of Col. Burr.

Mr. Wood's statement bears many marks of veracity and
candor, and if we maybelieve him, the Jacobins who furnished
hini with materials for his history, are the most deceitful of
mortals.

> Mr. Duane, (he says) sent me occasionally, in-
> formation as to characters and events, sometimes
> couched in the form of history, leaving it to my dis-
> cretion, whether to alter the language or not. Not-
> withstanding the active part which Mr. Duane had
> in the compilation of this history, he is pleased to
> assert in the Aurora of the 12th of July, (1802) that
> it *contains neither veracity nor dignity.* Such an
> observation would certainly have proceeded with
> more propriety from any critic than Mr. Duane, *for
> the facts furnished by him*, are well known to be the
> most false and libellous in the whole book.

p. 7.

Again, "All the circumstances furnished by Mr. Duane, in
his letters to me, proved afterwards to be the grossest false-
hoods, most probably fabricated by himself." p. 26.

43 By turning to the *Freeman's Journal*, of July, 1805, published
by Duane's former patrons and admirers, we shall perceive,
among other proofs of the want of principle of this flagitious
wretch, that he made oath to a falsehood about his having been
a long time a citizen of the United States.

Thy scoundrelship has not defamed,
And scarce a rogue, who ought to hang,
But may be numbered in thy gang.

With impudence the most consummate,
You publish all that you can come at,
To make, for discord's sake, a handle
Of private anecdote and scandal.[44]

Your rogue-ship's object seems to be
On "Liberty's tempestuous sea,"
To set our Commonwealth afloat,
Sans rudder, in an open boat.

'Twould ask some folios to unfold
The various lies which thou hast told,
Published with matchless impudence,
In face of thine own documents.[45]

---

44 In the pamphlet of Wood, above quoted, we find the following
    remark:

> A man, (to wit, Duane) who has partly the means
> of ransacking, in a clandestine manner the books of
> a public office, who did not hesitate to publish to the
> world the contents of letters, evidently intended for
> the post-office—who glories in being the discloser of
> secrets and the unfolder of private caucusses, ought
> to veil himself from society.

    p 82.
       Here we have Jacobin against Jacobin, and it is to be hoped
    that those who reject Federal testimony, will not refuse cre-
    dence to their own party.

45 This wretch continued to publish slanderous lies about the

Among the Catalines of faction,
None call more energies in action,
And, if not check'd in thy career,
Thou'lt make a second Roberspierre.[46]

And thou, audacious renegadoe,
With many a libellous bravadoe,
Assail'dst Columbia's Godlike son,

---

alledged defalcations of Mr. Pickering, while Secretary of the
Treasury, long after a committee, composed of Gallatin and
others, had acquitted Mr.Pickering of any malconduct in his
office. After as minute an investigation as could be made by
the eagle eye of party, these democrats themselves testified to
his innocence (see Vol. I, Note 53, page 135) still this factious
cur kept yelping against Mr. Pickering with as much virulence
as ever!!

46   In the *Aurora*, of March 21st, 1805, are the following expres-
sions, which shew what are the views of this would be tyrant:—

> ——They will petition loudly for a reprieve—they
> Mill stir up every interest in their power to procure
> their pardon—they will writhe, and twist, and turn—
> they know THEY ARE ON THE ROAD TO THE SCAFFOLD,
> AND MUST MEET THEIR FATE; but *that* FATE they will
> endeavour to procrastinate by their intreaties.—Re-
> publicans, be not novel by their intreaties.

> They look'd at the tree, they travers'd the cart,
> They handled the rope, but seem'd loth to depart.

These expressions; say the editors of the *Freeman's Jour-
nal*, are "diabolical." They most truly are so, but they present
nothing *new* to the Federalists. The Federalists knew from the
beginning, where Duane and the faction of which these gentry
composed a part would lead us. But Duane, M'Kean and co.
were then all Democrats, all Republicans.

The great, th' immortal WASHINGTON![47]

47 We shall trouble our readers with an extract from one of these libels. Although it has frequently appeared in fugitive publications, by way of testimony against the daring demagogue, by whom it was first penned, it ought to be again and again presented to those who pretend that the supporters of the present administration were the friends of Washington.

In the *Aurora* of March 6th, 1797, this favorite of Mr. Jefferson thus expresses himself:—

"Lord, now lettest thou thy servant depart in peace, for mine eyes have seen thy salvation," was the pious ejaculation of a man, who beheld a flood of happiness rushing in upon mankind—if ever there was a time, which would licence the reiteration of the exclamation, that time is now arrived; for the man, who is the source of all the misfortunes of our country, is this day reduced to a level with his fellow-citizens, aud is no longer possessed of power to multiply evils upon the United States. If ever there was a period for rejoicing, this is the moment—every heart in unison with the freedom and happiness of the people, ought to beat with high exultation that the *name* of WASHINGTON from this day, ceases to give a currency to political iniquity, and to legalize corruption—a new aera is now opening upon us, a new aera, which promises much to the people; for public measures must now stand upon their own merits, and nefarious projects can no longer be supported by a *name*.—When a retrospect is taken of the Washington administration for eight years past, it is a subject of the greatest astonishment that a single individual should have cancelled the principles of Republicanism in an enlightened people, just emerged from the gulf of despotism, and should have carried his designs against the public liberty so far, as to have put in jeopardy its very existence:— such, however, are the facts, and with these staring

Through patriotism's specious mask, all
Your own gang could discern the rascal,
But *tertium quids*, quoth spitting Matt,
Esteemed you none the less for that.[48]

Thus the Arch Fiend, the prince of lies,
Assumes, at will, an Angel's guise,
But with a Seraph's borrowed mien
The cloven-foot is always seen.

Though hunted through so many cHmes,
A very prodigy of crimes,
Your friends, the *quids*, still love youdearly.
And *spitting* Matt is yours sincerely.[49]

Dost thou remember much about a
Droll scrape of thine once, at Calcutta,
What time, invited to a breakfast,
In noose thou nigh hadst got thy neck fast.[50]

---

us in the face, this day ought to be a JUBILEE in the *United States*.

48 At least were willing to encourage him, and "give him money, all they could afford." See vol. ii. note 56. page 108.

49 See the conclusion of Matt. Lyon's letter to Duane, his "old friend," &c.

50 Duane is said to have set up the trade of a Patriot at Calcutta, and commenced his useful labours as Editor to a Newspaper, by exerting himself to foment aquarrel between the civil and military departments. Sir JOHN SHORE,* the English commander, paid so little regard to the *rights of man*, that he merely rewarded him with a fend of wooden-horsical promotion, which is not thought to confer very great honour on those who are the subjects of that kind of elevation. He then sent him

Sir John, however, on the whole,
Was wrong to set thee *on* a pole,
For such a patriot onght to ride
Suspended from the *under* side.

We next beg liberty to handle,
Another vile, imported Vandal,
A *Hatter*, who, by *intuition*,
Is a most *wond'rous* politician![51]

But highly merits being hung
For *murdering*—the English tongue,[52]

---

to England, from whence he was *imported*, to teach Americans liberty and equality, under the auspices of Emperor Jefferson. Duane says, that he was kidnapped by Sir John, having been invited to breakfast. But the man is so given to lying, that we wish our readers to place no dependence on that part of the story.

* This Gentleman, if I mistake not, is now Lord Teignmouth, and author of *Memoirs of the Life, Writings and Correspondence of Sir William Jones.*

51   We mean no reflection upon mechanics. But a man to be an editor of a newspaper, in a large city like New York, of a paper too, which boasts the patronage of government, ought, together with natural powers, to have possesed the means of information, and to have superadded culture to native luxuriance of genius. Even a "needy knife grinder," must serve some *apprenticeship* before he can *set up* for himself. But in our land of Liberty *ignorance may* be so qualified by *impudence* and *scurrility* as to entitle its happy possessors to the patronage of our first characters in the capacity of Newspaper editors, and thus to occupy the *most important* and *least responsible situations* in our government.

52   Had we nothing of more importance to command our attention,

Though that's among the smallest sins
Committed by our Jacobins.

To *honesty* he's no more claim
Than *Satan* to a *Christian* name;
Is no more bound in honour s fetters,
Than if he *stole* and *open'd letters.*[53]

Sometimes quite demon-like he swaggers,

---

we might point out hundreds of instances, in which this Mr.
"DAGGERMAN," has absolutely *assassinated* the English Lan-
guage. Sometimes Mr. Jefferson's *dress* is "TERSE," sometimes
he is not "*im*popular," sometimes we are told "Mr. Denniston,
another gentleman and me called on him at his house."—But
really we wish to get the creature oif our hands as quick as pos-
sible, and shall not therefore enlarge upon these minor faults.

53 *Somebody* once stole two letters, w'ritten at the City of Wash-
ington, one on the 6th and the other on the 7lh of December,
1801, by Richard Peters, Jun. Esq. both scaled and directed to
E. Bronson, Esq. editor of the *United States Gazette.* These
letters were on political topics, and were afterwards published
in the *Aurora.*

Mr. Bronson states a number of circumstances which seemed
to implicate one JAMES CHEETHAM, an Englishman, a hatter by
trade, and editor of a paper called *The American Citizen.*

The editor of the *New-York Evening Post,* after attending
to the evidence which appeared against this man, declares that
"he either stole the letters himself, or that he received them
from another, knowing them to be stolen. In the eye of the law
both are equally guilty." He afterwards invites this immacu-
late patriot to either sit down "infamous and contented," with
the reputation of being a THIEF or to appeal to the laws of the
land for redress. Patriot Jim. was best pleased with the former
alternative.

And threatens *sleeping men*—WITH DAGGERS![54]
The very next breath, to be sure,
No man has principles so pure.

And this is renegadoe Jim,
A patriot of the Godwin trim,
A useful tool in party strife,
A wicked, faction's butcher knife.

This man, the tale might well surprise one,
Deals but a daily dose of poison,
Most deleterious, and designed
To operate on the public mind.

The drivel of his dirty brains,
(And Demo's pay him for his pains)
Spins from his jobbernowl, and then
Displays it in the "Citizen."

For that is what he calls the paper,
Where he and faction huff and vapour,
But 'tis a s*ink of defamation*,
A *slaughter-house of reputation*.

---

54   This true imported, "*genuine republican*," in an unguarded mo-
ment fairly threw off the mask, and told the world what kind of
treatment his political opponents may expect, if he and his gang
should ever obtain their meditated ascendency. He declared in
the Citizen that the anti-revolutionists deserved to be assassi-
nated "in the unsuspecting moments of sleep." Can it be possi-
ble that such a ruffian is sutfered not only to go at large, but that
he and other incendiaries, of similar views, are patronized by
some of our most prominent political characters.

If it should suit his matter's "gestion,"
We'll put Sir Daggerman a question
Or two, that he may shew how fair
A character, some folks should bear.

Pray Jim. didst ever know a man
Who join'd a certain wicked clan,
That in their revels, every night,
Against the bible, aim'd their spite?

And as that fellow, it appears,
Still keeps *possession* of his ears,
Pray Sir, did *Justice* merely loan 'em
Or does he absolutely *own them!*

And, prithee give me leave to ask it,
Was't in a dirty, old clothes' basket,
Come! come! no quibbling, what a' ye 'fraid of)
Like Sir John Falstaff, that he made off?

Some say 'twas in a hatter's chest,
But I'm assur'd that *you know best*,
If that's the case, man, no denial,
Let's have the *whole truth* on this trial.

Did my informant tell me fibs,
Of Constables, and broken ribs?
A man knock'd down, who strove to quiet
A certain scoundrel in the riot.

Supposing half these things were true

Of some "imported rogue," like you,
Should not the vilest partizan
Be quite ashamed of such a man?

And can it be, this side the Atlantic
A faction now exists, so frantic,
They hire a wretch to print their papers,
Who is notorious for such capers?

Go, get your bread some honest way,
You can make decent hats, they say,
Go, and thank God you yet abide
Your former domicile's *outside*,[55]

Pray, reader, how dost like this show,
Of three *exotics* in a row,
Duane, and Gallatin, and Cheetham,
Dost think a score of fiends could beat 'em?

O! what a dirty, dirty faction!
What dirty tools they keep in action!
Worse than the rogues they offer daily
At shrine of Justice at Old Baily!

Let each Columbian hide his face,
And blush to own his native place,
If such a vile imported band

---

55 Patriot Jim was furnished with lodgings at the expence of
the Government of Great Britain, as a token of rtrgard for his
prowess exhibited in the nocturnal adventure, which termi-
nated in the demolition of the unfortunate Constable's ribs.

Must govern our *degraded* land.

But now the Muse of Satire bids
Us glance at certain *Tertium Quids*,
Who've run their skiff almost aground,
But lately tack'd for coming round.

Pray, how goes on your caterwaulling
With certain gemman of your calling,[56]
With whomy'embark'd in wondrous glee,
On "Liberty's tempestuous sea"?

Indeed, good Messrs. *Quids*, I think,
Unless you ply your pumps, you'll sink,
And, though I'm very loth to say't,
You almost merit such a fate.

But may you only *almost* drown,
Or, if you're *hung*, be soon cut down,
And never feel afflictions' rod
With greater force than Doctor Dodd.[57]

'Twas you, who first afforded aid

---

56 The Third Party gentry of Pennsylvania, a spawn from the same litter with the New-York Burrites, have made violent news-paper attacks on must of their quondam friends and associates, with whom they were formerly united in sapping the foundations of the Federal Government.

57 It has been said that this divine whose guilt, contrition and punishment have excited so much attention, after having suffered the penalty inflicted in England for the crime of forgery, was resuscitated, and lived in privacy a number of years.

To Duane in his lying trade,
But now he strives to take you all in,
You thwart him in his civil calling!

Had principle enough to hire,
Him, for an *ex officio* liar,
Knowing, for so old Matthew tells,
The man was good for nothing else.

Now, since you are the *sine qua non*
Of all the evils you complain on,
It would be Justice to a tittle,
To let such patriots swing—a little,

But as you have some claims to merit,
Have fought the Demagogue with spirit,
For that, and sure no other reason,
I'd cut your honours down in season.

Adversity's the best of schools,
For teaching vain men, Wisdom's rules,
And when you've suffered most severely,
You'll see your former folly clearly.

Thus Neb'chadnezzar was an ass
Until they turn'd him out to grass,
And Trumbull's Mack, in air suspended,
Found that his intellect was mended.[58]

---

58   Found that his intellect was mended,

     As Socrates of old at first did

Dear Democrats, now tell me, pray do,
How many a Tory renegadoe,[59]
You've rais'd, by crooked politics,
Above the Whigs of seventy-six.

Yet, inconsistent, lying prigs,
You call yourselves exclusive Whigs,
And oft, with other vicious stories,
Proclaim the Federalists old Tories!

First comes, the should-be hung, Tench Coxe,
A Jeffersonian orthodox,
Who gained immensity of glory
In the capacity of Tory.
Although, my fine sir, it was thy lot
To be the British army's pilot,

To aid Philosophy get hoisted,
And found his thoughts flow strangely clear,
Swung in a basket in mid ail:
Our culprit thus in purer sky,
With like advantage rais'd his eye;
And looking forth in prospect wide
His Tory errors clearly spied.

M. Fingal, Canto iii;

59 Among the numerous instances of the unblushing effrontery
of the dominant party, may be included their charging the
Federalists with having been enemies to their country during
the revolutionary war. This conduct evinces that hardihood in
guilt, which distinguishes the veteran offender from the mere
Tyro in iniquity. It is an attempt to fasten the dead weight of
Jacobin enormity about the neck of the Federalists, and to sink
the followers of Washington in the tempestuous sea of Jeffer-
sonian liberty. See note 52, page 117.

And lead Howe's myrmidons of thunder,
Your Countrymen to rob and plunder;

Since Jefferson began his reign,
The Democratic smoothing-plane,
In spite of all your Tory tricks, sir,
Has chang'd you to a *seventy-sixer*.[60]

Although fortreason erst attainted,[61]
Thou'rt now politically sainted;
Become a very proper man,
For Emperor Jeff' a partizan.

Good Democrats reward you now
For services you rendered Howe,
And feast you with the daintiest dishes
Of Governmental loaves and fishes.

Three thousand dollars, every year;
Three thousand precious dollars clear!
The rogues from labour's hard hand wrench,
To fill the purse of Tory Tench!

Next on our list is tory Danie!,[62]

---

60 Seventy-sixer, a cant word adopted by some of our mushroom
    patriots, to designate the men who first asserted American In-
    dependence in the year 1776.

61 This tory of the first water, who is moreover a most charm-
    ing Democrat, was attainted of treason, by the Legislature of
    Pennsylvania.

62 This man was appointed Navy Agent in the place of Mr James
    Watson. The latter was an officer in the Connecticut line, in the

And though I would not treat the man ill,
In name of Justice, common sense.
To office, what is his pretence?

How dare the fellow have the face
Toe rowd himself in Watson's place.
To batten thus on merit's spoils,^
And reap the fruit of glory's toils?

O! he's a thrifty sort of save-ally
Has woad'rous skill in matters naval.
Writes letters too, which would not sully
The reputation of old Tully.[63]

---

revolutionary war.

63 We shall trouble our readers with but a brief specimen of this
    gentleman's elegant epistolary stile.

    In an official letter to "Gen, Samuel Smith, Esq." dated
    New-York, May 13, 1801, occurs the following highly polished
    paragraph.

    > I had the honour of writing to you yesterday, to
    > which beg your reference. The hasty *result* of my ob-
    > servations respecting a navy yard are as follows. The
    > *situation combined* has, undoubtedly, advantages
    > for the purposes intended—one disadvantage most
    > striking to me is the exposure to an enemy landing
    > in the rear, the dangers of which 25 not so great on
    > reflection, and more in sound than in reality.

    The "result are" that, in the appointment of such an *ignora-
    mus*, in the "*situation combined*" there is "*one disadvantage*"
    which although "most striking" "the *dangers is* very great on
    reflection"!!

And there's a Mister Consul Erving,[64]
Who is so wondrous well deserving,
That sure his present elevation
Reflects high honour on the nation.

He kindled to our great man's glory,
That brill'ant blaze of oratory,
Which gave him nineteen times the odds
Of Homer's stoutest heathen Gods.[65]

And dealt in thunder and in lightening,
And cut a dash so very fright'ning,
And did the horrible such credit,
That our teeth chattered when we read it!

He is, indeed, a pretty chip
From Tory block, a kindred slip
Acion from a certain famous
Old Tory Counsellor Mandamus.[66]

A Mister Mansfield takes the place
Of General Putnam, in disgrace,
A warrior whig, O what a scandal!

---

64 This Gentleman has tasted of Mr. Jefferson's bounty in an appointment to a Consulship in London.

65 We have before had the honour to allude to a sublime specimen of this young man's eloquence in vol. 2; note I, p. 3.

66 The father of this sprig of Democracy was one of Governor Hutchinson's Mandamus Counsellors.

Supplanted by a tory Vandal.[67]

And one old Edgar stands confest[68]
A Democrat among the best;
What fits him nicely for such rank, he's
Accessory to scalping Yankies.

This fine old fellow found the Savages
With implements for making ravages.
Guns, Tomahawks, and Scalping Knives,

---

67 The cloven-foot of the vile faction was never more completely
displayed than in this infamous transaction.

Gen. Rufus Putnam served under Washington during the
revolutionary war. He had grown poor in his country's service,
and was obliged, in the decline of life, to migrate into the wilds
bordering on the Ohio, and endeavour to provide for a rising
family, by submitting ta the hardships of a first settler in a
dreary wilderness. Gen. Washington, in order to smooth the
path of his life's declivity, appointed him Surveyor General,
with a handsome salary.

He was, however, marked as a victim to the relentless ty-
rants now in power, and the war-worn veteran was displaced
to make room for Jared Mansfield, a *worthless old Tory*, but
a *good Democrat*. Yes, this same Mansfield was not only a no-
torious British partizan, but was active in the destruction of
some books, in New-Haven College Library, which were sup-
posed to be favourable to liberty.

Thus does Mr. Jefferson fulfil his promise of "injuring the
best men least," and placing the hand of power on "anti-revo-
lutionary adherence to our enemies."

68 This gentleman, tory, democrat, and tomahawk vender, has
been repeatedly honored with the confidence of the New-York
genuine republicans, &c. He has been chosen to represent that
party in the legislature; is one of the directors of the Manhat-
tan Bank and is in high repute, no doubt, for *revolutionary
services*.

For us, our Children, and our Wives.

Not only these, but well I wist,
Thousands might help to swell the list
Of vile old tories, fierce and flaming,
Now democratic honors claiming.

I might include with other lumber,
Judge Stevens, Wilson, and a number
Of such as Harrison and Warner,[69]

---

69 William Stevens of Georgia, was appointed Judge of the District Court by Mr. Jefferson. The amount of his claims for that station consist, we believe, in his being a good democrat; in his having been Chief Justice of the State of Georgia, and Lieutenant-Colonel of the Chatham county militia, in our revolutionary war, and while holding those offices of trust and confidence, deserting from the American service; receiving a British commission; being attainted for treason by the Legislature of the State of Georgia. Such are the men whom our pretended Republicans "delight to honour." Wilson is a tory Democrat, of Worcester, Massachusetts, advanced to office by the present administration. Harrison is in office by virtue of an appointment by the New-York tory hating democratic corporation, as a reward for his services as a midshipman on board one of his Britannic Majesty's ships, during the revolutionary war. This gentleman supplanted Mr. Jeremy Marshal, dismissed from office, for having been, as Governor Clinton (then General Clinton) affirmed of him, one of the most useful men in the American army. These are only a few of the many instances, which might be adduced to prove that our good Democrats have been, and still are, hostile to those who were found faithful in times which "tried men's souls."*

* For a more particular account of the proceedings of the New-York corporation, the reader will please to consult the *New-York Evening Post* of June 25th, in which the able and

For faith they swarm in every corner.

Alight swell our catalogue with various
Like idiotic Arcularius,
But cannot stoop in our progression,
To pick up every dirty Hessian,[70]

But though democracy now glories
In such a wondrous gang of tories,
With many fools, its knaves contrive,
To pass for whigs of seventy-five.

They pile their own abominations,
Enough to damn a dozen nations,
All on the simple harmless heads

---

indefatigable editor has exhibited in its just light, the man-
agement of this immaculate junto genuine Jeffersonians
and redoubtable seventy-sixers.

70 Philip Arcularius was appointed, by the New-York Corpora-
tion, Superintendant of the Alms-House. He is a Hessian by
birth, and, during the revolutionary war, kept a sutler's shop
for the supply of his countrymen in the British army. We can-
not, in this place, give a detail of the particular services which
recommended this man to our Democrats. To complete the
story, it is to be added, that he supplanted Mr. Richard Fur-
man, an American, who had served his country, both by sea
and land, during the whole war, and was several limes wound-
ed. This gentleman had been frequently employed by his fel-
low citizens in offices of trust and confidence, and had ever
approved himself a faithful public servant and worthy man. He
had been extremely useful in the office of Superintendant of
the Alms-House; but, as he was neither a Tory nor a Democrat,
he was obliged to give place to the fellow who has the honor of
a peg on our Gibbet.

Of passive inoffensive Feds,

Deprive them first of bread to eat,
And then their conquest to complete;
They hire the scum of foreign nations,
To blast their victims' reputations.

Tho' Burnet "fought in freedom's cause,"
He's doom'd to Cheetham's Harpy claws,[71]
And Spencer, having put down Foot,
Murders his character to boot.[72]

'Tis thus some canibals, 'tis said.
Still spite their enemies, though dead;
And worse, if possible than Cheetham,
Can't be contented *till they eat them!*

Here reader, is a pretty sample
Of rogues for *"negative example."*[73]

---

71   Captain Burnet, another of our revolutionary officers, and
one of the oldest post-masters in the United Slates, has been
turned out of employment by Mr. Jefferson.— Here again we
perceive the sincerity of Mr. Jefferson's declaration, that re-
movals from office should be thrown as much as possible on
"anti-revolutionary adherence to our enemies."

72   Mr. Foote was another revolutionary patriot who has been dis-
placed by the intolerant demagogues who are now dominant.
Foote had the misfortune to think with Washington on polit-
ical subjects, and was, of consequence, deprived of office, and
his reputation afterwards attacked, by way of palliating such
an iniquitous proceeding.

73   "We do not give you to posterity, as a pattern to imitate, but
as an example to deter—We mean to make you a negative In-

Cull'd from among some score of dozens
You'd think th' arch Democrats first cousins.

To this vile crew there might be added
Full many a hollow heart and bad head,
And some for infamy as famous,
As any history can name us.

Among the rest, fanatic preachers,[74]

---

struction to your successors for ever."

Junius to the Duke of Grafton.

74 We always possessed a violent antipathy to your bawling, itin-
erant, field and barn preachers; and having promised them a
dose, (P. 20. N. 24) we now proceed to administer a little of the
nitrous acid of Satire, which we hope may etfect a radical cure
of their disorder. Our medicine is as follows:

FANATICISM.

I HATE your hypocrltic race,
Who prate about pretended grace;
    With tabernacle phizzes;
Who think Omnipotence to charm,
By faces longer than my arm!
    O what a set of quizzes!

I hate your wretches, wild and sad,
Like gloomy wights in Bedlam mad,
    Or vile Old Baily culprits;
Who with a sacrilegious zeal,
Death and damnation dare to deal,
    From barn-erected pulpits.

I hate that hangman's aspect bluff,
In him, whose disposition rough,
    The porcupine surpasses;

Yourself-inspir'd, and self-taught teachers,

Who thinks that heaven is in his power,
Because his sullen looks might sour
    A barrel of molasses.

A stupid wretch, who cannot read,
(A very likely thing indeed)
    Receives from Heaven a calling;
He leaves his plough, he drops his hoe,
Gets on his meeting clothes, and lo,
    Sets up the trade of bawling.

With lenglhen'd visage, woe bedight,
An outward%\^n of inward light,
    He howls in dismal tone;—
"I say, as how, you must be d—d,
For Satan an't so easy shamm'd,
    And you're the devil's own!"

Fools, and old women, blubbering round,
With sobs, and sighs, and grief profound,
    His every tone respond, Sir,
O could I catch the whining cur,
The deuce a bit would I demur,
    To duck him in a pond, Sir,

If any of the canting race.
Are sent to visit any place,
    Adieu to all decorum;
To every virtue, now adieu;
Morality, religion true,
    Are blasted all before 'em.

A good old woman has the spleen,
And sees what is not to be seen,
    Or dreams of things uncommon;
Yea, ten times more than tongue can tell,
Strange things in heaven, and eke in h—ll,
    O, what a nice old woman!

Whose piety, so dark and mystical,
Is Godward *zealous*, manward—*twistical*.[75]

Creatures, who creep into your houses
Just to *regenerate* your spouses,[76]
With whom the spirit's operation,
Tends to a carnal termination.

Your New-York Democratic chickens,
Might make us most delightful pickings,
Avery pretty little brood!
For Satire's muse most charming food!

Straight by the sect 'tis blaz'd about,
That she's inspir'd beyond a doubt,
   And has her sins forgiven;
How tan the wretches hope for bliss,
Who palm such foolish stuff as this,
   Upon the God of Heaven!

Such doers of the devil's works,
Are sure than renegado Turks,
   Worse foes to real piety;
And though we would not persecute,
By dint of ridicule, we'll hoot.
   The wretches from society.

75 *Twistical* is a *Yankeyism*, which we liave introduced, by virtue
of our authority as a poet (*Poetica Licentia*.) The idea is bor-
rowed from an anecdote related of a countryman, who made
use of similar terms, in giving a character to a fanatic of his
acquaintance.

76 We have particular reference to certain notable Democrats of
our acquaintance, who make extraordinary piety a pretence
for "leading captive silly women."

We may, perhaps, hereafter hint on
The management of D. W. C——n
And, though the populace may stare,
May gibbet an intriguing Mayor.

If he and party must have pimps
From Palmer's and from Tom Pain'simps,
'Twill prove they're base birds of a feather,
Whose necks should ail be stretched together.

We might allude to money made
By virtue of a Governor's trade,
Might tell the world what kind of barter
Sometimes obtain'd a grant or charter.

Might cut down bankers, rank and f]Ie,and
Hang roguesbyhundreds in Rhode-Island,
Your patriotic Guinea-men— or[77]
Folks always drunk like G—r F—r.[78]

But worlds of folios were too few
To set forth half the crazy crew,

---

77 Some of the most fiery Rhode-Island republicans out of their
    superabundant regard to the "rights of Mail" are concerned in
    the slave trade. One Collins a violent Jacobin, and of consec-
    juence appointed a Collector for Newport, is a patriot of that
    description.

78 We are told that a gentleman who complained of the impro-
    priety of which a friend had been guilty, by in troducing him
    to his E———y while he was in a state of intoxication, was
    silenced by a reply, that it could not be otherwise, for his E—
    ——y, when awake, was never sober.

Of sharping knaves, and simple flats,
Who constitute good Democrats.

Besides, for credit of our nation.
We cease a while our "oppugnation,"
With these few gibbeted, 'tis best,
Perhaps to respite all the rest.

Some Democrats we meant to tickle,
(And still preserve a rod in pickle,)
May yet escape, upon condition
Of quick repentance, and contrition.

But those most hardened we'll exhibit.
On this, or something like this, *gibbet*,[79]
Hope yet to hang them every one,
A thing which ought, and shall be done.

---

79 We propose, "till time shall wear us out of action" to continue our strictures on certain flagitious demagogues, who have hitherto escaped our notice. We shall, however, probably publish them in such form that they may serve as a *continuation* to this work without their being blended with what we now place before the public.

CANTO VI

𝕸onition

ARGUMENT

We now, with due submission, tenture.
To make OURSELF *the People's Mentor,*
And boldly take the lead of those,
Who fain would lead them by the nose;
And, if their grand Omnipotences,
Have not entirely lost their senses.
By us forewarned, they'll shun the slavery,
Which waits on Democratic knavery.

Altho' not bless'd with second sight,
Divine inflation, or new light,
Have ne'er, in supernatural trance,
Seen through a mill-stone at a glance;

Ne'er danced with sprites at midnight revel,
Had never dealings with the devil,
Nor carried matters to such pitches,
As did the wicked Salem witches;—

Haven't made with t'other world so free, as
To go to H—ll, like one Æneas,[1]

---

1   For a particular account of this journey, See Book V. of the Æneid.

259

By virtue of divine commission,
For prospects bright in fields Elyssian,—

Cannot divine like Richard Brothers,
Miss Polly Davis, and some others,[2]
Who, in the world of spirits, spied
A gross of wonders—or they lied;—

Can't prophesy, as well as gingle,
Like 'Squire Columbus, or McFingal,[3]
And don't see quite so many glories,
As could be wish'd, now flash before us;

Though nothing more than mortal elf,
Good reader, very like yourself,
And therefore shan't, by any trope,
Presume to make ourself a Pope;

Yet ne'er was conjuror acuter,
In prying into matters future;—
No old Silenus, though in liquor,
Could tell you what would happen quicker.

We'll therefore venture to assume, a

---

2   Richard Brothers and Polly Davis, well known personages, whose missions and voyages, to the world of spirits, have caused much speculation among some very knowing ecclesiastics, whom one would suppose were rather of the lying than the standing order.

3   See Barlow's *Vision of Columbus*, and Trumbull's *McFingal*, in which the heroes of the poems respectively, after the manner of the ancients, take a peep into futurity.

Tone of authority, like Numas;[4]
And give such wondrous counsel, no man
Shall say, we fall beneath the Roman.

Good folks, of each degree and station,
Which goes to constitute our nation,
In social fabric who take place,
Or at the pinnacle or base.

With diligence, I pray, attend
To counsels of a *real* friend,
Who tells the truth, when he assures
You, that his interest is yours;[5]

Who hopes, that when you're plainly show'd
Your Democratic, downhill road,
Is dire destruction's dismal route,
You'll condescend to turn about.

Why should you hardily advance,
The highway, lately trod by France;
Nor take example, ere too late,
To shun the same disastrous fate.

---

4   Numa Pompilius was a King of Romans who pretended to inti-
macy with a female spirit, whom he named Egeria, and whose
monitions were probably as prophelic as those of our invisible
lady.

5   We have before observed, Vol. I. p, 10, that we have no private
nor party views to subserve in this poem. We have no *interest*
distinct from the good of our ccuntry and *no patron* but the
public.

(O, could I hope my rush-light taper
Might penetrate the Stygian vapour,
That you might see, and seeing miss,
The Democratic precipice.)

But now, methinks, you cry as one,
What shall be done! What shall be done!
What method hit on for defending,
Against such destiny impending?

Imprimis, cry down every rogue
Democracy has now in vogue,
Who thinks, by dint of wicked lies,
To cast a mist before your eyes.

Give power to none but honest men,
Long tried, and faithful found, and then
You will not flounder in the dark,
Still wide from real freedom's mark,

Distrust those wretches, every one,
Curses denounc'd by Washington;
Who have of late been busy, brewing
Their own, and other people's ruin.[6]

O had we built on that foundation,

---

6   Our lending Demogogues, are quite as likely to be offered as
victims at the shrine of Democracy as the Federalists. Governor
McKean, who was active in bringing about a Democratic order
of things in Pennsylvania, stands on very slippery ground, and
is in danger of being denounced by the Aurora-man, who is the
Wat Tyler of the Pennsylvania Democrats.

Laid by our late Administration![7]
The fabric of our Nation's Glory
Had never been surpassed in story.

---

7   To enumerate the most prominent measures of the Federal Administration, and the benefits which have resulted to the nation from the Federal system, would require volumes. We shall slightly advert to a few particulars, by way of elucidating this fact.

The Federalists found the country without permanent revenue, and without money in the Treasury sufficient to defray the necessary expences of Government; upwards of seventy-six millions in debt; the securities of Government selling at two shillings on the pound; the nation distracted at home and despised abroad—

> Like "some wreck'd vessel, all in shatters,"
> Scarce "held up by surrounding waters."*

Such was the state of things when they commenced their operations.

They liquidated the public funds for the extinction, of the national debt; punctually paid the interest and part of the principal.

They fortified our harbours.

They sought for and obtained indemnity for British and French spoliations.

They suppressed insurrections.

They built and purchased a Navy of thirty-six armed ships.

They secured peace abroad.

They established a Government at home.

They exalted our national character: under their auspices Agriculture flourished, Commerce was protected, a Revenue created without burthening the people, and Two Millions and an Half Dollars left in the Public Treasury.

* *McFingal.*

But ever sedulous in brewing
Their *own*, and other people's ruin,
Our Democrats have been at work
To lay all level, with a jerk.

Not Satan, breaking into Eden,
Could show more malice in proceeding,
Or tell more false, malicious stories,
Than these said Jacobin-French Tories.[8]

Sometimes the rogues were picking flaws

---

8   If any of our readers are not yet fully acquainted with the des-
    picable means by whkh our Jacobins attained the great end
    of destroying the Federal Administration, they are referred to
    Mr. Bayard's speech on the Judiciary Bill, spoken February 19,
    1802. We should be happy to insert that part of it which relates
    to a vindication of the measures of the Federal Administration,
    did not its length exceed our limits. One sentence, however,
    relative to the clamour, which the Antifederalists have raised
    against direct taxation, the abolition of which, according to
    Mr. Jefferson's late speech, (March, 1803) is one of the meas-
    ures so highly commendable in the gentlemen now at the head
    of our affairs, we cannot forbear to quote.

    > Will gentlemen say that the direct tax was laid in
    > order to enlarge thfe bounds of patronage? Will they
    > deny that this was a measure to which we had been
    > urged for years, by our adversaries, because they
    > saw in it the ruin of the Federal power?

    This is the way they have managed—cunningly clamoured
    the Federal Administration iuto measures, which they fore-
    jaw might be rendered obnoxious to the people, and then took
    advantage of the odium which such measures had excited! See
    P. 122. N. 55.

With Alien and Sedition Laws,[9]
The Constitution next attacking,
They sent the Federal Judges packing.[10]

With empty boasts of their surprising
Attention to economizing,
Thousands were thrown away, to show
How they could decorate the Berceau.[11]

And public money was such trash,
Two million dollars, at a dash,
Without descending to excuses,

---

9   These laws were among the measures of the late Administra-
tion, which were obnoxious to the tyrants in power, merely
because they were favourable to the rights of the citizen. The
Alien law provided for the deportation, under certain circum-
stances, of turbulent and seditious foreigners; thu latter gave
our citizens a right to publish the *truth* concerning the meas-
ures of government. See N. 12. P. 6.

10   No man whose head is not very weak, or his heart very wicked
can rontemplain, without emotions too vivid to be expressed,
the conduct of the Faction in their destruction of the Judiciary.
The sound arguments on the one side, and the flimsy sophisms
on the other side of that great national question, when con-
trasted, must convince every person, thal those men who laid
their sacrilegious hands on the ark of our safety, were prede-
termined not to be convinced, but to stick to their party, right
or wrong. See P. 119. N. 54.

11   More than thirty-two thousand dollars were expended in re-
pairing the French *Corvette Berceau*. The *Ganges*, an Amer-
ican ship of war of 26 guns, and all her stores, were sold by
administration for only 21,000 dollars, and most of the other
ships of the Federal navy, we believe, in the same proportion.

Their honours vote for private uses.[12]

The Feds chac'd down, the snarling elves.
At loggerheads among themselves,[13]
E'en cut and thrust, like gladiators,
For our amusement as spectators.

Resolv'd to prove the nation's curses,
They go from bad to what still worse is,
As females frail, by regular steps,
Are prostitutes from demireps.

Each wicked measure merely leading,
To more flagitious step succeeding,
Of late, their frantic innovations,
Have shook society's foundations.

Hot-headed Randolph's resolution
For cutting up the Constitution,
And that of Nicholson disclose,

---

12 See a resolve of Congress of November, 1803, that a sum of
    two millions of dollars in addition to the provision heretofore
    made, should be granted to the purposes of intercourse be-
    tween us and foreign nations.

13 Every body knows that Master Johnny Randolph has of late
    been attempting to *put off the monkey*, and *put on the tiger*,
    and to *bully* the nonconformists of his party into genuine Re-
    publicanism. But his essays in the *terrible*, have terminated in
    the *ludicrous*, for even Miss Nancy Dawson declares that *she*
    will not be frightened out of her *independence*, by this *whip-
    per*-in of the puppies of the party.

The rancour of its deadly foes.[14]

That "plague to G—d and man" Tom Paine,
Is at his dirty work again,[15]
The Devil's special legate sent,
And patroniz'd by Government!

But now, methinks, you cry as one,
What must be done! What must be done!
These growing evils to curtail,
And make our Demo's shorten sail?

---

14   it is well known that the Democratic party were formerly most
violent opponents of theFederal Constitution. Mr. Jefferson
declared that he "disliked, and greatly disliked" many parts of
it. We could, therefore, expect nothing better from the ene-
mies of the Constitution, than that they would endeavour to
destroy it. Some of the outworks are already demolished, and
the citadel is to be attacked the next session, (Nov. 1805.) It
is to be hoped that those Democrats, who are not rendered
quite frantic by the spirit of party, will be taught, from the en-
deavours of our Randolphs and Nicholsons, the impolicy of
placing the enemies of the Constitution of the United States
in situations where they can, with impunity, aim their blows at
its vitals. Would any man of a sound mind suffer his house to
be tenanted by persons, who, after having vainly opposed its
erection, had declared that its corner stones ought to be sub-
tracted from the building, and its principal pillars be laid pros-
trate? Yet such is the part which we have acted in trusting the
administratioa of the Federal Government in the hands of men
who were inimical to that government at its establishment,
and who, even now, neglect no opportunity for the display of
their hostility to the constitution by which it is administered.

15   To wit, scribbling newspaper essays for the Snyderites at
Pennsylvania.

Sirs, (our opinion to be blunt in)
The first step must be, "scoundrel hunting!"[16]
The minions of a wicked faction,
Hiss! hoot quite off the stage of action!

Next, every man throughout the nation,
Must be contented in his station,[17]

16   This may seem very harsh doctrine. The sense in which I use
the phrase quoted in this place, may, however, be explained,
by referring to N. 4. P. 4.

    I would not wish to hunt bad men with mobs, nor with mas-
tiffs, but I would hold them out to society in true colours, and if
the voice of the public does not consign them to infamy, Amer-
icans will pass from the "tempestuous sea" of licentiousness, to
the "dead calm of des pntism," with the embittering reflection
that they have merited their destiny. Thus, in France, after the
destruction of Fayette and others of their leaderss, who wert:
solicitous to reform the abuses of the old government, and
who were mostly well-meaning men, a succession of tygers,
in human shape, afflicted the nation, till the most ferocious
monster the kingdom afforded, was at lengh made Emperor.

17   There is, perhaps, no pride more preposterous than that
which impels so many, in the middle and lower classes in
society, to exert themselves to confer a collegiate education
on their children, not only *minerva invita*, but when the *res
angusta domus opposes* insurmountable impediments to
their progress. "What good end (says an English writer) can
it answer in these times, when every genteel profession is
overstocked, to rob our agriculture or our manufactures of so
many useful hands, by encouraging every substantial farm-
er, mechanic, or tradesman, to breed his son to the church;"
and he might have added, or any other learned profession. "If
now and then a very uncommon genius in those walks of life
discovers itself, there are seldom wanting gentlemen in the
neighbourhood, who are proud of calling forth, and if *neccs-
sary*, of supporting, by a subscription, such extraordinary
talents."

Nor think to cut a figure greater,

The multiplying of Academies, and poorly endowed Colleges, where that "dangerous thing." "a little learning" may be acquired, and frequently to the detriment of common Schools, in which that kind of knowledge is taught which is absolutely necessary for farmers, mechanics, &c. is, in our opinion, a great and a growing evil in America. Happy would it be for us if the number of that useful class of citizen?, who form the basis of society, was greater in proportion to the population of the country.

With all the freedom you can boast,
You cannot *all* be *uppermost*:

And where *subordination ends, tyranny hegins*; at first the *"tyranny of all"* which soon becomes the tyranny of the few, or the despotism of one. See P. 6. N. 8.

In the general scramble for political distinction, which takes place in America, in consequence of the door of office being open to every pretender, the basest means are resorted to, and the morals cf the people are corrupted by the example of those who are aspiring to take the lead in the community. This evil might, in a great degree, be remedied by lessening the number of competitors for offices. Let every man have a right to aspire to the highest stations, but let the pre-requisite qualifications, respecting age, education, talents, citizenship, but abore all *morals*, be such, that the number of competitors would be comparatively few.

Regulations of that kind would be perfectly consistent with freedom, the ascendancy of virtue and talents and the experience of ages.

These remarks apply, not only to the candidates for offices or emoluments under government, but to those who are crowding themselves into the learned professions, without those qualifications which ought to be considered as indispensable.

I know that Duane and the Jacobins of his school, maintain, that the learned professions, particularly that of Law, ought to be annihilated; and they may as well be annihilated, as to be

Than was designed for him by Nature.

No tinker bold with *brazen* pate,
Should set himself to *patch* the State,[18]
No cobbler leave, at Faction's call,
His *last*, and thereby lose his *all*.

No brawny blacksmith, brave and stout,
Our Constitution *hammer* out,
For if he's wise, he'll not desire
Too many *irons* in the fire;—

And though a master of his trade,
With politics on *anvil* laid,
He may take many a heat, and yet he
Can't weld a bye-law or a treaty.

No tailor, than his *goose* more silly,

---

crowded with witlings and unqualified professors. But it is to be hoped the good sense of Americans will resist the innovations of these Godwinian schemers.

Duane and his faction, may as well declare against watch-makers, tailors, or any other mechanics, as lawyers, or gentlemen of the other learned professions. They are each subservient to the happiness or convenience of all, and altogether constitute a civilized nation. But if what we have advanced in our exposition of the principles of Mr. Godwin, in Canto II. relative to the tendency of these and similar levelling tenets, should make no impression on the reader, we must turn him over to the demagogues of the day.

18 When tinkers bawl'd aloud to settle
Church discipline, for patching kettle, &c.
Hudibras, Part I. Canto II.

Should cut the State a garment, till he
Is sure he has the measure right,
Lest it *fit* awkward, loose or *tight*,

No farmer, had he Ceres' skill,
The commonwealth should think to *till*,
For many *soils* in human nature,
Would mock his art as *cultivator*.

The greatest number's greatest good,
Should, doubtless, ever be pursu'd;
But that consists, *sans* disputation,
In order and subordination.

Nature imposes her commands,
There must be *heads*, as well as *hands*,[19]

---

19   If our New School politicians are not too fastidious to peruse
with patience, even the Apocryphal part of the Bible, we would
beg leave to illustrate our ideas on this subject, by a quotation
from Ecclesiasticus, Chapter XXXVIII. V. 24, to the end of the
chapter.

> The wisdom of a learned man cometh by oppor-
> tunity of leisure: and he that hath little business
> shall become wise.
> How can he get wisdom that holdeth the plough?
> and that glorieth in the goad; that driveth oxen, and
> is occupied in their labours, and whose talk is of
> bullocks?
> He giveth his mind to make furrows; and is dili-
> gent to give the kine fodder.
> So every carpenter and workmaster that la-
> boureth night and day: and they that cut and grave
> seals, and are diligent to make great variety, and

give themselves to counterfeit imagery, and watch
to finish a work:

The smith also sitting by the anvil, and consider-
ing the iron work, the rapour of the fire wasteth his
flesh, and he fighteth with the heat of the furnace:
the noise of the hammer and the anvil is ever in his
ears, and his eyes look still upon the pattern of the
thing that hemaketh; he setteth his mind to finish
his work, and watcheth to polish it perfectly:

So doth the potter sitting at his work, and turning
the wheel about with his feet, who is always carefully
set at his work: and maketh all his work by number;

He fashioneth the clay with his arm, and boweth
down his strength before his feet, he applieth him-
self to lead it over; and he is diligent to make clean
the furnace:

All these trust to their hands: and every one is
wise in his work.

Without these cannot a city be inhabited: and
they shall not dwell where they will, nor go up and
down: They shall not be sought for in public coun-
sel, nor sit high in the congregation: they shall not
sit on the judges' seat, nor understand the sentence
of judgment: they cannot declare justice and judg-
ment, and they shall not be found where parables
are spoken.

But they will maintain the state of the world, and
[all] their desire is in the work of the craft.

It is impossible for any person who is truly a philanthropist
not to feel his indignation excited against the perverse philos-
ophists of the day, who, instead of inculcating *patience* and
tranquillity among mankind, are continually exciting that res-
tive and turbulent spirit, which is the bane of civilized society.
It is owing to their efforts that the hearts of the lower classes
in the connnunity are so frequently "Cankered with discon-
tent, that they consider themselves as condemned to labour
for the luxury of the rich, and look up with stupid malevolence

The man of body, "sonof soul,"
The former happiest on the whole:—[20]

For toil of body still we find.
Is lighter far than toil of mind,
And nought, perhaps, but tooth-ach pain,
Can equal "wear and tear of brains."

Blest is the man with wooden head,
Who labours for his daily bread,
More happy he, if truth were known,
Than Buonapart' upon his throne:

Yes, his advantage most immense is,
In all enjoyments of the senses,
If health and strength in him are joined,
With heaven's best boon, a tranquil mind.

Then think not Providence disgrac'd you,
If in some lower rank it plac'd you;
Think poverty no punishment.

---

towards those who are placed above them."*

* Johnson's *Rasselas, Prince of Abysinnia*.

20 He who has been in early life accustomed to laborious occupa-
tions, can rarely conform to sedentary pursuits: accustomed
to the *stimulus* of violent *corporeal exercise*, his frame will
be disordered, from its discontinuance. Listlessness, apathy,
hypochondriacal complaints, and not unfrequently madness,
swell the catalogue of disorders which await a transition of
that kind. Hence the impracticability of civilizing the aborig-
ines of America, who have, in early life, been inured to the toil
of the hunter state.

And be with competence content;

Do not assume of State the reins,
If you're but so so, as to brains,
Because you make yourselves vexation,
And but disgrace us as a nation.

Had Johnny Randolph known his place,
"He had not hunted Mr. Chase,[21]
Nor had the pubhc known him to be
A blundering and malicious booby.

Had Lawyer L——n staid at home,
His honour might have pass'd, with some,
For quite a decent country Squire,
And no bad Jury *argufier*.

And had our Governor that would be,
But been contented where he should be,
His Honour had not been the mark

---

21 The failure of this poor little "ghost of a monkey," in his im-
peachment of Mr. Chase, cannot but afford high satisfaction to
every friend to his country. We have reason to believe that had
Mr. Chase fallen, it was the intention of the stripling tyrant,
and his confederate mamelukes, to have destroyed all the Fed-
eral Judges, at "one fell swoop."

It was happily so ordered, that he made his attack on one
every way able to defend himself against the malicious and
vindictive assaults of the Faction, and who has not only re-
pelled the shafts of their calumny, but by his masterly vindi-
cation of his conduct, has done honour to Federalism and to
his country.

So often hit by D——r P——k.[22]

Had——somebody but known his station,
Perhaps his blasted reputation,
Stain'd by a multitude of sins,
Had 'scap'd the shafts of Young and Minns.[23]

So much for wiseacres, desiring
To show their folly by aspiring,
We turn to those who know their places,
And form our social fabric's basis.

I need not tell you, Sirs, how true 'tis,
That you have *rights*, as well as *duties*,
Have much at stake in preservation

---

22 The charges to which we here allude, are already before the
public. We offer no comments, but merely observe, that the
man, who, after having witnessed the developement of the
character of this candidate for the Gubernatorial chair will
give him his suffrage, has not *virtue* enough to qualify him to
be the citizen of a *free government*; and if a majority of the
citizens of Massachusetts are base enough to prefer this man
to Governor Strong, national freedom is at its last gasp, and
the character of the State is fast sinking to the lowest point of
degradation.

23 We allude here to the well known publication in the *New
England Palladium*, entitled, "The monarchy of Federalism,"
which gives in short hand, a correct idea of the man whom our
Democrats "delight to honour." The pamphlet, entitled, *The
Defence of Young and Minns*, which contains copies of the
documents, and statements of the facts alluded to in that pub-
lication, ought to be in the hands of every American freeman
who is not disposed to rush blindfold into the jaws of destruc-
tion.

Of Law and order in the nation.

But heed you notthe bawling clan,
Who prate about the "rights of man,"
Although like Thomas Pain, and Firm,
They fix no meaning to the term.[24]

See Elliot sick of the procedures[25]

---

24 Nothing can be more preposterous than the declamatory non-
sense ofthe demagogues ofthe day, who clamour about the
"rights of man." If these gentlemen wish to mix a little *knowl-
edge* with their zeal on this subject, they will diligently con
Judge Blackstone's Commentaries, particularly the first Chap-
ter of the first Book, which treats of the "Rights of Persons."

25 Mr. Elliot's letters to his constituents display very considera-
ble candor, and certain aproximations to rectitude, for which
he ought to receive a due degree of credit.

    This gentleman, together with many others, much his inferi-
ors in abilities and integrity, was elected to Congress by a party
who were opposed to the Washington and Adams administra-
tion; but perceiving that the views of the leaders of that party
were destructive to the Constitution, Laws and Liberty of the
Union, he appears *now* to halt between two opinions. He will,
by no means, acknowledge himself to be a Federalist, although
his political tenets appear *now* to be very nearly the same with
those *always* held by the Federal party. Perhaps, however, he
may hereafter observe of some other political subjects what
he has already remarked relative to a certain amendment of
the Constitution, that he "had never contemplated the subject
with a suitable degree of cool reflection and deep investiga-
tion."* No doubt a proper attention to contemplations of that
kind might induce him to become *altogether* a Federalist!

    We cannot, however, forbear to notice a slight inconsisten-
cy which appears in his "political creed," as expressed in his
11th letter to his constituents. Mr. Elliot says, "I believe that
Washington was the greatest warrior and probably the most

Of ourgood Democratic leaders,
Is *half* resolved on coming round,
And occupying Federal ground.

And others feel a foolish terror
'Gainst owning they have been in error,
And though convinced, are not so manly
As Butler, Elliot, and Stanley.[26]

Be not of good men over jealous,
Nor lightly trust the clamorous fellows,
Who'gainst yourtrue friendsset their faces,
Merely to crowd into their places.

There must be limits put to suffrage,[27]

---

correct statesman in our country, I believe Adams to be a man of integrity and talents, but the general system of his Administration was wrong." Now a "correct statesman" is not apt to give his sanction to wrong measures, but Washington did highly approve of Mr. Adams' Administration, as appears by his letter to Mr. Carrol. See N. 50. P. 115.

* See Mr. Elliots 3d *Letterto his Constituents.*

26 These gentlemen have all been of the Democratic party, but had honesty and independence enough to oppose the machinations of the Virginian junto.

27 It cannot be necessary in this place, to repeat what has been so often urged on the subject of "Universal Suffrage." borne qualifications as respects pioperty, residence, and cilizensnip, ever have, and ever will be found necessary in a civilized state of society, in ordur to entitle a man by his rote, to dispose of the property of others. What should we say of one, who assumed a right to direct the operations, and tax the shares of a private company of merchants, who held no stock belonging to

Although the step excite enough rage,
Lest men devoid of information
Andhonesty should rule the nation.

Your multiplying institutions,
Checks, balances andconstitutions,[28]
Which rogues can break down with impunity,
Will serve no purpose in community.

Thus Despotism France controuls,
In spite of Sieyes' pigeon holes,
And Revolutions every Moon,
Could not secure her Freedom's boon.

---

the company?

28 In that invaluable digest of the principles of our government
    entitled *The Federalist* we find the following apprehensions
    expressed on this subject.

> Experience assures us that the efficacy of *parch-
> ment barriers* has been greatly over-rated, and that
> some *more adequate* defence is indispensably nec-
> essary, for the more feeble against the more pow-
> erful members of the government. The Legislative
> department is every where extending the sphere of
> its activity, and drawing all power into its impetuous
> vortex.*

If this "m ore *adequate defence*" should not be found in
public opinion, our Constitution will fall,, our political and
civil rights wilt soon share its fate, and despotism in America,
as in France, will at length prove our only *asylum* from the
horrors of anarchy.

* The remarks of the eloquent Mallet Du Pan, on the fate of
Switzerland, corroborate these observations.

Let honesty and reputation,
Be passports to your approbation,
And ne'er support, with zeal most hearty,
A knave because he's of your party.

Remember, mid your party strife,
Whoso's a rogue in *private life*,[29]
If once he gets you at his beck
Will set his foot upon your neck.

Thus Mr. Burr, for aye intriguing,
With this side band with that side leaguing,
Has late contrived a scheme quite handy,
To make himself, for life, a grandee.[30]

---

29 One of the most dangerous errors of those among our demo-
crats, who are rather the *deluded* than the *deluders*, is an opin-
ion that our attention to the affairs of government ought to
be directed altogether to measures without adverting to *men*.
But an *evil tree* cannot produce *good fruit*, neither can igno-
rant wrongheaded and wicked men give origin and support to
measures which are beneficial to the public. Yet how often do
we trust those in *public station* in whom we could place no
confidence in *private life*, and how many democrats like Mat-
thew Lyon give countenance to your Duanes and Cheethams,
knowing them such as Lyon has described his "old friend,"
that is entirely destitute of common honesty. Such men de-
serve to be made "hewers of wood and drawers of water," as a
punishment for their stupidity, lack of political honesty, and
public spirit.

30 Mr. Burr's attempt to obtain the privilege of franking letters
is an indication of the kind of freedom with which be and his
party would favour the simpletons, who are capable of being
lulled to repose by the syren song of Liberty and Equality.

You next some method must be trying,
To stop the rage of party lying,
Which may be quickly done, provided
You will be honest and decided,

"When printers are to lies addicted,
And have most fairly been convicted;
For instance, men like Chronicleers,
Who should be thankful—for their ears.

From pillory though they are exempt,
You ought to blast them with contempt,
But now they find, by Faction's aid,
Lying a profitable trade.

But you can stop our Demo's dashing,
Bring honesty again in fashion,
Bring scoundrelism to disgrace,
Bid modest merit show its face.

Instead of sinking in despair,
Be as with WASHINGTON you *were*,
Revive the measures he approv'd,
RESTORE TO POWER THE MEN HE LOV'D![31]

---

31 Those men who were honoured with the confidence of their
fellow-citizens and appointed to office under Washington and
Adams' Administration, were selected from among their fel-
low-citizens, because they were known to be "honest and faith-
ful." Now the inquiry, as Mr. J——n's answer to the New-Ha-
ven remonstrance implies, is altogether whether the candidate
is of the right political sect. The demon of party brought for-
ward the Democrats, not any intrinsic merits of their own.

Then may you rationally hope
That *Liberty*, without a trope,
And all the virtues of hef train,
Will deign to visit us again.[32]

The same evil spirit which gave France her Marats, her Roberspierres, and her Buonaparte, has given America the tyrants who have put a period to the political existence of the Federalists, and who, as Duane has intimated, would lead them to the scaffold if they dared. If we have not virtue enough to retrace our steps and return to primitive men and measures, we may foresee in the fall of France what must be the termination of our struggies fox Liberty.

32 Many of our luke-warm Federalists, seem disposed to slide down the steep of Democracy, without an effort to save themselves and country, frem the *unlimited misery* which awaits such a career." They say, that Americans have not *virtue* enough to support a Republican Government, and that we had belter remain contented under the present state of our affairs, than by exertions which must prove fruitless, to hazard the introduction of a still worse order of things. But this is very foolish reasoning. As veil might a physician determine to give no medicine to allay the rage of a fever, because the disorder *will have its crisis*. If (he efforts of the Federalists should be unremitted, they will be, at least, able to muzzle the Mammoth of Democracy, and evade much of the evil which would inevitably ensue, should the monster be suffered to roam perfectly unrestrained. But we cannot better conclude this note, than with the remarks of the Editor of the *Utica Patriot*, an excellent Federal Newspaper.

"The cause of Federalism, we trust, has passed its most gloomy period. The ebb tide has arrived to its utmost point, and will shortly be succeeded by a flood, which will overwhelm its enemies in one prodigious ruin. The government again in the hands of the Federalists, the wounds which have been inflicted on the constitution, would be shortly healed, the government would convalesce from its preseat weakness, to perfect health and vigour, and the blessings of rational liberty would again be

But, my good sovereign friends, I now
Must make, alas, my parting bow,
Still humbly hoping, with submission,
That you'll attend to my Monition.

Take my advice, which not pursuing,
You're surely in the "road to ruin,"
For rul'd by men, and not by law,
Your rights will not be worth a straw.

FINIS

---

enjoyed in their pristine purity. Then let Federalists, knowing
the justice of their cause, and its importance to the salvation of
their country, be animated to exertion; and let each good man
and true patriot adopt for himself, the language of the Poet:

——Here I take my stand,
Here on the brink, the very verge of liberty:
Although contention rise upon the clouds,
Mix heaven with earth, and roll the ruin onwards,
Here will I fix, and breast me to the shock,
Till I or Denmark fall."

Index

M

Macon, Nathaniel 156
Madison, James 144
Madrid 132
Maine 130, 248
Mallet du Pan, Jacques 300
Manhattan Bank 272
Mansfield, Jared 272
Marat, Jean-Paul 303
Marie Antoinette 64
Marine Caslet Corps 35
Marshal, Jeremy 273
Marshall, John 29, 237
Marsh, Amos 132
Marsyas 104
Martin, Thomas 131
Maryland 132, 138, 177
Mason, D. D., John M. 123
McFingal (Trumbull) 282
McHenry, James 118, 247
Memoirs Illustrating the History of Jacobinism (Barruel) 38
Memoirs of the Life, Writings and Correspondence of Sir William Jones (Teignmouth) 261
Mercury (newspaper) 166, 243
Metamorphoses (Ovid) 85
Michigan 249
Middletown, CT 132
Miller, Henry 131
Miller, John 250
Milton, John 86, 87, 154
Minerva, The (newspaper) 195
Minns, William 297
Minot, George Richards 92
Mirabeau, Honoré Gabriel Riqueti, comte de 64, 66

Missisippi Territory 132
M'Kean, Thomas 106, 178, 258
Montauban 65
Montesquieu, Charles Louis de Secondat, Baron de La Brède et de 49
Moore, Thomas 105
Morris, Gouverneur 119, 143
Mount Ætna 208
Mount Vernon 138, 196

N

National Assembly (France) 57, 68
National Convention (France) 77
National Gazette 200
National Intelligencer 166
natural right 170, 182
Nebuchadnezzar II 267
Nero 111, 131
New England 24, 56, 84, 99, 125, 243, 297
New England manners 24
New England Palladium 243, 297
New Hampshire 131, 246, 247, 248
New Haven 132, 272, 302
New Haven College Library 272
New Orleans 134
Newton, Isaac 57
New York 19, 75, 87, 90, 91, 104, 132, 155, 195, 196, 256, 266, 270, 272, 273, 274, 278
New York Corporation 274
New York Evening Post 91, 203, 262